BIOGRAPHY

WRITING LIVES

GENRES IN CONTEXT

THE SHORT STORY
The Reality of Artifice
Charles E. May

FANTASY
The Liberation of Imagination
Richard Mathews

BIOGRAPHY
Writing Lives
Catherine N. Parke

THE SEA VOYAGE NARRATIVE
Robert Foulke

SCIENCE FICTION BEFORE 1900
Imagination Discovers Technology
Paul K. Alkon

SCIENCE FICTION AFTER 1900
From the Steam Man to the Stars
Brooks Landon

NATURE WRITING
The Pastoral Impulse in America
Don Scheese

THE FAIRY TALE
The Magic Mirror of Imagination
Steven Swann Jones

TRAVEL WRITING
The Self and the World
Casey Blanton

BIOGRAPHY

WRITING LIVES

Catherine N. Parke

Routledge
New York and London

Published in 2002 by
Routledge
29 West 35th Street
New York, NY 10001

Published in Great Britain by
Routledge
11 New Fetter Lane
London EC4P 4EE

Routledge is an imprint of the Taylor & Francis Group.

Originally published in hardcover by Twayne Publishers, an imprint of The Gale Group.
This paperback edition published by arrangement with Twayne Publishers.

First Routledge paperback edition 2002

Printed in the United States of America on acid-free paper.

10 9 8 7 6 5 4 3 2 1

Cataloging-in-Publication Data available from the Library of Congress.

ISBN 0–415–93892–9 (pbk)

#48435363

For Tom, Ann, Catherine
and in memory of John Wain

General Editor's Statement

Genre studies have been a central concern of Anglo-American and European literary theory for at least the past quarter century, and the academic interest has been reflected, for example, in new college courses in slave narratives, autobiography, biography, nature writing, and the literature of travel as well as in the rapid expansion of genre theory itself. Genre has also become an indispensable term for trade publishers and the vast readership they serve. Indeed, few general bookstores do not have sections devoted to science fiction, romance, and mystery fiction. Still, genre is among the slipperiest of literary terms, as any examination of genre theories and their histories will suggest.

In conceiving this series we have tried, on the one hand, to avoid the comically pedantic spirit that informs Polonius' recitation of kinds of drama and, on the other hand, the equally unhelpful insistence that every literary production is a unique expression that must not be forced into any system of classification. We have instead developed our list of titles, which range from ancient comedy to the Western, with the conviction that by common consent kinds of literature do exist—not as fixed categories but as fluid ones that change over time as the result of complex interplay of authors, audiences, and literary and cultural institutions. As individual titles in the series demonstrate, the idea of genre offers us provocative ways to study both the continuities and adaptability of literature as a familiar and inexhaustible source of human imagination.

Recognition of the fluid boundaries both within and among genres will provide, we believe, a useful array of perspectives from which to study literature's complex development. Genres, as traditional but open ways of understanding the world, contribute to our capacity to respond to narrative and expressive forms and offer means to discern moral significances embodied in these forms. Genres, in short, serve ethical as well as aesthetic purposes, and the volumes in this series attempt to demonstrate how this double benefit has been achieved as these genres have been transformed over the years. Each title in the series should be measured against this large ambition.

Ron Gottesman

We know the world by knowing people.
Robert Kelly

There is no meaning to the facts of life till the mind begins to play
upon them.
Walter Raleigh

Too much intelligence is often as pernicious to Biography as too
little; the mind remains perplexed by contradiction of probabili-
ties, and finds difficulty in separating report from truth.
Hester Lynch Thrale Piozzi

There is a seedy aspect to pawing through a life, but there is
merit in preserving fact and feeling and insight.
James Atlas

[T]here are so many millions always living and each one is his
own self inside him.
Gertrude Stein

Contents

Preface

B iography, of all the literary genres, might seem to be the one least in need of explanation, analysis, and justification. For biography, after all, tells the stories of our lives, combining the solid satisfaction of facts with the shaping pleasures of the imagination. We are born, live, and die in a world where event follows event. Biography narrates life, plotting the circle of existence from birth to death. As the secretary to our existence, biography might seem to have a self-evident poetics, a poetics inseparable from the genre, beyond words, or at least beyond words other than its own. Many practicing biographers have held this opinion. Readers' interest in this genre might also seem to share similar qualities of the self-evident. What should people be more naturally curious about, equipped for knowing, and in need of understanding than themselves and their fellow creatures? The fundamental social quality of human existence helps to account for the enduring and varied history of biography, for the way this form rivals fiction in its imaginative appeal to the most powerful emotions of hope and fear, desire and hate, attraction and repulsion, as well as for the fact that in its long history biography has identified issues and tackled problems endemic to life, which are in equal measure practical, metaphysical, quotidian, and mysterious, and which nearly every age, to date, has felt the obligation to rethink. For these reasons, among others, this most self-evident of genres invites examination.

Readers of this introductory study, even those who do not consider themselves practiced readers of biography, are probably more familiar with characteristics of the genre than they consciously know, so thoroughly does knowledge of biography infuse the common reader's habits. To demonstrate this general familiarity, I give the following short list of titles, which cut across the grain of biographical expectation and thus identify, by indirection, most readers' practical acquaintance with this genre: *God: A Biography, Biography of the Unborn, Biography of a Kangaroo, Biography of a Cathedral, Biography of an Idea: The Story of Mutual Fire and Casualty Insurance.* These titles ring changes on common expectations about life writing. It typically takes human beings as its subjects, not gods or kangaroos. It chooses people who have lived or are living in the world not those as yet unborn. These human beings may build cathedrals and have ideas about insurance or any number of other things, but these activities and accomplishments are not biography's sole reason for being.

Translated into questions, such matters do, however, motivate biographical research and subsequently challenge biographers to dramatize their findings in written form: How and why did a particular person do what she did, think what she thought, imagine what she imagined? How did the person's private and public lives relate to and influence one another? How did childhood affect the adult life? To what degree is the subject conscious of various shaping forces? How did cultural and historical events and context affect that life? How may these elements, organized as pattern by the biographical narrative, serve, in turn, to account for and explain a particular life and the forms it took? What makes one life more worth writing about than another? How and why does a particular biographer choose a particular biographical subject? How does a biographer reconstruct imaginatively the subject's inner life on the basis of available external evidence and how and why has imaginative reconstruction come to be understood as the principal aim of modern biography—at least in Western societies?[1] I will return to these matters in the historical overview in chapter 1 and in discussions of exemplary biographies in chapters 2 through 4.

Consider for a moment two anecdotes about biography conceived of in popular and readerly ways, not in scholarly or theoretical terms, which have their place later in this study. The first anecdote is set in the public library of a Midwestern town; the second is taken from the pages of a mail-order bookseller's catalog. In the Columbia, Missouri Public Library, biography and autobiography are catalogued together and shelved together, no distinction made between a life written in the first person by the one who lived it and a life written in the third person by someone other than the subject. Subject matter is the key to cataloguing life writing. Biographies and autobiographies are arranged alphabetically by the subjects' names, these names understood to be what is most important about these genres. Thus Henry Adams's autobiography, *The Education of Henry Adams*, is shelved beside Ernest Samuels's three-volume scholarly biography of Adams. The autobiography of Estée Lauder, founder of Lauder Cosmetics, *Estée: A Success Story*, her life told her way, is shelved next to the unauthorized biography, *Estée Lauder: Beyond the Magic* by Lee Israel, who debunks Lauder's account of herself. Pride of place goes to the biographical subject, not the author, though these, in the case of autobiography, are one and the same.

The life writing stacks stand next to fiction. This placement represents the library's understanding "of how popular these genres are," one librarian observed. "It also represents the fact," she continued, "that our users tend to think of these books together." She continued, "Both are, after all, stories of people's lives. Reference librarians, on the other hand, would prefer to have biography on the second floor next to history and near the telephone reference desk. When someone calls with a question about the Civil War, a librarian might want to turn to a biography of Ulysses S. Grant or Robert E. Lee. But," she concluded, "we shelve books with our patrons' reading habits in mind. That's why we put biography next to fiction."

My second anecdote is taken from a bookseller's catalogue. If all subject matter were equally salesworthy, a typical mail-order bookseller's catalogue of just under thirty-two newsprint pages, listing titles on forty subjects (Biography, American History, Crime and Criminals, Sports, Railroads, Business, Science Fiction, Gardening, Cookbooks, Self-Help, etc.), might devote three-quarters of a page to each subject. Biography fills, in fact, a disproportionate, if not surprising, three pages, second only to history's five-and-a-half pages. The biography section combines biography, autobiography, memoirs, letters, and diaries indiscriminately. History titles, by contrast, are divided into three subsections (Military, Civil War, and American) in addition to the general rubric.

These two anecdotes, taken as parables of biography, suggest that the common reader, at least as librarians and booksellers profile her, has certain expectations and habits regarding this genre. First, this reader has a general, even perhaps a generalizing appetite for the stories of other people's lives. Few readers, if any, would literally confuse biographical accounts of real people with novels about fictional characters, however closely novels may sometimes mimic life writing, written in third person or first person, in everything from title (*The History of Tom Jones, a Foundling; The Life and Strange Surprizing Adventures of Robinson Crusoe; Oronooko, or the Royal Slave*) to the plot-patterning which dramatizes by theme, symbol, and imagery "the progress of the protagonist from cradle to grave."[2] But readers may indeed find similar appetites aroused and satisfied by these two forms. Second, readers of history apparently have more specialized, discrete tastes in the kinds of history they read, while readers of lives have more ranging, eclectic, and encompassing tastes.

My two anecdotes also give an effective, if not subtle, historical overview of the relations among biography, fiction, and history, situated traditionally in a tug-of-war with biography in the middle. This placement gives a picture of biography's aims and challenges, assets and liabilities for writers and its rich complications and pleasures for readers. Reference librarians, who would prefer to have biography shelved near history, exemplify a tradition that identifies biography as a subgenre of history. The library patrons, who certainly know the difference between the biography of an actual person and a novel about a fictional character, tend, nonetheless, to associate the imaginative satisfactions offered by these two genres and the conventions employed to achieve them. I will turn to these matters in more detail, first in the general introduction and critical history and then in the close readings of exemplary titles.

This book is divided into five chapters. Chapter 1 gives an introductory critical-historical overview of biography from its beginnings in the preclassical period to the present. Chapters 2 through 4 give close readings of selected biographies. Chapter 5 surveys group and collective biographies and biographical series.

A bibliographic essay on the secondary literature and a selected list of recommended biographies conclude the study. The long central portion of this book, chapters 2 through 4, examines majority and minority biography. The terms *majority* and *minority biography* focus attention on several issues of difference and debate in the history and theory of biography: (1) the subject being or not being a member of the dominant culture (for our purposes, this means Anglo-American); (2) the author being or not being a member of the dominant culture; (3) the subject being or not being a conventional candidate for biography, i.e., one whose importance and interest go without saying; (4) construction of the subject's identity different from majority biography, often with greater emphasis on group contexts in which the subject lived and worked; and (5) implicit or explicit cross-examination of the manner, methods, and assumptions of majority biography. Minority biography has profound reasons to examine the degree to which "the prospects for biography in any society," as Noel C. Manganyi has commented, "are related to structural and institutional forces that define and sustain a culture," and hence to probe elements assumed in or repressed by the dominant form.[3]

Majority biography is exemplified by Samuel Johnson and Virginia Woolf, both of whom are important, influential biographers and theorists of the form, in addition to being subjects of many notable biographies. The examination of minority biography in chapter 4 takes Alice James and Langston Hughes as its subjects. The exemplary biographies chosen for discussion are all literary biographies, which is to say career biographies of writers.[4] I have made this choice, which like all choices involves assets and associated liabilities, to reflect the growing popularity of writers' lives. Over the past 200 years, professional writers have surpassed the former leading candidates of biographical interest in Western culture: royalty, saints, and military heroes. Writers, beginning in the late seventeenth century, became the new heroes of modern print culture and expanding literacy. Their lives also became templates for post-Renaissance notions of the relation between public and private self, the Western invention of individual identity, and the foundational concept of the reality of a psychological life.

Literary biography, in the Western tradition, particularly its Anglo-American manifestations, is the quintessential form of modern life writing, although authors might seem to be among the least likely unlikely candidates for biography, given how much time they must spend alone. By comparison with the externalized drama of an athlete's career "as it rises toward mastery and then declines with the symptoms of age" or of a politician's life involved in the visible sweep of events, writers, Andrew Delbanco observes, "may live in outward monotony."[5] Nonetheless, literary biography has achieved and maintained an emblematic predominance in Western European and Anglo-American traditions of life writing, particularly the latter, for which Richard Altick offers the following explanation:

> Until Boswell's time, most biographies, in the English tongue, at least, had been written about saints, divines, monarchs, statesmen, soldiers, retired courtesans, and highwaymen. But ever since, steadily edging out the pious, the powerful, and the perverse, one class had claimed the center of the biographial stage: the men and women who have created our literature. The life of the poet, as Lionel Trilling has remarked, nowadays is "the paradigm of all biography." For reasons that lie deep in social and cultural history, as well as in homely human preference, people have liked, and continue to like, to read the lives of authors. . . . Literary biography has shared in, and profited by, the general shift of literary interest from external action to the inner spectacle of the mind and feelings. . . . The peculiar attraction of literary biography is essentially that of the psychological novel and the confessional lyic.[6]

Altick identifies the pervasive effects of the Romantic revolution's guiding interest in the soul's interior drama, an episode in modern Western consciousness with substantial implications for a cultural explanation of how and why there are so many Anglo-American literary lives.[7] From this thumbnail sketch of biography, I turn, after a brief chronology, to survey the genre's history.

For reading all or parts of this manuscript, as they have read other work in the past, with their characteristically frank and informed intelligence, which I can only try to live up to, I am grateful to C. Haskell Hinnant, Fern McClanahan, Catherine N. Parke Sr., and Tom Quirk. My thanks to William L. Andrews, Wayne Barnes, Louis J. Budd, Theodore Dodson, Leon Edel, Tamara Guilford-Davis, Richard A. Hocks, Josephine Johnson, Barbara Krieger, Arnold Krupat, Xingzhong Li, Harald S. Naess,

Naomi Ritter, David Schenker, George C. Schoolfield, Martha Shirky, Tim Sougstad, Heather K. Thomas, Carla Waal, John Wesselmann, and Jeffrey Williams for valuable information. To Ronald Gottesman, series editor, my admiring gratitude for his ranging knowledge and graceful balancing of suggestions, corrections, and encouragement. To Tom Quirk, my husband, and Ann Neal Quirk, our daughter, thank you, as ever, for your fine minds and generous hearts.

Chronology

3rd millenium to 6th century B.C.E.,
Egyptian, Babylonian, and Assyrian kingdoms
        Earliest commemorative inscriptions

Mid to late 4th century B.C.E., Greece
        Isocrates, *Evagoras*; Xenophon, *Memorabilia*; Plato, *Dialogues*; Theophrastus, *Characters*

1st century B.C.E., China
        Szuma Chien, *Records of the Historian*

1st century B.C.E. to 2nd century, Roman Empire
        Cornelius Nepos, *Lives of Eminent Men*; Tacitus, *Life of Agricola*; Suetonius, *Lives of the Caesars*; Plutarch, *Lives of the Noble Greeks and Romans*; Arrian, *Discourses of Epictetus*

Late 1st century, Eastern Mediterranean
        Composition of the Gospels (probable order of composition: between ca. 70 and 110; Mark, Matthew, Luke, John)

Early 3rd century, Rome
        Philostratus, *Life of Apollonius*; Diogenes Laertius, *Lives and Opinions of Eminent Philosophers*

Early 6th century, Greece	Earliest use of *biographia* attributed to Damascius
9th century, Europe and England	Saints' lives, formerly written in Latin,begin being written in vernacular tongues
Ca. 1112–1214, England	Eadmer, *Life of St. Anselm*
Mid–14th century, Italy	Giovanni Boccaccio, *Life of Dante*
Early 15th century, Spain	Fernán Pérez de Guzmán, *Generations and Likenesses*, series of literary portraits
1545–1549, Switzerland	Konrad Gesner, *Bibliotheca Universalis*, early European bio-bibliographical dictionary, published in Latin, Greek, and Hebrew
1550, Italy	Giorgio Vasari, *Lives of the Most Excellent Italian Architects, Painters, and Sculptors*
Mid–16th century, England	William Roper, *Life of Sir Thomas More* (in MS until 17th century); George Cavendish, *Life of Cardinal Wolsey* (circulated in MS, first printed 1641)
1554, France	John Foxe, *Actes and Monuments* (English edition by John Day at Strasbourg, 1563)
1559, France	Jacques Amyot, first translation of Plutarch's *Lives*
1573, France	Antoine Du Verdier, *Prosopographia*, lives of illustrious persons since the beginning of the world, published at Lyons
1579, England	Sir Thomas North, translation of Plutarch's *Lives*
1591, England	Sir Henry Savile, translation of Tacitus's *Agricola*

1605, England	Francis Bacon, *The Advancement of Learning* identifies biography as a distinct kind of historical writing
1606, England	Philemon Holland's translation of Suetonius's *Lives of the Twelve Caesars*
1643–1786, Belgium	*Acta Sanctorum*, lives of saints and martyrs compiled by John Bolland and later Bollandists
1662, England	Thomas Fuller, *History of the Worthies of England* introduces the word *biographist*
1640, 1651, 1665, 1670, 1678; England	Izaak Walton, lives of John Donne, Sir Henry Wotton, Richard Hooker, George Herbert, Bishop Sanderson
1673, France	Louis Moréri, *Le grand dictionnaire*, first to include biographical section
1683, England	John Dryden, *Life of Plutarch*, prefatory to translation of the *Lives*, uses *biography* in the modern sense of "the history of particular men's lives"
Late 17th century, England	John Aubrey, *Minutes of Lives* (later entitled *Lives of Eminent Men*; better known as *Brief Lives*, published 1813; fuller editions 1890 and 1931)
1691–1692, England	Anthony Wood, *Athenae Oxonienses*, biographical dictionary of authors and bishops
Ca. 1718–1730s, England	Roger North, *General Preface* and *The Lives of Francis North, Dudley North, John North*, 1742–1744; Augustus Jessop edition, 1890
1744, England	Samuel Johnson, *Life of Richard Savage*
1750, 1759; England	Johnson, *Rambler* No. 60 (13 October 1750) on biography; *Idler* No. 84 (24 November 1759) on autobiography

1763, England	James Boswell meets Samuel Johnson (16 May 1763) and shortly thereafter decides to write his biography
1774, England	William Mason, *Memoirs of the Life and Writings of Thomas Gray* introduces substantial familiar correspondence into the biographical narrative
1777, England	Johnson contracts with London booksellers to write *Prefaces Biographical and Critical to the Works of the English Poets* (also published separately as *Lives of the English Poets*)
1779–1781, England	Johnson, *Lives of the English Poets*
1785, England	Boswell, *The Journal of a Tour to the Hebrides with Samuel Johnson, LL.D.*, experiments with techniques used in the subsequent *Life of Johnson*
1786, England	Hester Lynch Thrale Piozzi, *Anecdotes of the Late Samuel Johnson*
1787, England	Sir John Hawkins, *Life of Samuel Johnson*
1791, England	Boswell, *Life of Johnson* (important 3rd rev. ed. 1799; G. B. Hill, rev. L. F. Powell, 1934–1964)
1835–1900, Europe	Multivolume dictionaries of national biography undertaken in various European countries. Sweden (1835–1837), Holland (1852–1878), Austria (1856–1891), Belgium (begun 1866), Germany (1878–1900)
1836, England	*Johnsoniana: Anecdotes of the Late Samuel Johnson LL.D.*, ed. Robina Napier (1886 rev. ed.)
1837–1838, England	J. G. Lockhart, *Life of Sir Walter Scott*; 1848 popular abridgment also by Lockhart
1841, England	Thomas Carlyle, *On Heroes, Hero-Worship and the Heroic in History*

1843–1865, France	*Biographie universelle ancienne et moderne,* ed. M. Michaud
1850, United States	Ralph Waldo Emerson, *Representative Men*
1856, England	Thomas Macaulay, *Samuel Johnson* (rpt. in *The Encyclopaedia Britannica* until 1965)
1856, Argentina	Bartolomé Mitre, *Biographical Studies*
1857, England	Elizabeth Gaskell, *The Life of Charlotte Brontë*
1865, United States	Lydia Maria Child, *The Freedmen's Book*
1885– , England	*Dictionary of National Biography,* founded by George Smith, 1882, ed. Leslie Stephen and later Sidney Lee (1885–1901), 22 vols., with later supplements, now every five years
1897, United States	*Chambers Biographical Dictionary* (most recent revision, 1969)
1908, 1933; United States	Gertrude Stein, *Three Lives, The Autobiography of Alice B. Toklas, Four in America*
1909–1952, England	A. L. Reade, *Johnsonian Gleanings,* 10 vols.
1910, Germany	Sigmund Freud, *Leonardo da Vinci and a Memory of His Childhood*
1914, 1916, 1922, 1932; United States	Gamaliel Bradford, *Confederate Portraits, Union Portraits, American Portraits 1875–1900, Biography and the Human Heart*
1917, United States	First Pulitzer Prize for Biography (or Autobiography) awarded to Laura E. H. Richards, Maud H. Elliott, and Florence H. Hall for *Julia Ward Howe* (1916)
1918, 1921; England	Lytton Strachey, *Eminent Victorians, Queen Victoria* (James Tait Black Memorial Prize for Biography in Great Britain)
1918, United States	Charles Eastman, *Indian Heroes and Great Chieftains*

BIOGRAPHY

1919, England	First James Tait Black Memorial Prize for Biography awarded by the University of Edinburgh for *Samuel Butler, Author of Erewhon (1835–1902)—a Memoir* by H. Festing Jones
1927, England	Harold Nicolson, *The Development of English Biography*
1928– , United States	*Dictionary of American Biography*, originally 21 vols., with later supplements
1928, 1933, 1939, 1940; England	Virginia Woolf, "The New Biography," and *Orlando, Flush,* "The Art of Biography," *Roger Fry: A Biography*
1923, 1928, 1952; France	André Maurois, *Life of Shelley, Aspects of Biography, Life of George Sand*
1940– , United States	*Current Biography* (monthly publication of biographical sketches and obituary notices of people prominent in their fields)
1941, 1955, 1970, 1979; United States	James L. Clifford, *Hester Lynch Piozzi (Mrs.Thrale), Young Sam Johnson, From Puzzles to Portraits: Problems of a Literary Biographer, Dictionary Johnson: Samuel Johnson's Middle Years*
1947, 1952, 1971; France	Jean-Paul Sartre, lives of Baudelaire, Jean Genet, Gustave Flaubert
1948, 1959, 1971, 1973, 1987; England and United States	Richard Ellmann, *Yeats: The Man and the Masks; James Joyce; Literary Biography; Golden Codgers: Biographical Speculations; Oscar Wilde* (Pulitzer Prize)

1953–1957, United States	Ernest Jones, *The Life and Work of Sigmund Freud*, 3 vols.: vol. 1, *The Formative Years and the Great Discoveries, 1856–1900*; vol. 2, *Years of Maturity, 1901–1919*; vol. 3, *The Last Phase, 1919–1939*
1953–1973, 1957, 1962, 1984; United States	Leon Edel, *Literary Biography*; *The Conquest of London* and *The Middle Years*, vols. 2 and 3 of the five-volume *Henry James* (Pulitzer Prize); *Writing Lives: Principia Biographica*
1958, 1959, 1975; United States	Erik H. Erikson, *Young Man Luther: A Study in Psychoanalysis and History*; *Identity and the Life Cycle*; *Life History and the Historical Moment*
1959–1965, United States	George D. Painter, *Proust*, 2 vols.
1962– , United States	*Contemporary Authors: A Bio-bibliographical Guide to Current Authors and their Works*
1971, England	First Whitbread Literary Award for Biography awarded by the Booksellers Association of Great Britain for *Philip Larkin: A Writer's Life* by Andrew Motion
1972, United States	Quentin Bell, *Virginia Woolf: A Biography*
1974, England	John Wain, *Samuel Johnson: A Biography*
1975, United States	R. W. B. Lewis, *Edith Wharton: A Biography* (Pulitzer Prize); First National Book Critics Circle Award for Biography/Autobiography to *Mary McCarthy and Her World* by Carol Brightman

1977, United States	W. Jackson Bate, *Samuel Johnson* (Pulitzer Prize); First Edgar Allan Poe Critical/Biographical Award to the *Encyclopedia of Mystery and Detection*
1978– , United States	*Biography: An Interdisciplinary Quarterly* (Biographical Research Center, University of Hawaii); *Dictionary of Literary Biography*
1979, 1979, 1994; United States	Frederick R. Karl, *Joseph Conrad: The Three Lives; Franz Kafka, Representative Man;* Editor, *Biography and Source Studies*
1979–1982 United States	*American Women Writers: A Critical Reference Guide from Colonial Times to the Present*, 4 vols.
1980, United States	Jean Strouse, *Alice James: A Biography*
1981, United States	First International Symposium on Biography, Biographical Research Center, University of Hawaii
1986–1987, United States	Arnold Rampersad, *The Life of Langston Hughes*, 2 vols., *Volume 1 1902–1941, I, Too, Sing America* (1986); *Volume 2 1941–1967, I Dream a World (1988)*
1990– , United States	*Biography* series on Arts & Entertainment Network (profiles including Josephine Baker, Princess Diana, Amelia Earhart, Alfred Hitchcock, Muhammed Ali)
1994, United States	Joan Hedrick, *Harriet Beecher Stowe: A Life* (Pulitzer Prize)
1996, United States	New York University Master of Arts concentration in Literary Biography

Chapter 1

BIOGRAPHY:
AN OVERVIEW OF THE GENRE

The words *biography* and *biographer* in English and their related forms in modern European languages, from the Greek roots *bios*, life, and *graphein*, to write, do not appear until the mid-seventeenth century.[1] The writing of lives, however, and the impulses and aims that have inspired such writing date back several thousand years. The twin urges for immediate fame and subsequent immortality inspired the earliest records of powerful people's lives. Commemorative writings aimed to reach beyond, if not entirely to circumvent, the finitude of human life, while their subjects, materials, and audiences served simultaneously as constant reminders of the flux and mutability inspiring biography's memorializing function.

In ancient Egypt the formulaic accounts of Pharaohs' lives praised the continuity of dynastic power. Although typically written in the first person, these pronouncements are public, general testimonials, not personal utterances. This practice continued in Babylonia and later in Assyria, where it took the form of chronicles, introducing temporality into the genre and diverging from such earlier atemporal or transtemporal formulas as,

"I am the king, I am the lord, I am the exalted, the great, the strong, I am famous, I am the prince, I am the noble, the powerful in war, I am a lion, I am a hero of youthful strength."[2] However much modern readers may wish to flatter themselves that biography has progressed in subtlety of technique, variety of forms, and self-awareness about its aims, methods, and responsibilities since the appearance of these ancient documents, it would be a mistake not to recognize that the primary urges to celebrate, commemorate, and immortalize, the impulse of life against death, have continued to be among the chief motives for writing lives.

Classical Greece and Rome developed flourishing biographical traditions. Portraits of eminent statesmen and generals appeared in the historical writings of Herodotus, Thucydides, Xenophon, and Polybius in Greece and in work of the Roman historians, Livy, Tacitus, and Dio Cassius. The first century B.C.E. Chinese Grand Historian, Szuma Chien, composed *Records of the Historian* (104–91 B.C.E.), a series of biographies narrating an official history. Szuma Chien's portraits introduced a new form of highly realistic historical writing in China. The biographer broke with formulaic utterances, used vernacular language, and interwove anecdote, conversation, and illustrative detail.[3] He concludes each portrait with interpretive summary, usually including a moral, exemplified in this passage from the life of Han Hsin:

> *When I visited Huaiyin, the local people told me* that even while a common citizen Han Hsin was not like ordinary people. At the time of his mother's death he could not afford to give her a funeral, yet he found a high burial ground with room enough for ten thousand households to settle. *I visited his mother's grave and confirmed that this was true. . . .* Had Han Hsin followed the Way [of Confucius] and been more modest instead of boasting of his achievements and glorying in his ability, all would have been well. . . . But instead he attempted to revolt when the empire was united. To have his family wiped out was no more than he deserved. (Szuma Chien, 286–87, my emphasis)

Szuma Chien's remarks also demonstrate the operations of biographical skepticism and primary research, which twentieth-century biography cannot claim to have invented.

As early as the fourth century B.C.E. in the Western tradition, biography began to be distinguished from general history as a separate rhetorical form. Two principal lines emerged: historical biography chronicling the subject's entire life, and popular biography recounting notable incidents and sayings with little or no attempt to establish chronology or to depict the subject in historical context. Among the earliest accounts of an individual life is *Evagoras* (ca. 365 B.C.E), a discourse on the King of Cyprus (ca. 411–374 B.C.E.), written by the Attic orator and teacher Isocrates. This life was followed shortly by the *Memorabilia*, Xenophon's homage to his teacher Socrates. This late-fourth-century B.C.E. text consists of separate pieces, later combined, though not by Xenophon. The *Memorabilia* includes an account of Socrates's philosophy and personal anecdotes about this famous man, organized topically and beginning with a lengthy critique of the state's charges against Socrates for rejecting the gods and corrupting youth.

Though not formal biography, the *Memorabilia* introduced several subsequently important characteristics of the genre. First, Xenophon's choice of Socrates as his subject departed from conventional subjects since Socrates was a man of popular interest chiefly in and for himself, not a king or general. Second, Xenophon placed a new exploratory emphasis on the subject's work in relation to the life. Third, he used anecdotes, which include conversation, though of uncertain reliability, to enliven the portrait, as, for example, in the opening of book 2, where Socrates exhorts Aristippus to practice temperance in all things, beginning with the question: "Tell me, Aristippus, if you were required to take charge of two youths and educate them so that the one would be fit to rule and the other would never think of putting himself forward, how would you educate them? Shall we consider it, beginning with the elementary question of food?"[4]

Plato who, like Xenophon, knew Socrates personally, collected his teacher's lectures. By contrast with Xenophon's depiction of a "wise, simple, friendly, moral instructor," Plato depicts a "provocative disturber of mental and civic rest and assumption."[5] Plato's late-fourth-century B.C.E. *Dialogues,* while not a formal narrative biography, is generally agreed to present a coherent, dramatic portrait of Socrates the thinker, particularly in the early dialogues, the *Charmides, Euthyphro,* and *Ion,* where Socrates is less the lecturer and more the dramatic inquirer.

These two early instances of personal acquaintance between biographers and their subjects introduce an issue with a long history of actively debated pros and cons. Acquaintance is still con-

BIOGRAPHY

sidered by many biographers and readers alike to be an empowering qualification, if not an essential one, for writing a life. Much
of the power and authority of the four New Testament Gospels—
aside from considerations of the historical complexities of actual
authorship—are understood to derive from their being written
by men who knew the historical Jesus. In the mid-Renaissance
William Roper announced his competence to write the *Life of Sir
Thomas More* (ca. 1570) on the basis of being More's son-in-law
who had lived in More's house for more than fifteen years. Four
centuries later Tom Clark, Rock Hudson's publicist and house-
mate of twenty years, argues the authority of *Rock Hudson, Friend
of Mine* (1989) by recounting how friends encouraged him to
write this book, drawing on his intimate knowledge of the man,
in order to correct sensational errors in other Hudson biographies. Eric Lax in *Woody Allen: A Biography* (1991) claims authority
for his book based, in part, on having spent four years watching
Allen make movies and talking with friends and intimates whom
Allen instructed to speak frankly with the biographer.

If biographers' and their subjects' personal acquaintance is
often considered a significant resource for life writing, its accompanying liability of nearly unavoidable bias has almost as often
been viewed as a challenge, sometimes even an outright obstacle,
to the modern ideal of skeptical objectivity. In chapter 2 on
Samuel Johnson I will return to this matter.

Theophrastus, the Greek philosopher of the fourth and late
third century B.C.E., applied to the art of verbal portraiture his
teacher Aristotle's proposition that character, the root word
meaning a mark or stamp, as in the impression on a coin, is best
revealed by acts. The *Characters* is a book of ideal types illustrated
by specific behavior. Theophrastus's types include the irascible
man, the complaisant man, the suspicious man, the boor, the
miser, and the man of petty ambition. Scholar-critics generally
agree that Theophrastus probably drew on acquaintance and
personal experience to compose these portraits. Yet his types are
not informed by the idea of inner individuality so familiar to the
post-Renaissance mind.[6] The *Characters*, revived and translated
into English beginning in the late sixteenth century, influenced
verbal portraiture in drama, poetry, and the newly developing
genres of fiction and nonfiction prose from the Renaissance on.

Biographical writing flourished along with the growth of the
Roman Empire. Inspired by Greek models and adapted to suit

the Roman version of the Greek tradition of family pride, the genre was also applied to express the new politics of imperialism. Tacitus, Suetonius, and Plutarch were the three most popular and important biographers of the first and second centuries and again later, when their work was revived in Renaissance translations. These three writers' achievements identify three distinct aspects of method, form, and subject matter still relevant to the modern theory and practice of biography.

Cornelius Tacitus wrote the life of the soldier-statesman Agricola, who was also his admired father-in-law. Historians of biography have noted the continued predominance of conventional panegyric in this life. Tacitus, for instance, announces as his aim "to publish the records of virtue" to an age hard in spirit and "cynical towards virtue."[7] Yet the biographer's laudatory account of Agricola's career, also notable for its description of the conquest of Britain, is enlivened by the biographer's personal acquaintance and close observation of Agricola, as, for instance, in this passage on his son's death: "In the beginning of the summer Agricola suffered a domestic blow: he lost the son born a year before. He took the loss neither with bravado, like most strong men, nor yet with the lamentations and mournings of a woman. Among other things, he turned for comfort to fighting" (Tacitus, 219).

Suetonius, a contemporary of Tacitus, wrote the highly popular *Lives of the Caesars*. By virtue of the biographer's industrious gathering of facts, anecdotes, and sayings, and the celebrated or infamous reputations of his subjects, these lives have been called the first tell-all biographies. Light on interpretation and understanding but full of riveting, often scandalous detail about famous people, Suetonius's life of Gaius Caligula is perhaps the most dramatic of all the portraits. The biographer depicts Caligula's melodramatic cruelty and viciousness, including incestuous relations with his sisters, fascination with executions and torture, chronic gluttony, adultery. He gives hideous details about the emperor's dark-spotted corpse, froth at the mouth, and a heart that withstood cremation, suggesting to contemporaries his having been poisoned by one of the many people who had reason to despise him. Suetonius, whose *Caesars* was translated into English by Philemon Holland in 1606, also began writing another collective biography, the lives of the eminent grammarians, rhetoricians, and poets, apparently never completed.

BIOGRAPHY

The work of Tacitus and Suetonius, translated into most modern European languages during the Renaissance, assuredly influenced life writers of both their own and later periods. But it was Plutarch's *Parallel Lives* (forty-six Greek and Roman biographies of military and political leaders, including Lucullus and Cimon, Alexander and Caesar, Demosthenes and Cicero, each Greek paired with a Roman to shed light on one another), composed around the beginning of the second century, that stands as the distinct predecessor of modern biography, which subsequently branched out into the lives of other professionals in the arts and sciences. Plutarch, like his predecessor Cornelius Nepos, the first-century-B.C.E. author of an earlier important collection of *Lives of Eminent Men,* which survives only in part,[8] announced a clear distinction between history and biography. History describes what people do, Plutarch affirms, while biography reveals who they are. Since their primary aim was not to write history but to dramatize character, both Nepos and Plutarch emphasized the selective presentation of anecdote and detail rather than an exhaustive chronological narrative. In the following passage Plutarch illustrates Alcibiades's "mightiest passions," his "love of rivalry and love of preeminence," in the following story recorded of the Athenian statesman and general's childhood: "He was once hard pressed in wrestling, and to save himself from getting a fall, set his teeth in his opponent's arms, where they clutched him, and was like to have bitten through them. His adversary, letting go his hold, cried: 'You bite, Alcibiades, as women do!' 'Not I,' said Alcibiades, 'but as lions do.'"[9] Plutarch's identification of a distinct formal and conceptual space for biography is a key event in the history of the genre. Chiefly a moralist, his guiding notion was the image of the virtuous man, which is to say the heroic man, and he wrote lives to dramatize this idea.

Plutarch was not a scholar first and foremost, as scholar would come later to be defined in terms of responsibility to historiographical standards, generally agreed upon methods, and criteria for gathering, assessing, interpreting and judging evidence. But he was highly conscious of the distinctive project he had undertaken. Plutarch was an artist who considered biography to be both educationally substantive and imaginatively pleasurable. His enduring reputation, his revival during the Renaissance, and influence on subsequent major writers, including Shakespeare and Dryden, all

6

testify to Plutarch's success as a biographer who, by Ralph Waldo Emerson's estimate, "will be perpetually rediscovered from time to time as long as books last."[10]

Other notable classical biographers of the first three centuries were Arrian (*Discourses of Epictetus*, the stoic philosopher with whom Arrian had studied, ca. 60), Philostratus (life of Apollonius, the philosopher Tyana, composed from oral and written sources and from the *Lives of the Sophists*, early third century), and Diogenes Laertius *(Lives and Opinions of Eminent Philosophers*, also early third century).

The Christian era applied biography to its educational mission of dramatizing the life and spreading the teachings of Jesus. The four Gospels, thought to have been composed between ca. 70 and 110, combine depictions of the earthly and spiritual aspects of Jesus's life with an explication and exhortation of his teachings. Reminiscent of their pre-Christian predecessors, including popular biographies of Epictetus, Apollonius, and Socrates, the first three Gospels (Mark, Matthew, and Luke), which present similar but not identical accounts of their subject, praise their protagonist, gather and interpret his best sayings, and, in so doing, attempt to convince readers that studying Jesus's life, works, and words is essential to their spiritual welfare. The Gospel of John, less readily recognizable as a biographical narrative, is a philosophical and visionary meditation on the meaning of Jesus's life and death.

As time passed and the Apocalypse, originally predicted to arrive before the second century, did not come, the early Church began making institutional plans for a prolonged earthly mission. These plans included commemorating lives of saints and martyrs, first in the form of saint's-day calendars, then gradually developing into narrative accounts. The ninth century marks a significant divide between the lives composed in Latin and Greek, intended for clergy who could read, and the production of more explicitly didactic lives written in the vernacular. These latter hortatory biographies, often intended as materials for sermons delivered to nonreaders, may also possibly have been read by a larger lay audience.

Students of biography generally agree that the early Christian era was an unhappy digression from the line of development of modern biography stretching back to Plutarch. This lineage defines the genre as the reconstructon of an individual life in historical context, combining thorough scholarship with skeptical assessment of evidence and sympathetic engagement. Modern biography's chief aim is understood to be neither praise nor blame, at least not explicitly so, nor is didacticism understood to be its driving motive. Medieval hagiography, when judged by post-Medieval standards informed by the scientific revolution of the seventeenth century, may seem incompetent, naive, or both. Yet there is, of course, as with all such issues, another side to the story. Sacred biographers saw no necessary contradiction between the worlds of fact and legend. Both fact and legend were for them signs of fundamental truth about the nature of things in relation to the realm of the spirit. These were different evidentiary signs from those which the modern scientific world of the sixteenth century and after would find convincing. But in terms of this period's standards and beliefs, these signs were understood to reveal unimpeachable and indispensably educative truth. The sacred biographers' aim of instruction recognized imagination as an accurate lens to focus on essential, which is to say holy, truths. Popular lives of St. Christina, for instance, describe a scene in which the protagonist's faith and purity are tested by enemies tossing poisonous snakes on her head and shoulders. The snakes are miraculously changed into "small infaunts" who suckle from St. Christina's breasts and "custe hure" (kissed her).[11]

The perceived interconnections among reason and fantasy, imagination and truth, and the earthly and spiritual realms that characterize the world view underwriting sacred biography were severely scrutinized during the early modern scientific period of the sixteenth and early seventeenth centuries. Distinction and commensurability became more highly valued ways of thinking than fusion and the identification of symbolic interconnections. These changes informed the ways in which life was conceived of and recounted. The subsequent Enlightenment emphasis on distinguishing reason from fantasy and common sense from imagination resulted in skeptical discounting of medieval sacred biographies. The word *hagiography* has became synonymous with biographical irresponsibility, as, for example, in these remarks on a life of the baseball player Ted Williams: "The only other creditable full length biography [of Williams] has been characterized even by novelist John Updike, a truly unreconstructed Williams fan, as a 'hagiography.' Williams deserves something other . . .

than sainthood."[12] The Middle Ages might not have made Williams a saint, but it would not have agreed that a human being could deserve something better than sainthood. And in this difference it is evident how cultural beliefs and values essentially inform biography.

One culture's ways of thinking may appear foolish, ignorant, or self-deluded to people living in another time or place, judgments which would doubtless surprise the original thinkers. Thus there is often much to be learned about a particular period by studying the ways it tells lives and the purposes it conceives for biography. When, for example, the twentieth-century biographer James L. Clifford recounts the anecdote of how Agnellus, mid-ninth-century Bishop of Ravenna, prayed to God and fellow believers to provide missing documentary evidence to complete a series of saints' lives, Clifford finds fault with the bishop's scholarship. But the bishop held himself accountable to other values and criteria than the secular, skeptical standards which were to become methodological commonplaces of post-Enlightenment biographical research.[13] Modern biography holds itself accountable to standards of objective scholarship, as exemplified in this passage from a biography of Dizzy Dean written for young readers: "Some anonymous railroad conductor (his name cannot even be determined at this late date) saw Diz pitch, either for the Twelfth Field Artillery or for the Public Service Corps. Whoever he was, he knew a pitcher when he saw one and he reported his find to Don Curtis."[14] Regarding the two issues of evidence reported in this passage, the small but meaningful details of the railroad conductor and the first team Dean pitched for, the biographer goes no farther than documentation can support.

The scientific and humanistic revolutions of the Renaissance and following did not bring an immediate end to saints' lives, which continued to be written into the sixteenth and seventeenth centuries. Among the most famous is John Foxe's *Actes and Monuments*, better known as the *Book of Martyrs*, a history of the Christian Church told through the lives of martyrs (Latin edition, 1554; first English translation, 1563), and the *Acta Sanctorum*, undertaken by the Flemish Jesuit John Bolland, which began appearing in 1643 and continued into the next century. The latter has been identified as the first biographical dictionary compiled in Europe.[15]

A few generally agreed upon exceptions to modern scholars' typically low assessment of medieval biography include the early-twelfth-century life of St. Anselm, Archbishop of Canterbury, written by the English monk Eadmer, called by Harold Nicolson "the first 'pure' biography" written in England;[16] and secular lives, such as a ninth-century life of Charlemagne by the Frankish noble and historian Einhard. These lives diverge from formulaic patterns, demonstrate the authors' commitment to factual accuracy, if not a thoroughgoing skepticism, and exhibit a distinct consciousness of their genre.

The hallmark of the fourteenth-century Italian Renaissance was humanism's ranging, temporal, secular curiosity, which revived interest in Greek and Roman achievements, biography central among them. Humanism also placed a distinctive new emphasis on the individual that renewed fascination and experimentation with this genre. Giovanni Boccaccio's life of Dante and Filippo Villani's *Lives of Illustrious Florentines* exemplify modern developments that trace back to the two main tendencies of early Hellenistic and Roman biography: (1) individual lives developing out of the rhetorical techniques of praise and criticism, more often the former than the latter; and (2) collective biographies of philosophers, painters, musicians, grammarians, and other practitioners of specialized skills and arts, developing out of the Peripatetics' encyclopedic interest in knowledge and technical skill.[17] Villani's late-sixteenth-century lives are a collection of sketches of successful secular figures, artists, scholars, soldiers, and politicians. This early modern collective biography, a form increasingly popular beginning in the Renaissance, examines the subjects' lives in relation to their work.

Collective biography and dictionaries of biography, more fully treated in chapter 5, such as Villani's and his fellow Italian Giorgio Vasari's *Lives of the Most Excellent Italian Architects, Painters, and Sculptors* (1550), tend to develop during periods of nationalistic and imperialistic expansion, such as characterize Anglo-European history from the sixteenth into the late nineteenth centuries. Noteworthy examples are Konrad Gesner's *Bibliotheca Universalis* (Geneva, 1545–1549), the earliest European bio-bibliographical dictionary of authors and their writings in Latin, Greek, and Hebrew; Antoine du Verdier's *Prosopographia, ou description des personnes insignes* (Lyons, 1573), a universal biographical dictionary listing as its chief categories patriarchs, prophets, religious figures, heads of state, philosophers, orators, poets and inventors; Pierre Bayle's *Dictionnaire historique et critique* (1697; English translation 1734), an important early work of scientific biography and critique of religion and legend, with entries including actual historical figures, typically those who had not been treated adequately in other sources (Lacydes, the Greek philosopher, Arngrimus Jonas, the sixteenth- and seventeenth-century Icelandic historian, Joseph Hall, the seventeenth-century English prelate), sects and movements (Manicheans, Paulicians, Mammilarians), and mythico-religious figures (Jupiter, Chrysis, Abimelech, David); and finally Samuel Johnson's *Lives of the English Poets* (1779–1781).

Johnson, late in his career, was approached by a group of London publishers to write biographical-critical prefaces for an edition of the works of the English poets—Addison, Butler, Cowley, Dryden, Gray, Milton, and Pope, to name only a handful of the fifty-two authors included. This publishing venture was calculated to rival an edition already in production by a Scottish firm. This commission indicates the publishers' assessment of the project's marketability, especially when combined with Johnson's biographical prefaces. Johnson's fifty-two essays on Restoration and early-eighteenth-century writers narrate collectively a history of the early years of modern professional writing, unfolding in the new world of the printed book and expanding literacy.

Other group biographies, such as Bartolomé Mitre's collection of short biographies of Argentine national heroes, *Biografías estudios* (1856), were sometimes written to support independence movements or other nationalistic agendas. Throughout Europe, beginning in Sweden with the publication of the twenty-three volume Swedish dictionary of national biography (1835–1857), the new nation states, including Holland, Austria, Germany, and England, published multivolume works to narrate national history through the lives of its major participants. Lydia Maria Child, a white abolitionist, wrote *The Freedmen's Book* (1865), a textbook for use in freedmen's schools, which contains, among other pieces, short biographies of exemplary figures, Toussaint L'Ouverture, Benjamin Banneker, Phillis Wheatley, and Frederick Douglass notable among them. The author, in her dedication "To the Freedmen," describes the project in the following way that demonstrates how biography's ethical-exemplary-historical dimensions have remained vigorous since its origins: "I have prepared this book expressly for you, with the hope that those of you who can read will read it aloud to others, and that all of you will derive fresh strength and courage from this true record of what colored men [sic] have accomplished, under great disadvantages."[18]

The history of modern translations of Plutarch's collection of famous Greeks and Romans gives one measure of the Renaissance's energetic interest in biography. By the mid-sixteenth century Plutarch had been translated into French by Jacques Amyot (1559). Shortly thereafter a version by Sir Thomas North (1579) appeared in English, followed by Sir Henry Savile's translation of Tacitus's *Agricola* (1591) and Philemon Holland's *Suetonius* (1606), all within a half century.

The composition of original, contemporary lives accompanied this flurry of translation from the classical period of biography. Distinguished examples include William Roper's mid-sixteenth-century life of his father-in-law, Sir Thomas More, and, in the same period, a life of Cardinal Wolsey written by his gentleman usher, George Cavendish, circulated in manuscript but not printed until 1641. Cavendish's work exemplifies Johnson's later observation that "More knowledge may be gained of a man's real character by a short conversation with one of his servants, than from a formal and studied narrative, begun with his pedigree, and ended with his funeral."[19] While praise and commemoration still seem to be Roper's and Cavendish's chief motivations, both biographies bear lively marks of intimate familiarity between author and subject. Two hundred years later, James Boswell would recombine these elements of commemoration and intimacy with agile self-awareness, bravado, and literary sophistication in the *Life of Samuel Johnson.*

During the early modern period the assumptions and methods of the new science distributed its effects among other disciplines and arts. Historians of biography typically assert that the new science, with its emphasis on experience, the inductive search for truth in a world of particulars, and the critique of traditional authority, combined with Christian humanism's and Puritanism's valuing of the individual conscience and consciousness to constitute a new world view distinctly hospitable to biography. During this period biography and autobiography, little distinction being made between the two until after the seventeenth century, were metonymies for vital cultural revolutions. Life writing was not merely the result of but also the signifier and vehicle of changes that ushered in the modern era of the seventeenth and eighteenth centuries. Among these changes were new conceptions of personal and cultural identity associated with the notion of the secular individual, the explosion of print culture and other technologies of mass production, increased literacy, imperialistic exploration, new global trade and commercialism, and a heightened interest in childhood as a distinct phase of existence, all of which combined to produce new senses of what constitutes a life, its possibilities and meanings, and the reasons for and ways of telling a life story.[20]

Biography now became a fully separate branch of literature, the record of a life used not merely as an opportunity for celebrating certain ideal qualities or as an occasion for discussing broad philosophical, religious, or historical ideas and issues but examined for its own sake, Edmund Gosse observes, in its singleness, even its singularity.[21]

At the outset of the seventeenth century, biography began to shift its creative center of gravity to England, as this nation entered its most active period of commerical, technological, and cultural global expansion, matters whose generative relations with life writing I will return to at the end of this chapter. Sir Francis Bacon, in *The Advancement of Learning* (1605), proposed a three-part distinction among the kinds of history, biography being one of these. He catalogued history as *chronicles* (representing time), *lives* (representing people), and *narrations* or *relations* (representing action). Of these forms, he prefers lives, noting that "if they be well written, propounding to themselves a person to represent in whom actions both greater and smaller, public and private, have a commixture, must of necessity contain a more true, native, and lively representation."[22] Bacon encouraged life writing, noting this genre's curious scarcity in an age when active empirical investigation in other areas should also have motivated similar scientific interest in biography. Whether or not directly traceable to Bacon's urging, many more lives were being written by the end of his century than at the beginning.

The first appearance of the word *biographer*, in the variant form *biographist*, is attributed to Thomas Fuller's *History of the Worthies of England* (1662). Fuller notes the "want of honest hearts in the

Biographists of these Saints, which betrayed their pens to such abominable untruths."[23] The biographer's primary responsibility to truthfulness appears early in the history of the poetics of this genre.

John Dryden's *Life of Plutarch*, prefatory to a translation of *Plutarch's Lives* (1683) by several hands, provides the earliest, most developed description of the genre in English: "[In] *Biographia*, or the history of particular men's lives . . . all things here are circumscribed and driven to a point. . . . [H]ere you are led into the private lodgings of the hero; you see him in undress, and are made familiar with his most private actions and conversations."[24] Dryden's remarks focus on the distinguishing particularity of the life and the intimacy of the evidence. He admires Plutarch for displacing the public record as sufficient source of evidence for a life.

The new science's fascination with empirically verifiable evidence fueled the antiquarian and scholarly inquiries of such writers as Anthony Wood, a contemporary of Dryden and author of the first English biographical dictionary of authors (1691–1692). John Aubrey, Wood's assistant, also wrote a collection of lives. Though less devoted to authorized facts, these biographies recreate a felt sense of life, personality, and circumstantial particularity that account for the enduring appeal of Aubrey's work better known by its later title, *Brief Lives*.

Izaak Walton was the third major biographer of the seventeenth century. Walton, in his lives of the poets and clerics John Donne (1640) and George Herbert (1670) and of the theologians Richard Hooker (1665) and Bishop Sanderson (1678), gave nearly equal attention to accurate detail regarding character and career and to satisfying narrative which includes substantial accounts of people formatively significant in his subjects' lives. Walton, in the *Life of Herbert*, for instance, describes Herbert's mother in what he refers to as "my promis'd account." He characterizes Lady Herbert's understanding of her children's temperament as being so astute to the need to balance instruction and pleasure that she managed the education of her oldest son "without rigid sourness." In addition, she became a valued friend and correspondent of Donne (Walton inserts the detail that he possesses some of their correspondence) and the subject of Donne's poem "Autumnal Beauty."[25] It is no happenstance that Johnson, the great eighteenth-century theorist and practitioner of biography, admired Walton's *Lives* and planned, though never completed, a new edition.

The history of biography from the eighteenth century to the present is dense and complex, so firmly has the form identified itself with modern Western consciousness and culture. To begin a survey of the past three hundred years it is useful to return briefly to Plutarch, specifically to his two main points about the biographer's reponsibility to method and genre. For though chiefly a moralist and artist, not a genuine scholar as we would recognize the activities involved in that occupation, Plutarch did identify two definitive tenets of the modern form: First, the biographer is responsible for gathering accurate facts.[26] Second, history and biography are not identical. Plutarch makes these distinctions about the form in which he is writing in the *Lives*: "For it is not Histories that I am writing, but Lives; and in the most illustrious deeds there is not always a manifestation of virtue or vice, nay a slight thing like a phrase or a jest often makes a greater revelation of character than battles where thousands fall, or the greatest armaments, or sieges of cities."[27] Plutarch's paired emphases on accurate facts and the interpretation of character have become touchstones of modern biography. Arnold Rampersad, authorized biographer of Langston Hughes, has, for instance, elaborated these criteria in his observation that contemporary biography is characterized by "exhaustiveness of research, an appreciation for accumulated, verified detail . . . and a relative certainty that the life of the subject can be absolutely understood, usually through the application of psychological schemas largely derived from Freud."[28]

Eighteenth-century England produced the first substantial body of critical writings on biography to foster the burgeoning genre. This criticism was motivated by many of the same impulses of experimentation and skepticism that inspired the new science. Johnson, who assimilated and revised the best elements of earlier biographical tradition, became the foremost biographer of his age. His distinctive formal and theoretical contributions, discussed thoroughly in chapter 2, are exemplified in this well known passage from *Rambler* No. 60 (1750), one of his two important essays on biography:

> Those parallel circumstances, and kindred images, to which we readily conform our minds, are, above all other writings, to be found in narratives of the lives of particular persons; and therefore no species of writing seems more worthy of cultivation than biography, since

none can be more delightful or more useful, none can more certainly enchain the heart by irresistible interest, or more widely diffuse instruction to every diversity of condition.[29]

Johnson identifies biography as a particular kind of writing with distinctly powerful psychological effects and widespread ethical uses. This genre appeals first to the reader's emotions, while its chief aim and hence the biographer's chief responsibility is instruction. Like Bacon before him, Johnson urges the "cultivation" of biography.

Johnson's most noteworthy contribution to the poetics of modern biography appears in his observation that "there has rarely passed a life of which a judicious and faithful narrative would not be useful." With this statement he expands the traditional qualifications of the biographical subject (formulaic virtue and conventional greatness), widening the field to include many possible subjects beyond the rich, royal, famous, infamous, and holy.[30]

Johnson wrote biography throughout his career from the late 1730s into the last decade of his life. His *Life of Richard Savage* (1744) was based on personal acquaintance. His *Prefaces Biographical and Critical to the Works of the English Poets* (1779–1781), published also as a separate collection under the more familiar title, *Lives of the English Poets*, was based on a lifetime of reading, writing, and observing human behavior. With Johnson's *Lives*, it is often noted, modern literary biography was underway.

Johnson valued primary materials most highly, the authenticated personal details and evidence such as letters and autobiographical documents, anecdotes, and contemporary accounts which he thought revealed the subject's character most precisely and engaged the reader most pleasurably. He regretted, for instance, that so little of Alexander Pope's authenticated conversation remained even shortly after the poet's death in 1747. In regretting this lack, Johnson identified what has proved to be a perduring modern interest in personality and the documented social and private life of the artist. Johnson's biographer, James Boswell, was alert to the challenge of preventing such losses in the case of another great writer. He decided, not long after meeting Johnson, to begin gathering materials for a life and to interweave the generic and social arts of biographical documentation and friendship in order to write a definitive life of Johnson.

Johnson's theory and practice of biography, underwritten by his profound sense of human frailty (both the subject's and the biographer's), identified by Ellmann as the key to great biography, were brilliantly assimilated by his friend and protégé Boswell.[31] Well read in previous biographies, willing, as he said of himelf, to "run half over London in order to fix a date correctly," a tireless recorder and recreator of conversation, which he understood to be the chief value of his life of Johnson, Boswell set out to write a life to supplant all other lives of Johnson, past, present, and future. His self-announced emphasis on painstaking primary research continues to be a major criterion of the genre. When Robert Creamer opens his life of Babe Ruth with the mock-serious confession "I apologize for not having talked to everybody," he places himself in an investigative tradition tracing back directly to Boswell, who, in turn, credits Johnson for his education in biography.[32]

Boswell masterfully scripts the biographer's double role as part invisible secretary, part self-spotlighted, self-aggrandizing director, in equal parts subservient and managerial. He also recognized the necessity of the reader's co-creative imaginative participation. Even his detractors usually agree, if grudgingly, that Boswell wrote the first definitive modern biography. A wholehearted admirer of Boswell and herself a masterful biographer, Gertrude Stein, acknowledges him as an invaluable mentor. Yet Boswell established a model which, while it may have inspired many, has rarely, if ever, been precisely imitated.

The main difference between Johnson and Boswell as biographers centers on their respective viewpoints regarding the question of what biographers should do to and with their materials. Should they write "biography pure and simple," to borrow George Saintsbury's phrase, in which all the collected materials are passed through the mind of the biographer, few if any materials appearing except in altered, digested, and interpreted form?—which is Johnson's manner. Or should biography be essentially a collection of primary documents (letters, sayings, conversations, anecdotes) connected by minimal narrative or other transition devices provided by the biographer but otherwise unaltered?—which is Boswell's manner. Once established as a question by the appearance of Johnson's and Boswell's fundamentally different kinds of biographical writings, debate on this issue has continued. Technical and conceptual differences aside, Johnson and Boswell would almost certainly have agreed on the fundamentals of the following definition of the genre, a definition all but inconceivable before the eighteenth century: the history of an individual, not a type or exemplar, depicted accurately and fully in domestic and other private settings, set in historical, circumstantial context, and examined skeptically, though not without sympathy.

The work of Johnson and Boswell had been anticipated in their own century by the innovative biographer Roger North. North wrote lives of his three brothers and an essay on biography (ca. 1718 through 1730s), much of this work remaining in manuscript until the nineteenth century and thus probably unavailable to either Johnson or Boswell. North, in the "General Preface," proposes a quintessentially modern poetics of biography based on the greater usefulness of biography over history:

> The history of private lives adapted to the perusal of common men is more beneficial (generally) than the most solemn registers of ages and nations, or the acts and monuments of famed governors, statesmen, prelates, or generals of armies. The gross reason is because the latter contain little if anything comparate or applicable to instruct a private economy, or tending to make a man either wiser or more cautelous [cautious] in his own proper concerns.[33]

The striking similarities among North's, Johnson's, and Boswell's conceptions of biography, again readily apparent in the passage below, lend support to the notion, hardly a surprising one, that the development of modern biography in the eighteenth century, though pioneered by individuals, arose from factors more generally distributed throughout the culture:

> No man at large, who is not expressly qualified, can fairly take upon him to write the life of any other man. They may make gatherings and excerpts out of letters, books, or reports concerning him, but those are memorials, or rather bundles of uncemented materials, but not the life, and it is obnoxious to this shrewd failing that all these gatherings, and the conjectures built upon them, are of course taken as positive truths, of which much or the greatest part most commonly are utter mistakes, and without a due check make a strange history. . . . a man's character is not, and scarce can be, justly represented by mere words in the way of history without some specimens derived from himself, either of his writing, or some speaking testimony of things remaining, and referred to. (North, 77, 80)

North's assertion that to write biography requires training, along with his emphasis on the necessity of autobiographical materials in genuine biography, recurs in Johnson's and Boswell's work only a few years later.

The eighteenth century saw the rise of the professional biographer in the literary marketplace, the cultivation by publishers of an avid reading public, and the appearance of a body of critical writings on the genre. This period's unique equilibrium whereby, as Donald A. Stauffer observes, both the individual and the world were for a time valued as equivalent realities, conditioned contemporaneous developments in the related form of the novel. The novel and biography ran on parallel tracks, borrowing from, imitating, and mutually inspiring one another in the dramatic depiction of the progress and pattern of the protagonist's life in a world of circumstance and contingency. A multitude of novels have titles that blur distinctions between historical life writing and fiction, many of these novels written in the first person: *The Fortunes and Misfortunes of the Famous Moll Flanders* (1722); *The Life and Opinions of Tristram Shandy* (1760–1767); *Evelina, or the History of a Young Lady's Entrance into the World* (1778); *Jane Eyre: An Autobiography* (1847). These fictions, sometimes purporting to be actual life histories, often included quasi-documentary materials, such as letters and diary entries, that were also becoming evidentiary staples of factual biography. Borrowing also occurred in the other direction, as biography adapted techniques from fiction, and both genres learned from drama how to depict scene and character.[34]

While the origins of biography and the novel are substantially allied, the use of fictional techniques and the possibility of soundly interweaving the two forms have been points of chronic dispute. The novelist Henry James, who also wrote biography, believed that only fiction could capture the otherwise elusive qualities of life. "The art of the biographer—devilish art!—is somehow practically *thinning*. It simplifies even while seeking to enrich—& even the Immortal[s] are so helpless & passive in death."[35] Classical and early modern biography, which aimed to commemorate the glorious or edifying meaning of a person's life, took on a simpler task than has modern biography, at least as James here defines it: to find words which, though not the equivalents of life, since this is presumably impossible, are adequate imaginative correlatives of that life. Biography, being nonfiction, could not, according to James, approximate the virtual reality of the imagination.

Less than fifty years after Johnson and Boswell had convincingly argued that panegyric and commemoration are inappropriate aims for modern biography and thus had seemingly put that issue to rest, an emphasis on respectability and the forms of politenesss, associated with Queen Victoria's reign (1837–1901), reintroduced these decorums as responsible proprieties of the genre. When the new biographers of the early twentieth century, Strachey and Woolf among them, looked back on the preceding century, they saw muffled, lifeless, distractingly detailed compilations of sanitized facts or portraits of improbable goodness. Yet as in the case of medieval hagiography, there is at least one other side to the story.

Robert Southey's lives of Admiral Nelson (1813) and John Wesley, the famous Methodist preacher and hymnist (1820), are two exemplary biographies of the early nineteenth century. Subsequently J. G. Lockhart's seven-volume *Life of Sir Walter Scott* (1837–1838), the popular novelist, was both successful and highly regarded as a specimen of the genre in its own time and later in reprints and Lockhart's abridgment. Some critics have praised Lockhart over and above Boswell for his thoroughness and attractive style. Yet this life also met with criticism from contemporary readers, Thomas Carlyle, himself a notable biographer, among them. Carlyle criticized Lockhart for writing a mere compilation of facts, not genuine biography. For Carlyle, to whom I will return shortly, biography must be based on ideas not driven by data. Lockhart, ten years after the first edition of his life of Scott, produced at his publisher's request an abridgment which he described as "more strictly narrative" than the original.

The novelist Elizabeth Gaskell wrote the important *Life of Charlotte Brontë* (1857). This biography, commissioned by Patrick Brontë, Charlotte's father, announces as its aim to depict Brontë the model daughter and wife, not Brontë the professional writer. In spite of its decorum, this biography bears the imaginative energy of Gaskell's fiction in its depiction of scenery and character, frequent citation from primary documents, including juvenilia and especially letters, and its insights into the Brontë family psychology, particularly the Brontë sisters' relations and their artistic collaboration, described in moving detail in the following passage:

It was the household custom among these girls to sew till nine o'clock at night. At that hour, Miss Branwell generally went to bed, and her nieces' duties for the day were accounted done. They put away their work, and began to pace the room backwards and forwards, up and down,—as often with the candles extinguished, for economy's sake, as not,—their figures glancing into the fire-light, and out into the shadow, perpetually. At this time, they talked over past cares, and troubles; they planned for the future, and consulted each other as to their plans. In after years, this was the time for discussing together the plots of their novels. And again, still later, this was the time for the last surviving sister to walk alone, from old accustomed habit, round and round the desolate room, thinking sadly upon the "days that were no more."[36]

The combination of material detail and psychological acumen produces an insightful group portrait.

James A. Froude is the late-Victorian biographer most often credited with reintroducing Boswellian detail and candor. Carlyle appointed Froude to be his literary executor in 1871, providing him with memoirs and correspondence with his wife, Jane Welsh Carlyle, and others. Froude's two-volume *Thomas Carlyle: History of the First Forty Years of His Life* (1882), followed by its two-volume sequel, *Thomas Carlyle: History of His Life in London* (1884), was considered indecorous, even scandalous in its own time, for the biographer's frankness regarding Carlyle's personal life, particularly his sexual dysfunction.

In the United States, the early history of biography was dominated by the Mather family in the seventeenth and early eighteenth centuries. No American family, except the Adamses, Daniel B. Shea Jr. observes, "rivaled the Mathers in an hereditary inclination toward biography and autobiography."[37] Mather sons regularly wrote their fathers' lives: Increase Mather wrote a biography of Richard (1670), the first American Mather; Cotton Mather wrote the life of Increase (1724); and Samuel wrote the life of Cotton (1729). Cotton Mather's major work, the *Magnalia Christi Americana, or the Ecclesiastical History from Its First Planting in the Year 1620, unto the Year of Our Lord, 1698* ("The Great Achievements of Christ in America," 1702), includes a series of character portraits focusing on exemplary spiritual features of the founders of New England. Mather depicts these early clergy and governors as soldiers of Christ, during the first seventy-eight years of the Plymouth and Massachusetts colonies.[38] The following passage from

21

the chapter on Edward Hopkins, governor of the Connecticut colony, gives a specimen of Mather's biographical ethos:

> When the great God of heaven had carried his *peculiar people* into a *wilderness*, the *theocracy*, wherein he became (as he was for *that reason* stiled) *the Lord of Hosts*, unto them and the *four* squadrons of their *army*, was most eminently displayed in *his* enacting of their *laws*, *his* directing of their *wars*, and his electing and inspiring of their *judges*. . . . Now among the first *judges* of New-England, was EDWARD HOPKINS, Esq. in whose time the *colony of Connecticut* was favoured with *judges as at the first*; and put under the power of those with whom it was a maxim, *Gratius est pietatis Nomen, quam potestatis.*[39]

Just as divine will directs the general unfolding of history, so too it guides and manifests itself in the individual life of a chosen soldier of the Lord. The subsequent history of American biography in the early nineteenth century was also dominated by clergy and educators. The genre was motivated by moral purpose, combined with the sense of civic responsibility, to forge a new nation by instructing citizens in worthy public and private behavior. This agenda discouraged what would be considered, by present-day standards, responsibly skeptical inquiry.

Best known among early American biographers are Jared Sparks and Mason Locke Weems (Parson Weems), whose popular *Life of [George] Washington* (1800–1808) appeared first as the eighty-page *Life and Memorable Actions of George Washington* about a month after Washington's death on December 14, 1799. Weems's life of Washington was substantively revised in 1806 to include two new anecdotes: the famous but unsubstantiated cherry tree anecdote involving the young Washington and his father ("I cannot tell a lie") and the story of George's father planting cabbage-seed secretly so that, when it sprouted, the letters spelling his name would appear. Weems then enlarged this short biography into the 200-plus-page *Life of George Washington; With Curious Anecdotes, Equally Honourable to Himself and Exemplary to His Young Countrymen* (1808). Weems's biography portrays an exemplary hero who converts a lie into an immediate demonstration of virtue by confessing it. This volume was edited and reprinted some eighty times between 1806 and 1927, evidence that Weems offered what readers wanted.[40] Jared Sparks, editor of Washington's letters, who improved his subject's style and grammar, also wrote a life of Gouverneur Morris (1832) and both edited and contributed to *The American Library of Biography* (25 vols., 1834–1838; 1844–1847).

By as early as the mid-nineteenth century, a secular and more skeptical consciousness began to appear in American life writing. Complexities of form, issues of evidence, and criteria for selection and discrimination of the real and important facts of a life began to be identified as problems and challenges. The following passage from an 1856 issue of *The Southern Literary Messenger* aptly illustrates this change: "A little reflection will show that half a dozen different narratives of the same life may be constructed, each of which shall contain facts and facts only, while none of them shall furnish either a true account of the man's life or a true picture of his character."[41] Even Jorge Luis Borges in his playful speculations on the various hypothetical biographies that could be written of an individual, "a history of a man's dreams . . . or of the organs of his body; or of the mistakes he has made; or of all the moments when he imagined the Pyramids; or of his traffic with night and with dawn," has only elaborated a statement that precedes him by more than a century.[42]

Another energetic questioner of the use of facts, Ralph Waldo Emerson, undertook to inform biographical theory and practice with Transcendentalist principles and methods. Emerson's profound belief in the power of biography to clear the mind of cant and demystify illusions, thus liberating spirit in earthly life, is memorably summarized in this passage from his essay, "Experience" (1844): "Let us treat the men and women . . . as if they were real; perhaps they are."[43] *Representative Men* (1850) proposes six types of greatness: Plato, the philsopher; Swedenborg, the mystic; Montaigne, the skeptic; Shakespeare, the poet; Napoleon, the man of the world; and Goethe, the writer. For Emerson these figures embody archetypal powers available to us by contemplating the significant details of their lives. Significant details do not include, for Emerson, the trivial data of birth, family, schooling, career, marriage, etc. Rather he sought symbolic facts drawn from the archetypal figure's work and ideas. Thus the materials for authentic biography reside in the spiritual autobiography of great achievements. Shakespeare's plays provide the opportunity, Emerson suggests, for readers to experience the poet's life in his own words. This encounter introduces readers not only to the poet as creative-spiritual agent, but also to Shakespearean aspects of themselves. *Representative Men*, undertaken in part as response to Carlyle's *On Heroes, Hero-Worship, and the Heroic in History* (1841), emphasizes the importance of actively using empowering figures in our own lives, rather than passively worshipping them from afar.

Gamaliel Bradford made distinctive contributions to the line of American biography developing from Emerson. His "psychographs" aim to identify the essential, "permanent habits of thought and action that constitute what we call character" in such a way as to suggest "all the varied and complicated stages of life and character that have preceded."[44] While interested in other people's lives in and for themselves and for the opportunity they provide to escape from "the hampering prison of the *I*," Bradford also believed that in the characters of representative men and women lay the "personal clues" at the heart of all great movements in literature, art, science, and religion.[45] During the first third of the twentieth century, he wrote a number of popular lives, Robert E. Lee, Aaron Burr, P. T. Barnum, Thomas Paine, Henry Wadsworth Longfellow, Charlotte Cushman, and Grover Cleveland, to name only a few.

Bradford's work shares family resemblances with the biographical experiments of his near contemporary, Gertrude Stein. Stein undertook to invigorate biography by emphasizing the genre's alliances with imaginative writing—no less playful than fiction, yet scientific, not the mere secretary to fact, yet empirically based. In *Three Lives* (1908), Stein, who had studied psychology with William James at Harvard, creates three fictional characters, "The Good Anna," "Melanctha," and "The Gentle Lena," whom she examines as case studies in trouble and unhappiness. *The Autobiography of Alice B. Toklas* (1933), written by Stein and not by Toklas, blurs the referential distinction between biography and autobiography. *Four in America* (1947) again cross-examines the notion of the simple, unitary facts of identity by reimagining George Washington as a novelist, Henry James as a general, the Wright brothers as painters, and Ulysses S. Grant as a religious leader who subsequently became a saint. Through these imaginative transformations, Stein reexamines the operations of creativity, freshly explores the relationship among personality, gifts, and genius, and applies all her findings to the question of what it means to be an American.

The innovative characteristics of American biography evident in Emerson, Bradford, and Stein continued to serve the nation's project of inventing a set of new markers of identity, grounded imaginatively in the country itself, in its distinctive psychological, geographical, historical, and ethnographic characteristics. This movement was allied with other civic and educational projects for self-improvement and self-identification distinct from English and European forebears. The interest in biography took other forms, as well, notable among them the founding of the first academic departments of biography by Professor Ambrose White Vernon in the late nineteenth century, first at Carleton College, later at Dartmouth.

Developments in adjacent cultural contexts also profoundly influenced biography. These include the work of Charles Darwin, Karl Marx, Sigmund Freud, and those who broke from or elaborated aspects of Freud's work, most notably Carl Jung, who developed the idea of universal archetypes, the symbol system of a collective unconscious, and Erik Erikson, who proposed a developmental model of identity that focuses on key moments of ego formation in relation to historical context as well as personal circumstances. Darwin's paradigm of natural selection and determinism, Freud's topography of the unconscious and notions of early childhood psychosexual formation, and Marx's cultural-material description of history were appropriated into the subject matter and methods of the genre. Each of these movements makes individuals paradoxically both more and less important to and central in their own lives: whether mere cogs in the great wheel of materialism and unequally distributed wealth or potential revolutionaries; whether creatures subject to unconscious drives by which they are ambushed in dreams and slips of the tongue; or heroes making a psychoanalytic descent into the underworld of unknown drives and forces. These three twentieth-century paradigms promised, each in its distinctive way, to make biography more scientific, which is to say more skeptical, secular, and objective, while at the same time creating surrogates for earlier models of heroism and the dramas of the soul and imagination.

Of these three movements depth psychology has had the most profound effects on biography. Freud's predominant legacy, the "conviction that a secret life is going on within us that is only partly under our control,"[46] focuses biographical inquiry on the private, unconscious motivational drives, particularly those imprinted in childhood, understood to shape public, conscious life. If Boswell had written his life of Johnson after Freud, John Wain proposes, "he would never have had so little to say about Johnson's childhood."[47] He would have felt compelled to analyze the childhood drama rather than gather all available materials and present them to the reader to analyze. Lacking information about Johnson's early life equivalent to data he had collected about the last twenty years, Boswell moves through these years quickly in order to arrive at the period when anecdotal information and accounts of conversation are abundant, the biographer's personal acquaintance with his subject begins, and hence a personal portrait of Johnson can emerge to complement readers' familiarity with the author's writings.

By contrast with the multiplicity of evidence on which Boswell draws, Freud's watershed psychoanalytic study of Leonardo, *Leonardo da Vinci and a Memory of His Childhood* (1910), depends heavily on a single recollected dream about a kind of bird known as a kite, though renamed by Freud a vulture, to help explain the artist's homosexuality in relation to his work.[48] (In psychoanalysis, slim evidence does not hinder interpretation.) Freud was confidently enthusiastic about the "domain of biography [becoming] ours," so he wrote in a letter to Carl Jung in 1909. He defended writing a pathography of Leonardo, Peter Gay notes in *Freud: A Life for Our Time*, "on the ground that ordinary biographers, 'fixated' on their hero, succeed only in presenting a 'cold, strange, ideal figure instead of a human being to whom we might feel ourselves distantly related.'"[49]

So profoundly did the founder of psychoanalysis influence twentieth-century notions of who we are, how we develop, our degrees of self-awareness, and the need for psychoanalytic insight to become conscious of these processes that, after Freud, no responsible biographer can justify knowing nothing about psychoanalytic interpretive methods, though like any other interpretive or investigative methods, its assets and liabilities, insights and blindnesses, even its very presence, must be consciously examined. Anthony Storr remarks that ideas and concepts originally derived from psychoanalysis have, for instance, "become so incorporated into intellectual discourse that biographers automatically employ them without always realizing whence they came." He also comments that psychoanalysis, "although liberating in some ways . . . has made us suspicious of virtue. There is little room for altruism, for self-sacrifice, for unselfishness, or for generosity in the Freudian scheme."[50]

Beginning around the turn of the twentieth century and on through the years during and following World War I, almost every complacent verity, habit of thought, and spiritual belief, public and private, was called into question. The genteel discretion of Victorian biography was thoroughly scrutinized by the self-styled "new biographers." These innovative writers brought the following tenets to their revisionist work: brevity, skepticism, a commitment to psychoanalytic notions of the unconscious, and a belief that no one is well served, neither reader nor biographical subject, by suppressing the complexities of the human psyche. These last two insights could have been learned equally well from the great Victorian novelists whose insights into the shadowiness and indecipherability of so much of human behavior Freud would have been the first to acknowledge.[51] These ideas were energetically developed and applied to life writing by Lytton Strachey, perhaps the twentieth century's most notorious biographer, and Virginia Woolf, the subject of chapter 3, arguably this century's most varied and imaginative biographer.

Strachey's *Eminent Victorians* (1918) sketches iconoclastic, yet not unadmiring portraits of four Victorian culture heroes: Florence Nightingale, Cardinal Manning, General Gordon, and Thomas Arnold. Strachey, as one reader has observed, balances "sympathy with mockery, and economy with vivid dramatic sense."[52] He "released biography from Victorian respectability and earnestness," comments biographer Michael Holroyd, "and returned it to what he saw as the Johnsonian ideal of finding private motives behind actions."[53] Strachey's poetics of biography waved off the scholarly obligation to undertake painstaking primary research and to include massive amounts of information. He took his facts from other biographers and reinstituted the principle of radical editorial exclusion, a tenet which, in the wake of Boswell's powerful example, few had been willing to accept.

Strachey distinguished his work from conventional life-and-times panegyric biography by ousting notions of the writer's and reader's dutiful responsibility to respectful decorum and plodding thoroughness, emphasizing instead pleasure and even "whimsy." He argued that only by selecting, omitting, and avoiding "the direct method of a scrupulous narration . . . row[ing] out over that great ocean of material, and lower[ing] down into it, here and there, a little bucket, which will bring up to the light of day some characteristic" can the past be seen clearly, unclouded by intervening myths or, to use Strachey's word, "visions," which settle in between us and our predecessors.[54]

Yet in spite of his announced iconoclasm, or perhaps curiously in support of it, Strachey's poetics of the "new biography" recalls the classical idea of virtue with a modern heterodox turn: "It is perhaps as difficult to write a good life as to live one." He intended not crudely to debunk admired figures, to demonstrate that they were, after all, merely human, or to refer to them as "mere symptoms of the past." Rather he aimed to demonstrate that mere humans can become heroic and that their value is always "independent of any temporal processes" (Strachey, 10). Strachey's thoughtful distinctions have sometimes been lost on his successors who misread him as mere iconoclast or muckraker. While Strachey's work genuinely invigorated early-twentieth-century biography, after more than fifty years of weighty Victorian panegyric, it has also been misdirected to produce heavy-handed iconoclasm and crude gossip in hands less skillful than the originator's. A similar fate has sometimes overtaken Freud's insights into the dark underside of consciousness, resulting in some of the following famous critiques of biography: Oscar Wilde's witty observation that the prospect of being the subject of a biography added new terrors to death, James Joyce's reference to the *biografiend*, and Joyce Carol Oates's coinage *pathography*.

The relation between art and fact, imagination and truth, fiction and nonfiction became the preoccupying issues of the twentieth century's ways of thinking about biography. Woolf says it best: "The biographer's imagination is always being stimulated to use the novelist's art of arrangement, suggestion, dramatic effect to expound the private life. Yet if he carries the use of fiction too far, so that he disregards the truth, or can only introduce it with incongruity, he loses both worlds."[55] In other words, the biographer is, to use Desmond McCarthy's frequently cited phrase, an "artist on oath" who must give equal emphasis and simultaneous attention to aesthetic shaping and scholarly responsibility.[56] Woolf was as pessimistic about the possibility of truly knowing another person as she was strict about the biographer's responsibility to accuracy. She once reminded a friend of the difficulty of separating our own feelings and intentions from those of other people. More likely than not, she feared, our knowledge of others is mere "emanations of ourselves." Woolf's firm belief in this fundamental human responsibility to treat other people as if they were real and thus separate from ourselves drew her repeatedly to the challenge of biography.

By now in this introduction it may almost go without saying, yet still be worth emphasizing, what has been implied throughout, namely that biography is not a monolithic term. There are various ways to divide up this generic territory. One way is to discriminate among (1) popular biographies narrating the lives of current celebrities—movie stars and sports heroes, for instance; (2) historical biographies emphasizing their central and influential figures' relations to and effects on their times; (3) literary biographies recreating the life and personality of artists, attempting to account for the particular bent of their talent and sometimes, as in critical biographies, interpreting and assessing their work; (4) reference biographies, also called collective biographies, consisting of alphabetically arranged, relatively brief entries on notable figures, associatively collected by several factors, such as profession, notable achievement, and geographical-historical coordinates of their lives; and (5) fictional biographies taking factual materials about real people and events and developing them by applying fictional narrative techniques.[57]

Another taxonomy, proposed by James L. Clifford, identifies categories conceived more explicitly from the writer's point of view regarding the practice of biography, including the relative proportions of attempted subjectivity and objectivity, the kinds of research involved, and the respective proportions of artful imagination and historical fact. Clifford names the following kinds of biography: (1) the "objective" biography which, though it cannot entirely omit subjective choices (even the ordering of data involves personal decisions), attempts to keep them to a minimum; (2) the "scholarly-historical" biography, characterized by the "careful use of selected facts, strung together in chronological order, with some historical background; (3) the "artistic-scholarly" biography, for which the author does all the homework required for scholarly-historical biography but presents these materials "in the liveliest and most interesting manner possible" while not altering or adding to the facts; (4) the "narrative" biography, for which the author collects all the evidence and "turns it into a running narrative, almost fictional in form," though still not adding material; and (5) "fictional" biography, for which the author relies on secondary sources and treats the life of the historical subject as a novelist would treat a character, adding and inventing as the author sees fit for the effects she is trying to create.[58] The biographer's talents and inclinations, the imagined audience for the biography, and, to some degree, the qualities of the biographical subject all enter into the writer's choice of research methods and compositional form for a life.

If, as this introduction has suggested and the following chapters will examine in more detail, the biographer's task is complex and challenging, while the reader's engagement is intricate and demanding, there is one overarching fact about the function of this genre to which discussion must always return, namely its appeal to the imagination. Richard Ellmann, one of the twentieth century's greatest literary biographers, identifies how the collaborative work of writers and readers of biography is motivated by fundamental, life-defining urges of the imagination: "The effort . . . to make out of apparently haphazard circumstances a plotted circle, to know another person who has lived as well as we know a character in fiction, and better than we know ourselves, is not frivolous. It may even be, for readers as for writers, an essential part of experience."[59] This notion of biography being an essential part of experience is justified by its varied, durable history over many centuries, while for the individual reader, the experience of reading biography over a lifetime may serve as an analogous personal education in the genre's enduringly indispensable uses and pleasures. Such is, at least, the view under Western eyes since biography began in Western culture to satisfy curiosity about the exceptional individual and how he (usually a "he") came to be that way.[60]

This overview would be incomplete without noting explicitly, however, that biography is not a universal genre nor one whose fundamental validity has entirely gone without saying. On the latter issue, postmodern theory and critical practice date emblematically from two seminal essays by Roland Barthes, "Death of the Author" (1968) and Michel Foucault, "What Is an Author?" (1969), which jointly deconstructed the modern hypostatized and commercialized notion of author. Foucault's question infers readers' and writers' responsibility to "reexamine the empty space left by the author's disappearance . . . along its gaps and fault lines."[61] In spite of the profound influence of Foucault and Barthes, at least among academics, the author as a practical concept and hence literary biography as a successful commercial genre, so Walter Kendrick notes, continue to thrive. They seem "likely to endure," Kendrick elaborates, precisely because "at their best, literary biographies never catered to a simplistic desire to ride herd on writing and rein signification in." From the genre's origin in the late eighteenth century, he concludes, "it has taken a subtler, more intelligent approach to its subject than Foucault's overbearing 'author' would sit still for."[62]

Biography has proved to be remarkably "'immune' from deconstruction," which is not to say that theory has no place in the biographer's project, since theory by default or design informs every genre.[63] Jürgen Schlaeger describes biography as "fundamentally reactionary, conservative, perpetually accommodating new models of man, new theories of the inner self, into a personality-oriented cultural mainstream, thus always helping to defuse their subversive potential." By contrast with autobiography, which Schlaeger describes as "a discourse of anxiety," biography is "a discourse of usurpation." Autobiographers take as their chief rhetorical responsibility being true to themselves and to the image they wish to present to their audience, while for biographers the "truth-criterion does not consist in the authenticity of an inside view but in the consistency of the narrative and the explanatory power of the arguments."[64] This distinction between *inside* and *outside* views correlates with the two different narrative positions of autobiography and biography, respectively, and may help us understand why minorities gravitate toward autobiography until such time as their group politics and position become, either in their own or other people's eyes, better served by the rhetoric of argument than of confession or witnessing. Such revision is not to be confused necessarily with improvement, but it almost certainly coincides with growing formal traditionalism and also perhaps political conservatism.

With regard to the Western origin of biography, it is important to underscore the fact implied in this chapter's overview of the genre, namely that life writing did not develop worldwide or transhistorically. It is indigenous to the Western world, associated developmentally with the ethos of Christianity and Renaissance humanism, with Western technologies of science and print, the new commercial world, the spread of empire, and Western class structure based on indigenous economic coordinates. Biography has been shaped by and in turn gives form to the values and perspectives of empiricism, the centrality of literacy, the romantic revolution's invention of the individual's interior life as the new preoccupying drama of the self-examining soul, and the subsequent inventions of psychology and psychoanalysis. Biography is, in other words, culture specific. Even the Western world's aggressive exportation of its distinctive materials, methods, politics, and values to indigenous cultures both within and beyond our borders cannot infuse directly into oral cultures or into cultures where individualism is not the measure of all things the perceptions and assumptions of Western life writing.

It is beyond the scope of this chapter or this book to discuss the forms of life writing worldwide. But let me conclude with three specific instances of non-Anglo-Euramerican societies within whose cultural-historical matrices biography is not a given, where it did not precede autobiography, as it did in the West, and where stories other than the drama of "psychological man" have been more compelling to writers and readers alike.

In Japan, biography did not begin until the seventeenth century when Ohta Gyuichi's *Records of Prince Nobunaga* initiated the genre of lives of *samurai* heroes. There did exist, however, another much earlier tradition of lives, the "nikki," dating from the tenth century. Nikki, meaning diary or journal, are secular tales of romance, of marriage, of fidelity and infidelity, told by women, with an emphasis on the expression of personal emotions and the values of intimacy. In the Western tradition, by contrast, biography precedes autobiography by many centuries; St. Augustine's *Confessions* (fifth century) is usually identified as the original autobiography that started the form off on the spiritual, soul-searching path it has continued to follow.[65] In addition, in the West women did not have the first say, nor were scenes of domestic life and emotion, from a female point of view, the first subjects.[66]

In Southern Africa the historical confluence of two major cultural streams, the Euro-Africans who have sustained a dominant Eurocentric culture and the Africans and other black groups who have struggled to maintain an indigenous culture, has had profound effects on life writing. The latter group associates itself with the oral tradition that flourished before European colonization. This oral tradition, with its emphasis on the eponymous epic hero, a representative but not an individualistic culture hero, was subverted, seduced, and subdued by the intersection of colonizing ideologies of Christianity and empire which, during the

1930s, produced Western-style biographies of the elite. Black nationalistic movements of the 1950s and 1960s produced autobiography in which writers typically present themselves as representatives of their race and culture, not as figures "preoccupied only with the vicissitudes of the individual self" but as people concerned instead "with the individual *and* the historical moment" (my emphasis).[67]

The value of some books on the lives of Native Americans, Paula Gunn Allen proposes, perhaps with some extravagance, may be best appreciated by measuring the degree to which "'they make no sense'" to non-Native Americans, resisting these readers' attempts "to sag back into the usual habits of sense-making, heaving melancholy sighs and thinking knowing thoughts, forcing ourselves with sentimentally condescending appropriation into the circle of their imagination as we have forced our way otherwise into their lives."[68] On a related note, Patricia Nelson Limerick exhorts nonminority biographers of minority subjects (Limerick's instance is a life of Sitting Bull) not merely to avoid historical distortions of pointless guilt but even to minimize reflections on the possible reasons and motives for either white or Indian actions. The subjective world of Sitting Bull, Limerick observes, "what he really thought and felt," remains "well shielded from the inspection of intruders, obscured by the passage of time, the distinctiveness of his culture, and the absence of a consistent written record."[69]

Fantasies of the master race play out in all areas of culture, Ward Churchill observes, literature not exempt, even those genres, like life writing, that are primarily responsible to fact. From the outset of colonial invasions of North America, Churchill continues, "it was necessary to alter indigenous realities in order to assuage the invading colonial conscience" and subsequently "to alter these realities to assure the maintenance of empire."[70] Vine Deloria Jr. makes the case that "underneath all the conflicting images of the Indian one fundamental truth emerges: the white man knows that he is alien and he knows that North America is Indian . . . [though] he thinks that by some clever manipulation he can achieve an authenticity which can never be his."[71] From these and other cultural complications, including the fundamental fact that Anglo-European colonists arrived in the New World "burdened with the cultural baggage of the old World," which inescapably shaped and arguably distorted their view of indigenous culture, derives the indispensable value of autobiography taking precedence over biography in the literary history of an oppressed people.[72]

Though these issues may have particular relevance to minority biography, to which I return in more detail in chapters 4 and 5, they are also relevant, in varying degrees, to all biography. The basic requirements and extraordinary difficulties of getting the facts right, finding the appropriate form for presenting them, and understanding the significance of another person's life, even a person of the same gender, race, economic class, and historical period as both the biographer and reader, are never less than a complex challenge.

Chapter 2

MAJORITY BIOGRAPHY 1:
SAMUEL JOHNSON

I have often thought that there has rarely passed a life of which a
judicious and faithful narrative would not be useful.

Johnson, *Rambler* No. 60 (1750)

Samuel Johnson, Biographer

M odern literary biography that takes as its chief aim to identify the ways a mind "negotiates with its surroundings to
produce literature" begins with Samuel Johnson, who occupies
this genre's original ground in several senses.[1] Johnson wrote the
Lives of the English Poets (1779–1781), the first series of modern literary lives in the English language. Second, he is the subject of
the best known and, many would say, most important literary
biography in the English language, Boswell's *Life of Johnson*
(1791), whose author acknowledged Johnson as his admired
model and teacher. And third, Johnson has continued to be the
subject of important biographies. These elements, combined with

the fact that all biographers after Johnson and Boswell write somehow in their shadow, make these two biographers a useful pair to examine.

Johnson wrote lives throughout his long career as a professional writer. Among his early biographical pieces, which developed out of journalistic work involving translation and heavy paraphrase, are eight short lives published in the *Gentleman's Magazine* (1738–1742): biographies of Father Paolo Sarpi, Venetian priest, scholar, and reformer; Herman Boerhaave, Dutch physician and scientist; Louis Morin, French physician and botanist; Pieter Burman, Dutch scholar; British Admirals Robert Blake and Sir Francis Drake; German scholar J. P. Baratier, and British physician John Sydenham. These lives, written during his first years after moving to London, do not exhibit Johnson's distinctive biographical style soon to emerge. But knowing the subsequent importance of biography in his career, one is tempted to see in this work early signs of later developing interest. Certainly these commissions give evidence of the genre's popularity and exemplify its new subject matter: lives of scientists, explorers, and scholars—all men, it might be noted.

The great original biography of Johnson's early career, the *Life of Richard Savage* (1744), the profligate, self-destructive writer and friend of Johnson, appeared just two years after the last of these earlier journalistic lives was published. After Savage's death, Johnson decided to write the life of his gifted, charming, unsuccessful, self-destructive acquaintance. Johnson's decision turned out to be one of those events marking the intersection of external circumstance and personal calling that sometimes focus indispensably a writer's latent interests and talents. Johnson wrote to set the record straight on the life of a man whose abilities, failings, and fate he felt qualified, responsible, and emotionally committed to recount and assess, the latter for reasons that include several qualities and characteristics shared by the subject and his biographer.[2]

The *Life of Savage* is a case study in factors contributing to blighted talent and a wasted life. Johnson and Savage shared intense passions, frustrations, intelligence, perhaps gifts, and memories of unhappy childhoods. Savage claimed to be the unacknowledged bastard of the Earl of Rivers and the Countess of Macclesfield, a claim unsupported by evidence. He accused the countess of ruining him by denying her maternity with unnatural cruelty. Johnson translates Savage's indictment into a portrait of the countess as the archetypal wicked mother. For reasons which are perhaps difficult to dissociate from his own unhappy childhood life (a strong, discontented mother, a father less successful in business than his wife had hoped for), Johnson seems uncharacteristically unskeptical about the validity of Savage's claim.[3] Johnson was, after all, a man who once remarked that an inaccurate story is a story about nothing. Johnson's assessment of Savage's situation creates, however, a powerful pathos and a compelling plot, so effective and rhetorically well shaped that this life has appeared, on at least one occasion, in a collection of eighteenth-century novellas.

The *Life of Savage* takes a writer as its subject. But it is neither a literary nor a critical biography, as these forms would be recognized today, in part because Savage did not fulfill his early promise as a writer and thus left only a small body of work to be examined; in part, too, because Johnson identified the tragedy of Savage's life as a lesson in dangers of self-destructive irresponsibility. Johnson presents his subject as a man victimized, yet still accountable for his failure. He interweaves anecdote, personal knowledge, and excerpts from Savage's personal writings into a psychologically and morally probing narrative which powerfully invokes the reader's self-examination. The narrative concludes with a complex set of instructions about the lessons to be learned from the example of Savage's life:

> Those are no proper judges of his conduct who have slumbered away their time on the down of plenty, nor will any wise man presume to say, "Had I been in Savage's condition, I should have lived or written better than Savage."
>
> This relation will not be wholly without its use if those who languish under any part of his suffering shall be enabled to fortify their patience by reflecting that they feel only those afflictions from which the abilities of Savage did not exempt him; or those who, in confidence of superior capacities or attainments, disregard the common maxims of life, shall be reminded that nothing will supply the want of prudence, and that negligence and irregularity long continued will make knowledge useless, wit ridiculous, and genius contemptible.[4]

Johnson offers no simple, complacent moral. Here, as in his other major biographical writings, he gives moral and psychological form to the narration of a life but not by reducing the actual complexities or elevating the biographer above the subject.

In 1750 and again in 1759, Johnson wrote two important essays on biography. The first essay, *Rambler* No. 60, examines biography from ethical, psychological, and rhetorical points of view, in this order of importance, interweaving the operations of these three elements while establishing clearly a hierarchy among them. He describes the emotional identification linking human beings through the agency of imagination that fundamentally defines this genre, discussed in chapter 1. The imagination operates more strongly in proportion to the probability that the objects it contemplates are real and to the degree and proximity of their relation to the perceiver.

In the tradition of Plutarch, Johnson distinguishes the "general and rapid narratives of history" from the educative specificity of biography, introducing the key observation that "there has rarely passed a life of which a judicious and faithful narrative would not be useful." Johnson defends this democratization of subject matter by invoking a measure of value based on usefulness. He defines usefulness, in turn, in secular, practical, day-to-day terms regarding how the greatest number of people may be benefited either by reducing their misery or increasing virtuous pleasure. Since the many are, by definition, not the distinguished few, the majority of people are best served by reading lives of people such as themselves. Johnson recommends that biographers pass "slightly over those performances and incidents, which produce vulgar greatness, to lead the thoughts into domestic privacies." These minute details of daily life, "invisible circumstances," Johnson calls them, "whether we read as inquirers after natural and moral knowledge, whether we intend to enlarge our science, or increase our virtue" are "more important than public occurrences" to depict character.

Character is, in turn, the touchstone of biographical instruction. Factually accurate information, gathered with a discriminating eye to distinguish important details (details that exemplify character) from unimportant details (accidental qualities unallied with character), is the biographer's chief responsibility. It is uninformative, Johnson observes, to distinguish Joseph Addison, the early eighteenth-century essayist, poet, and playwright, from other men by "'the irregularity of his pulse,'" as did one biographer. But to note the Roman politician Catiline's walk was "'now quick, and again slow,' as an indication of a mind revolving something with violent commotion," is illustratively informative.[5] Johnson had already put this poetics of biography into practice in his use of detail in the *Life of Savage*, as in the following passage:

> He had the peculiar felicity that his attention never deserted him: he was present to every object, and regardful of the most trifling occurrences. He had the art of escaping from his own reflections, and accommodating himself to every scene. . . . His method of life particularly qualified him for conversation, of which he knew how to practise all the graces. He was never vehement or loud, but at once modest and easy, open and respectful; his language was vivacious and elegant, and equally happy upon grave or humourous subjects. He was generally censured for not knowing when to retire, but that was not the defect of his judgement, but of his fortune; when he left his company he was frequently to spend the remaining part of the night in the street, or at least was abandoned to gloomy reflections, which it is not strange that he delayed as long as he could; and he sometimes forgot that he gave others pain to avoid it himself. (Johnson, *Savage*, 2:429–31)

Johnson assembles these details about Savage's conversation into a succinct portrait of this man's temperament, gifts, and financial plight.

Johnson's second essay on biography, *Idler* No. 84, elaborates the previous discussion of how the genre's imaginative appeal derives from readers recognizing its applicability to their own lives. Curiosity is more actively engaged by veracity than by mere invention, however artful that invention may be. Johnson directs this emphasis on the power of the circumstantially real toward constructing an argument on behalf of lives written in the first person: "Those relations are therefore commonly of most value in which the writer tells his own story." Autobiographers presumably have the primary qualifications of knowing the truth about themselves and of, certainly, being self-identical with the subject. There is as little reason to suspect their partiality as to suspect the biographer's bias, since biographers are usually either friends or enemies of their subjects and thus equally tempted to falsehood.

In 1777, Johnson was approached by a group of thirty-six London publishers to write forematter to an edition of works by Restoration and eighteenth-century British authors. As Johnson wrote this series of biographical-critical prefaces, some developed into substantial examinations of 15,000 words or more—Joseph Addison, Abraham Cowley, John Dryden, John Milton, Alexander Pope, and Jonathan Swift among them, whom Johnson judged to be the first-generation makers of modern English literature. Taken together, these longer lives compose a literary history of the period immediately preceding Johnson's generation, the writers with whom he felt powerful affinities, differences, familiarities, and allegiances in the development of his own career.[6] Johnson's *Prefaces Biographical and Critical to the Works of the English Poets* were also published separately under the later more familiar title, *Lives of the English Poets*. These lives embody Johnson's deeply held belief that a nation should take pride in its great writers, his fascination with the workings of the creative imagination, and his sense of the importance for literary and intellectual history of identifying the intersection of genius and historical circumstance.

The *Lives* introduced innovation into English criticism. Heretofore lives of writers and their work had typically been considered two separate entities, a distinction also evident throughout the nineteenth-century tradition of life-and-times biographies.[7] To the degree that each of Johnson's prefaces opens with an account of the poet's life, often taken from earlier biographies, proceeds to a chronology of the works, and concludes with an interpretive assessment of the writer's character and accomplishment, Johnson retains this traditional distinction. Yet particularly with the poets whom he examines most thoroughly and intensively, the aim of describing how the writer and his writing are imaginatively and cognitively interrelated and distinctly of their age, though not, if they are truly great, time bound, emerges clearly. Johnson in the longer lives characteristically identifies the intersection of creative intelligence, character, and accomplishment in the new era of the professional writer. Believing as he did that it was by their intellects that these writers were due their biographies, Johnson sketches a mental picture of his subjects filtered through his own subjective but not merely private intelligence.[8]

The *Lives of the Poets* may also be read as group biography in the peripatetic tradition of examining a field of knowledge by collecting and portraying a group of its practitioners, here representatives of the new profession of writing. The cumulative narrative structure of the *Lives* is all the more compelling for having been written by a writer who himself actively participated in the history he narrates and whose focus and emphases, being distinctively his own, add an intensifying autobiographical element to the commentary.

Johnson succeeds in the basic but nonetheless most difficult challenge of biography, namely to make the subjects seem once actually to have lived in a world of choices, to have experienced the vagaries of accident and contingency, and thus not to be fore-ordained to have achieved what they achieved and become who they became. Johnson actively dramatizes character and precludes viewing these writers' lives exclusively in light of their conclusion. Yet overall, Johnson, like Aristotle, consistently subordinates character to plot. Plot in the *Lives* predominates over and serves as the informing context of character. By this choice Johnson simultaneously asserts a thesis about the individual's responsibility to be useful, argues the subordination of self to the achievement left for posterity, and acknowledges the biographer's interpretive role in fashioning an explanatory narrative.[9]

Johnson and His Biographers

James Boswell aimed to be and succeeded in becoming the biographer most thoroughly associated with Johnson in the popular mind. Yet Boswell is by no means the sole creator of the Johnson image, and before turning directly to his life of Johnson, I will survey other of Johnson's contemporary biographers. Between the time of Johnson's death, in 1784, and the publication of Boswell's benchmark biography in 1791, at least eleven other lives appeared, testimony to the public's interest in Johnson, in particular, and biography, in general.

These other lesser-known biographies divide along two main lines in their depictions of the man: Johnson the writer and Johnson the moralist, a familiar division well through the nineteenth century.[10] They differ on two other main matters: how well the biographer knew Johnson and the manner and intent of constructing Johnson's persona (hero and exemplum, on the one hand; human being who overcame weaknesses and adversity to achieve greatness, on the other).

Active controversy over this latter issue unfolded in contemporary reviews of these lives, which accused some biographers of apotheosis, others of indiscretion and betrayal. In an age of secular skepticism, it was becoming increasingly difficult to reconcile heroism with humanity.[11] Lives of courtesans, rogues, highwaymen, and other low-life characters were increasingly popular since the mid-seventeenth century. But as in the novel, a moral lesson dramatized in the life of the main character was essential. Boswell, Sir John Hawkins, and Hester Lynch Thrale Piozzi, Johnson's foremost biographers, were all criticized on grounds of their frank examination of the dark side of his personality, though in the psychoanalytic twentieth century their accounts may seem evasive, incurious, or naive about Johnson's unconscious and the possibility of explaining his behavior in psychosexual terms.

Early biographers of *Johnson the writer* did not write critical biographies as twentieth-century readers would recognize this form. They neither read his work as a way of explaining his character (or to use the twentieth-century word *psychology*) or vice versa, nor did they explore the interrelation of character, drives or motivations, and the forms of his creativity. These writers variously portray Johnson as a literary giant whose accomplishments serve as a professional model. They also record contemporary information about him and his career, such as lists of Johnson's writings, invaluable to later scholars.

Biographers of *Johnson the moralist*, while they praise his literary accomplishments, place primary emphasis on character. To Thomas Tyers and William Cooke, for instance, Johnson is most noteworthy for his moral influence. While Tyers praises Johnson's virtue, he does so by dramatizing the man he knew personally in easy, conversational style so that the man's goodness appears engaging, not merely uplifting. Contrasting with Tyers's attractively casual style is Cooke's graver tone and more formally organized presentation of Johnson's life, modeled on the structure of each biography in the *Lives of the Poets*. Both biographers spotlight Johnson's conversation, Cooke emphasizing its substantive worth, Tyers, its liveliness.

Particularly notable among these early lives of Johnson the moralist, for its statement on decorum, is an anonymous biographical essay, *The Life of Samuel Johnson, LL.D.* (1786). The writer criticizes previous biographers for the damage done by "the enmity of injudicious friendship" and for pursuing a "new and base species of intellectual anatomy" harmful to the living and dead alike, giving "instability to every humane opinion," diffusing "uncertainty and suspicion through every human attachment."[12] Such notions of biographical decorum and breaches of decorum, which moved center stage in the nineteenth century, were overturned in the early twentieth century, only to be renewed, or at least reviewed, in the late twentieth century.

Turning to Boswell, the best way to begin examining his achievement is to compare his and Johnson's respective attitudes toward plot and character. Johnson valued plot over character and thus made narrative his organizing principle. Boswell valued character over plot and thus made character the organizing principle of his *Life of Johnson*. Boswell's *Life*, though not lacking in summarizing judgment and narrative form, announces that its valuable originality lies in the biographer's refusal to melt down into a homogeneous mass his painstakingly gathered, checked, and double-checked materials. Boswell claims that the heterogeneity of his collected data is this biography's greatest asset as a record of Johnson's life.

Fifty years earlier, Conyers Middleton, in his preface to *The Life and Letters of Marcus Tullius Cicero* (1741), had defended citations from Cicero's work for the way "the subject's own words" give "luster" and "authority" to the biographical account.[13] He promised not merely to sew on patches of citation but to weave them into the biographical narrative. Boswell, by contrast, emphasizes the variety of genres and voices within his biography. He works centrifugally toward multiplicity and variety and away from the notion of a single or unified evaluative or explanatory center.[14]

Describing his biography of Johnson as "more of a life" than had ever before been written, Boswell presumably refers to the sheer amount of material gathered. This material, he in turn asserts as a good empiricist, supports the validity of his investigation. Readers of the *Life*, Boswell proceeds to claim, have the opportunity to know Johnson better and to experience the force of his character more powerfully even than those who actually knew him, thanks to the biographer, because this life assembles multiple points of view.[15]

Boswell does not present Johnson's character in the making, since, being a man of his age, he believed that the child is the adult in miniature. Nor, does Boswell succeed in his claim to depict Johnson's personality, warts and all, especially the bouts of powerful melancholy—at least as measured by twentieth-century psychoanalytic standards of candidly explicit sexual interpretation—though Boswell believed himself to be thoroughly candid. Even by twentieth-century standards, however, he describes Johnson in acute sensory detail, cueing the reader palpably to imagine how the man actually looked and sounded when he spoke the words recorded by his biographer, as in this passage from *The Journal of a Tour to the Hebrides with Samuel Johnson, LL.D.* (1785), Boswell's first portrait of Johnson in which he experimented with techniques used later in the *Life*:

> *While therefore Doctor Johnson's sayings are read, let his manner be taken along with them*. . . . His person was large, robust, I may say approaching the gigantick, and grown unwieldy from corpulency. His countenance was naturally of the cast of an ancient statue, but somewhat disfigured by the scars of that evil, which, it was formerly imagined, the royal touch could cure. He was now in his sixty-fourth year, and was become a little dull of hearing. His sight had always been somewhat weak; yet, so much does mind govern, and even supply the deficiency of organs, that his perceptions were uncommonly quick and accurate. His head, and sometimes also his body, shook with a kind of motion like the effect of a palsy: he appeared to be frequently disturbed by cramps, or convulsive contractions. . . . He wore a full suit of plain brown clothes, with twisted-hair buttons of the same colour, a large bushy greyish wig, a plain shirt, black worsted stockings, and silver buckles.[16]

Readers of any biography encounter nothing more or less than a representation, however complex that representation may be. Boswell's Johnson, however fully described, is not the man himself but a captured and hence necessarily restricted version. This point, though perhaps self-evident, is perhaps worth recalling, from time to time. Philip Toynbee makes this point especially well: "But even if there were a million pages this figure would still be constricted as the real Johnson was never constricted. . . . [A]t every second of his life he was, as we all are, infinite, unseizable, imponderable." The hero of a biography, like the hero of a novel, as a result of this artificial, albeit unavoidable, constriction, Toynbee concludes, "*differs violently* from the living people we know."[17]

Boswell's attempt to overcome, or at least to compensate inventively for, these limits of language, to "picture the varieties of mind," to portray the biographical subject as it exists in the mind of the biographer and others who knew the subject has remained compelling to two centuries of readers (Krutch, 358). He dramatizes anecdote, particularly emphasizing recreated conversation, in order to reanimate the past. Boswell's emphasis on recording Johnson's spoken words perhaps took inspiration from Johnson's observation about the unfortunate lack of Pope's recorded conversation. Johnson was scarcely naive about conversation's potential for revealing unmediated truth, the genuine, as opposed to the artful, side of the writer. Yet in biography's attempt to depict the subject's mind, the more evidence from the more sources, the better. An accurate record of conversation is, Johnson believed, potentially of great use and certainly of more engaging interest to a reading public newly interested in the writer as celebrity and culture hero.

Boswell describes his sense of the biographical usefulness of recorded conversation and its written equivalent, letters: "I am absolutely certain that *my* mode of Biography which gives not only a *History* of Johnson's *visible* progress through the World, and of his Publications, but a *View* of his mind, in his Letters, and Conversations is the most perfect that can be conceived, and will be *more* of a Life than any Work that has ever yet appeared."[18] Elements from this personal letter reappear in the full title of the *Life of Johnson*, which comprises the main points of Boswell's poetics of literary biography:

> *The Life of Samuel Johnson LL.D., comprehending an account of his studies and numerous works in chronological order; a series of his epistolary correspondence and conversations with many eminent persons; and various original pieces of his composition never before published: the whole exhibiting a view of literature and literary men in Great-Britain for near half a century during which he flourished.*

This title describes an alternating close-up and wide-angle focus on life, works, and the subject's surrounding and radiating contexts, personal, historical, and cultural. Two centuries later Boswell's conception remains recognizable. Seidel's earlier-mentioned biography of Ted Williams, for instance, announces that a "full and fair record" of this athlete's life can be presented only in the complete context of "the temper of major league baseball in America in the 1940s and 1950s" (Seidel, xi). The monumental life-and-times Victorian biographies, modeled to some degree on Boswell, came under fire from the revisionist biographers Strachey and Woolf, who valued brevity, depreciated historical background material, and argued on behalf of biographers' equality with their subjects. In spite of Strachey's and Woolf's influence, the latter discussed in chapter 3, readers have never been convinced that a life can be comprehensibly depicted entirely apart from historical context, though the manner and amount of contextualization may vary widely from one biography to another.

Boswell, then, to underscore my earlier point, believed that the most valuable part of his work was its full and accurate record of Johnson's conversation. Conversation, in turn, contributes to the dramatic recreation of his felt presence, the sense of an actual, individual mind at work, precisely because these are among life's most evanescent and, as perceived by modern sensibilities, revealing qualities.

Boswell functions predominantly as an interviewer, measured not so much by the sheer amount of text within quotation marks as by the forcefulness of his case for conversation being this biography's greatest value. Sometimes he introduces an issue, makes an assertion, or asks a question. Sometimes he motivates Johnson's remarks entirely verbally by announcing a topic under which heading he then assembles a number of Johnson's remarks. Occasionally he arranges or participates in an event, or *in-vent*, as one might name the elaborately arranged dinner party meeting between Johnson and an arch-rival, the republican John Wilkes, an arrangement made without Johnson's knowledge, on which the biographer prided himself. Boswell introduces the anecdote with a combination of puckish troublemaking and suspense:

> I am now to record a very curious incident in Dr. Johnson's Life, which fell under my own observation . . . . My Desire of being acquainted with celebrated men of every description, had made me, much about the same time, obtain an introduction to Dr. Samuel Johnson and to John Wilkes, Esq. Two men more different could perhaps not be selected out of all mankind. They had even attacked one another with some asperity in their writings; yet I lived in habits of friendship with both. . . . But I conceived an irresistible wish, if possible, to bring Dr. Johnson and Mr. Wilkes together. How to manage it, was a nice and difficult matter.[19]

Boswell's techniques, though not always so dramatic as in the Wilkes episode, aim to recreate cumulatively the felt sense of Johnson responding and reacting to his biographer. Boswell intends to suggest the active, transactional nature of thought and language initiated and exchanged in the form of questions and answers. Energy and spontaneity are evoked, the total effect being to help the reader imagine Johnson as a living person and his biographer as a participant-observer in Johnson's life, not his coroner.

While Boswell's recreation of Johnson's talk asserts the substantive importance of the man's remarks, it also implies the complementary assertion that the value of each conversational episode lies also in the existential moment, which is to say in the listener's having been in Johnson's presence. Johnson's body, the sound of his voice, even his silences seem sometimes to signify more than his words. Thus the biography, in creating a simulacrum of Johnsonian moments, reminds readers that they were, in fact, absent from the original events.

To summarize, Boswell uses Johnson's talk in three principal ways: first, as a fund of interesting, useful topics and opinions of a great man, which he believes to be perennially educative and fascinating; second, as the essential dramatic technique to depict the living man; and third, as an index of Johnson's character and evidence of his genius.

Boswell's accuracy and his motives for creating the character Johnson the talker have been called into question by scholars and critics. He has been criticized most harshly by Donald Greene, discussed more fully later in this chapter, for creating the image of a pompous, self-satisfied conservative, for editing heavily and even making up things, though never finally convicted on any of these counts. But no one has, to my knowledge, successfully argued that Johnson's conversation is not the core of the *Life*, or convinced readers that this conversation is uninteresting. I will return to Boswell shortly in the context of his two chief rival biographers of Johnson, Sir John Hawkins and Hester Lynch Thrale Piozzi.

The manner and method of Boswell's depiction of Johnson proved to be sufficiently convincing that a supplement, *Johnsoniana* (1836), was published, containing anecdotes and sayings of Johnson, gathered from publications of Johnson's intimates and friends, including Piozzi, Hawkins, Tyers, Arthur Murphy, and

Frances Burney. The aim of this biographical supplement to Boswell's *Life* was to gather materials by and about Johnson from other publications, too unwieldy to be included as notes to the *Life*, materials, so the Advertisement claims, "essential to the completion of the intellectual portrait of Johnson." The word *essential* suggests the degree to which even self-announced contributors to Boswell's portrait could make their additions only by contesting his absolute authority. In her collection of previously published anecdotes by Piozzi, Richard Cumberland, Burney, and others, Robina Napier comments: "We sometimes fancy that another hand might give a different, not a better or a fuller representation than Boswell's." Napier describes the purpose of her collection as being "to afford satisfaction to this feeling and gratify the desire to know all that can be known about so great a man."[20]

A scholarly collection of all the writings included under the general title *Johnsoniana* was subsequently edited by G. B. Hill, at the request of Sir Leslie Stephen, editor of the *Dictionary of National Biography* and also a Johnson biographer. Hill's two-volume scholarly work, *Johnsonian Miscellanies* (1897), includes Johnson's prayers and meditations, the brief remaining portion of Johnson's autobiography of his early years, Piozzi's *Anecdotes*, and Murphy's *Essay on the Life and Genius of Samuel Johnson*, along with extracts from memoirs and lives by Hawkins, Bishop Percy, Sir Joshua Reynolds, and others, in addition to letters by Johnson, some of which appear for the first time.

The three chief contemporary contenders among late eighteenth-century Johnson biographers, Boswell, Piozzi, and Hawkins, make a fascinating case study in comparative biography. Friends of Johnson, contemporaries and rivals, they wrote different lives of the different man each knew. This historical episode of the publication of Piozzi's *Anecdotes of the Late Samuel Johnson* (1786), Hawkins's *Life of Samuel Johnson* (1787), and Boswell's *Life* give ample evidence of the significance of the biographer in constructing the biographical subject and of the complexities involved in authorized lives.

Hawkins was an old friend of Johnson, executor of his estate, and the man whom a group of London publishers, within a few hours of Johnson's death, invited to edit Johnson's works and write a prefatory life.[21] Even before Johnson's funeral, a London newspaper announced that Hawkins and Boswell were chief contenders for the role of official biographer. Immediately after the funeral, Hawkins's publishers advertized their projected edition, emphasizing the "authentick" life, which would accompany it, and warning readers against lives from less competent sources. A few weeks later a series of anonymous letters, which turned out to be written by an enemy of Hawkins, began appearing in the *St. James Chronicle*, arguing the superior qualifications of Boswell as biographer. The claims centered on issues now associated with authorized versus unauthorized biographies: "It is evident from the Conduct of the late Dr. Johnson, that he designed Mr. Boswell for the sole Writer of his Life. Why else did he furnish him with such Materials for it as were withheld from every other friend?" (Hawkins, xii). Boswell, acknowledging Hawkins's significant rival claim, challenged him directly in the Advertisement to the first edition of the *Life*. Hawkins was Boswell's principal competitor, as Boswell knew only too well, because Sir John had been appointed Johnson's executor. Hawkins thus had first access to Johnson's papers, including the autobiographical fragments, only subsequently available to Boswell. These papers, Boswell comments, if developed by Johnson into a full-length life, would have made unnecessary a third-person life of Johnson since, by Johnson's standards, every person is his own best biographer, a qualification intensely heightened in the particular case of Johnson. Since Hawkins's seeing the papers first located him within the first circle of Johnson's acquaintances, a proximity crucial to Boswell's defense of his own authority, Boswell felt obliged to establish a different ground of authority for his own writing.

He constructs his unique authority by revising the grounds of authority from a consideration of mere priority to validity of interpretation and tonal accuracy. Hawkins, Boswell asserts, lacks "that nice perception which was necessary to mark the finer and less obvious parts of Johnson's character" (Boswell, *Life*, 1:27). Hawkins's biography is a "farrago . . . swelled out with long unnecessary extracts from various works . . . a very small part of [it] relates to the person who is the subject of the book" (Boswell, *Life*, 1:28). Yet more damning than either the biographer's imperceptiveness or his triviality is "the dark uncharitable cast of the whole" (Boswell, *Life*, 1:28). Thus the key evidence in Boswell's case does not involve reliance on primary materials, oral and written, the preservation of a mass of particular details about the biographical subject, or Hawkins's method. With the exception of

Boswell's criticism of his rival's digressions, he finds Hawkins's materials and method generally supportive of his own. Rather, the question becomes one of Hawkins's temperament and disposition for writing about Johnson and the degree to which the two men are, or are not, as Boswell, claims, well matched as biographer and subject.

Boswell presents himself as sympathetic, without being uncritical, a trusted personal friend yet not sycophantish, a man tireless in checking and double-checking his evidence, and most of all one whose education in biography has come from the preeminent biographer of the age who also approved this biography.

At first well reviewed, Hawkins's life of Johnson was soon criticized for being inaccurate, malevolent, spiteful, filled with digressions and legalisms. It has resided, since that time, in Boswell's shadow. Both Boswell and Hawkins aimed to set their subject in his time and explore his personality. Both promised not to write mere panegyrics. Both presented a great man who was not unbelievably or inimitably heroic. Their different temperaments and styles, their respective ages (Boswell was in his mid-thirties when he began systematic work on the *Life*, while Hawkins was in his late sixties), and the different lengths of their friendships with Johnson (twenty years for Boswell, fifty for Hawkins) produced, not surprisingly, different books. Boswell's easier, more familiar, and less judicial style, along with his emphasis on recreating scenes in Johnson's life has enjoyed much greater favor with readers.

Different though their lives of Johnson are, Hawkins and Boswell shared the modern sense of an "obligation to include" and the extreme unwillingness to exclude anything relevant to the subject.[22] This responsibility to be compendious informs Boswell's journal entry, "sorted till I was stupefied," written while organizing materials for the *Life*.[23] Motivated by the desire to write "more of a life" than had ever before been written and to retain primary sources, such as letters, diaries, and anecdotes in their full particularity, Boswell thoroughly established a tradition of "mixed" biography, as opposed to biography "pure and simple" in which all evidence is recounted narratively by the biographer.

Boswell's method was complex. He took rough notes shortly after a meeting with Johnson, then transferred them with elaborations and revisions into a journal. Arguably, Boswell's journal is the text that encompasses his *Life of Johnson*, rather than the *Life* being the end and aim of his life of writing. In one journal entry Boswell notes that he will try to live no more than he can hope to transcribe in his journal. Although people joked both at the time and after about Boswell's trailing after Johnson, pen and paper in hand, the two men, over their twenty-year friendship, spent cumulatively something less than one year together. The extant papers indicate his actual method of telegraphic note taking followed by elaborations which, when materials exist to compare the two, prove to be accurate. Boswell's aim was to recreate the Johnson whom he and others knew, and Johnson's effect, his *factual effect*, one might say, upon them. Boswell did not intend, as some have claimed, to "improve on the record but to make it more accurate" (Krutch, 381).

Boswell did not write a critical biography, a form which tries to shed light on and interpret an author's writings in context of the life, though he does comment briefly on Johnson's writings within the encompassing chronology of his life. Boswell's choice not to place more emphasis on Johnson the writer is part and parcel of his expressed aim to depict the man. It may also be evidence of his inability to imagine a time when it could not be assumed that readers would not be familiar with Johnson's work. Boswell intended his biography to be an adjunct to the reader's experience of knowing Johnson the writer. It is also important to note that for all literary biographers since Boswell one of the central and most challenging issues remains the question of how much to quote from their subjects' writings and to say about them.[24] No definitive formula exists to guide this decision, and biographers' decisions are typically either vindicated or condemned on the basis of their subjects' subsequent reputations, to which important biographies may make their own contributions.

Piozzi's *Anecdotes* is a different kind of book from either Hawkins's or Boswell's life. Next to autobiography, the most valuable records written about a person are, presumably, accounts by intimate contemporaries who may, of course, be wrong but who have the unassailable resource of firsthand knowledge. Among the several differences between Piozzi's account and the other two, size is most striking. Hers is a slim memoir. Like Hawkins and Boswell, Piozzi was a personal friend of Johnson. Their acquaintance began when she was married to Henry Thrale, also a close friend of Johnson. Both Mrs. Thrale and Boswell knew Johnson during the last two decades of his life. Piozzi's and Johnson's friendship ended after Henry Thrale died and Hester subsequently married, much to her family's and Johnson's distress, Gabriel Piozzi, an expatriate Italian musician and teacher.

Johnson's friends in life, Hawkins, Boswell, and Piozzi competed for the reading public's interest, belief, and allegiance in their respective biographies after his death. Each knew Johnson as the other two did not and in ways that their differences of personality, mind, temperament, gender, and age help explain, surely the case with most intimate friendships. Piozzi, whom Johnson knew as Hester Thrale during her first marriage, was a woman, wife, and mother. She was bright, able, attractive, a successful hostess, an energetic mother, nurturing, attentive, and solicitous to Johnson. Boswell, when he first met Johnson, was a young Scotsman from a titled family, living in London, trying to decide on a career and to make a break from his overbearing father. He was alternately melancholy, ebullient, unreliable, dependent, overly imaginative, and self-indulgent. He later took up law, his father's profession, married, and had a family. To Boswell, Johnson was a surrogate father who combined encouragement with love and tutorial discipline in equal parts. With Thrale, he could behave differently, being by turns childlike, fatherlike, and suitorlike, his behavior ranging from the confessional to the demanding, the brusque to the passionate. Boswell's and Piozzi's accounts depict different, though interrelated, aspects of the man's makeup. Boswell's multivolume work contrasts with Thrale's slim, pocketable book. The difference in size alone makes different assertions about the writers' authority, assertions conventionally related, though not solely related, to their respective genders.

These differences also motivate different readerly responses to that authority.[25] All three writers share the assumption that biography is essentially a social form. As Ellmann observes, "For the biographer, who himself represents the outside world, the social self is the real self, the self only comes to exist when juxtaposed with other people."[26] Yet, as these three depictions of Johnson demonstrate, if the biographer "represents" the outside world, there will be, depending on the biographer, different emergent worlds.

Piozzi's preface to the *Anecdotes* describes the author's anticipation that many readers will criticize her for insufficiently praising Johnson. She challenges these critics, noting that, if she has "described his manners as they were," the truth claim taking precedence over panegyric, she has equally depicted his "superiority to the common forms of common life."[27] Then, in a passage uncannily predictive of Strachey's preface to *Eminent Victorians*, she remarks that "too much intelligence is often as pernicious to Biography as too little" (Piozzi, 61); the biographer must select and edit radically details of the subject's life. Piozzi concludes by noting that if Johnson had not asked her to write a memoir and without similar requests from others, she would never have undertaken this project.

For all of Johnson's contemporary biographers and their audience, the chief issue at stake is the question of their respective authority to write this life. Piozzi recounts, in support of her book, a 1773 conversation with Johnson. To Johnson's question about who she thought would be his biographer, she answered, "Goldsmith." Johnson agreed with her that Goldsmith could write it best, if only he would, adding that Goldsmith had malice toward him and was not careful about truth. Piozzi replied that Johnson's friends would see to it that he told the truth. Johnson then named several others who knew him well, especially in the early years (John Taylor, William Adams, and Robert James, along with John Hawkesworth whom, Johnson said, he had known for many years preceding his introduction to the Thrales). He concluded that he would either make Mrs. Thrale write his life in collaboration with Taylor, who could provide information from the early years, or "do it myself, after outliving you all" (Piozzi, 70). By citing this anecdote Piozzi edges out her preeminent competition, Boswell and Hawkins.

Though Piozzi characterizes her account as a "mere *candle-light* picture" of Johnson's latter days, she promises the reader the pleasures of encountering "little specimens of the rarities" of this great man's conversations enjoying the social pleasures of the Thrales' home at Streatham Park. Yet, like Boswell and Hawkins, she also frankly describes his "disordered health and spirits," diseases "incident to the most vivid and fervent imaginations," and the pains she and her husband took to "sooth or repress . . . his uneasy fancies" (Piozzi, 156).

Murphy begins his biographical-critical *Essay on the Life and Genius of Dr. Johnson* (1792) by noting how thoroughly Johnson has been scrutinized in the many literary biographies published during the eighteen years since his death. He has been examined to a degree that "perhaps never was a human being of whom more may be known by those who have had no oppportunity of personal acquaintance."[28] Such thorough familiarity with a writer certainly has drawbacks, particularly, Murphy notes, in the opportunities indirectly provided for unfounded speculation and malicious exaggeration. Yet there is apparently no stopping the interest in Johnson who provides at least as many questions as answers, thus inviting repeated examinations of his life.

Murphy makes several comments that give evidence of the essential continuity of literary biography's informing principles since the eighteenth century:

> That the history of an author must be found in his works is, in general, a true observation; and was never more apparent than in the present narrative. Every area of Johnson's life is fixed by his writings. . . . There may, perhaps, be a degree of sameness in this regular way of tracing an author from one work to another, and the reader may feel the effect of a tedious monotony; but in the life of Johnson there are no other landmarks. (Murphy, 1:48, 54)

Literary biographers have continued searching for authors' histories in their works and interpreting their writings as instances of conduct by which the biographical narrative is organized and hence character revealed.

Yet significant rival claims have arisen, challenging the commonsensical and seemingly self-evident value of conscious conduct as the principal datum for biographical analysis. Psychoanalysis and other depth psychologies have asserted competing emphases on indirect revelation of unconscious motives and the formative effects of early childhood psychosexuality. Psychoanalysis, by positing dream and fantasy as perennial psychic functions, defines the compensatory channeling of unconscious motives and desires into art as a special case of a general phenomenon of existential pathology. Artists thus becomes quintessential types of pathologized humanity, though their pathology presumably expresses itself with formal symbolic power.

Like formalist criticism, its near contemporary, psychoanalytic approaches to creativity revise the place of the creator in the work, though each displaces the artist in a slightly different way. The degree of their combined and interrelated impact on twentieth-century literary biography can be inferred from Leon Howard's description of the way his *Herman Melville* (1951) departs from conventional biography in the "amount of attention paid to the writing of Melville's books as a series of important events in his life."[29] Acts of the creative imagination, according to Howard, cannot be successfully explained or construed merely as self-expression or unconscious emanation, tracing back directly or indirectly to the author's personal life (the process model), or as studied rhetorical art (the product model). They are events, nothing more or less, and thus must be recounted and explained as such in the biographical narrative.

Boswell's sparse account of Johnson's early years, a distinct liability from the psychoanalytic point of view, motivated the scholarly biographical work of A. L. Reade in his ten-volume *Johnsonian Gleanings* (1909–1952). Subsequent Johnson biographers have expressed their debt to Reade for the substantial materials he discovered relevant to this period. Two excerpts from prefaces to two of these volumes are especially pertinent to a discussion of the poetics and method of modern biography.

Reade observes in the volume entitled *Francis Barber: The Doctor's Negro Servant* (1912):

> While this series intends to "provide material for the student [rather] than entertainment for the general reader, yet it is possible that the present volume may, to some extent, bridge the gulf that often separates dry research from human narrative. . . . There must be few readers of *Boswell* who do not feel a generous curiosity as to the Doctor's humble negro servant, who won so warm a place in his affections, and who inherited almost all [of Johnson's] modest fortune."[30]

Constructing this kind of bridge between the facts of scholarship and the projects of the imagination, which are the main topic of chapter 3, has become a matter of increasing interest to twentieth-century biographers.

In *The Doctor's Boyhood* (1922), Reade comments on the purpose of gathering and analyzing the various printed accounts of Johnson's boyhood, including Johnson's youth, along with additonal information researched by Reade himself, "not only for the actual light it throws upon his early life, its formative circumstances and surroundings, but also as an example of how much can be achieved by introducing determined and orderly method into the province of biographical research" (Reade, part 3, preface, iii–iv). Reade concludes by observing that the "art of biography is the gift of the few, but the science of biography can be advanced by anyone schooled to the pursuit of truth" (Reade, part 3, iv).

This issue of the opposing claims and methods of science versus the imagination are a recurring motif in modern discussions of biographical method with the debate typically resolving in favor of collaboration. The best practicing biographers generally agree that their conclusions, while based on previous experience, knowledge, and the scientific approach of a trained mind, trained particularly in psychology, are intuitive in the manner of a medical diagnosis that perceives meaningful pattern in a multitude of details. While thoroughly grounded in objective science, such perceptions involve the pattern-making creativity and connective leaps associated with art.[31] As Jay Martin comments in his life of Henry Miller, a book twenty-three years in the making, the biographer is responsible for gathering all the data possible ("where [Miller] lived and how, what he ate and what he wore, whom he spoke to and where, and what he said") and reading all extant manuscript materials. But this work is prologue to the purpose of the investigation, "since the 'facts' of his life become the most interesting—and perhaps the most true—just at the edge of mystery."[32]

No Johnson biographer after Boswell could fail to write in response or, to some degree, escape the shadow of this original modern life writer. Thomas Babington Macaulay's "Samuel Johnson" (1856), which also served as *The Encyclopaedia Britannica* entry on Johnson until 1965, initiated two major modern trends in the depiction of Johnson and his biographer. First, Macaulay presents Johnson as a writer whose memory remains alive thanks to his legendary personality, not his writings. This personality is, in turn, owed largely to Boswell's *Life*. Having denied Johnson the fame of authorship and granted Boswell the fame of writing a remarkable biography, Macaulay then proceeds to identify Boswell as a fool who accidentally wrote a great book, a writer who succeeded not in spite of but because of his weaknesses.

This two-part thesis, each half of which gives and simultaneously takes away from Boswell and Johnson, though flawed by illogic, has significantly affected both men's reputations. Macaulay describes Boswell as a "slave and idolator," whose "mind resembled those creepers which the botanists call parasites, and which can subsist only by clinging round the stems and imbibing the juices of stronger plants" who "in a happy hour fastened himself on Johnson." He refers to Boswell's method, in the passive voice: "In this way were gathered the materials, out of which was afterward constructed the most interesting biographical work in the world."[33] Boswell's method could have been known only partially at this time, since his working papers were not discovered until the twentieth century. Yet Macaulay's syntax robs Boswell of artistic consciousness and agency, while curiously granting him the prize of being the "first of biographers."[34]

Macaulay grants Boswell the dubious prize of being a trivial man who wrote a great book. He simultaneously grants Johnson the prize of being one of the most remarkable men, thanks to Boswell's depiction, which keeps Johnson's works alive through another man's account of him. Macaulay concludes his *Life of Johnson* with the following depiction of eccentric personality and virtuous character as Johnson's greatest, most memorable achievements:

> The old philosopher is still among us in the brown coat with the metal buttons and the shirt which ought to be at wash, blinking, puffing, rolling his head, drumming with his fingers, tearing his meat like a tiger, and swallowing his tea in oceans. No human being who has been more than seventy years in the grave is so well known to us. And it is but just to say that our intimate acquaintance with what he himself would have called the anfractuosities of his intellect and of his temper serves only to strengthen our conviction that he was both a great and a good man. (Macaulay, 578)

Sir Leslie Stephen contributed a biography of Johnson to the *English Men of Letters* series (1878). He continued in the line of Macaulay's characterizations of Johnson and Boswell, the two figures now associated as something like halves of a single persona. Stephen depicted Johnson the conversationalist and focused on the writings that reflect his excellent talk, the *Lives of the Poets* chief among them.

Sir Walter Raleigh's *Six Essays on Johnson* (1910) marks a distinctive revision of the nineteenth-century image of Johnson and hence, though not a systematic biography, deserves attention in this genealogy of Johnson lives. This series of interrelated critical-biographical inquiries cumulatively examines the man, his works, and Johnson's several depictions by Boswell, Piozzi, Hawkins, Tyers, Shaw, and others. Raleigh's observation in the introductory essay that Johnson's "life is inseparable from his works" revises the nineteenth-century trend of valuing Johnson's character over his writings.[35] By emphasizing the inseparability of life and works and hence directing readers to consider how these elements shed light on one another, Raleigh turns biography's attention to the creative process. To this end he tries to give Boswell his due by pointing out Macaulay's illogic in identifying Boswell as a fool who accidentally wrote a great book, while also, in the centerpiece essay, "Johnson without Boswell," focusing on Johnson separate from the biographer who had become part of his subject's persona.

"Johnson without Boswell" examines comparatively Boswell and his predecessors. Raleigh writes not in order to detract from Boswell's achievement but rather to place it in the historical context so radically constricted by the nineteenth century. He asks a series of questions that indicate the way the new biography was examining this genre and redefining its tasks: What would we know of Johnson if Boswell had never written? Is Boswell's account confirmed by the testimony of others? Is Boswell's narrative in any respects biased, partial, or erroneous? In answer to the first question, Raleigh asserts that even without Boswell, we would know more of Johnson than of any other writer of his time. In answer to the second, Boswell's great merits, Raleigh observes, include his careful depiction of context, his love of Johnson, and his accuracy. Raleigh says that Boswell's is the best life among those written by Johnson's contemporaries because "he loved Johnson better than they did" and because the man he loved "was worth it" (Raleigh, 72, 73).

Joseph Wood Krutch describes his life of Johnson as a book intended "to give the general reader a running account of Johnson's life, character, and work as they appear in light of contemporary knowledge and contemporary judgment" (Krutch, vii). Though not a conventional scholarly biography, *Samuel Johnson* (1944) is scholarly and learned. Though not a critical biography as such, it provides a substantial running commentary on the writings viewed through the lens of life. Krutch discusses Johnson's writings in substantial detail, some works occupying entire chapters (*Rasselas*, the edition of Shakespeare's plays, and the *Lives of the Poets*). But in a manner reminiscent of Leon Howard's method in *Herman Melville: A Biography*, Krutch presents these works as events in the life of a writer who subsequently became the reigning professional man of letters of his day. Krutch's remarks on

Johnson's depiction of Shakespeare, as "the people's Shakespeare rather than either the Shakespeare of learned critics or the Shakespeare of the aesthete" well describe the Johnson intended by Krutch for the educated nonspecialist reader (Krutch, 336). This biographer's chief aim is to propose a convincing explanation of Johnson's existence defined in terms of the paradoxes of his personality. A "pessimist with an enormous zest for living" (Krutch, 1), a man whose appetites for learning, literature, good company, and food ran as deep as his belief that all is vanity, Krutch's Johnson is a construction of powerful, systemic opposites.

Recognizing how central Boswell has become to the idea of Johnson, Krutch introduces him directly into the biography in a chapter entitled "Enter James Boswell." While not uncritical of Boswell, Krutch defends him against the charge, still not put to rest, of being a fool who happened to write a great biography. He argues that Boswell, though neurotic, possessed and furthermore developed three characteristics strategic for a great biographer: his "genuine admiration for intellectual greatness; an almost unrivaled sense of what words or gestures or actions reveal of personality; and a passionately industrious habit of writing down whatever seemed to him memorable" (Krutch, 230).

Clifford, in *Young Sam Johnson* (1955), the first volume of a two-volume life of Johnson from childhood until he meets Boswell, sets out to write what the author calls an artistic-scholarly biography. *Young Sam* and its sequel, *Dictionary Johnson* (1979), discussed later in this chapter, involve the same thorough research and primary allegiance to factual accuracy as scholarly-historical biography. But the artistic-scholarly biography differs in the way the writer conceives of himself as an imaginative artist, in addition to being a historian.[36]

Young Sam, as the title predicts, addresses the challenge of reversing the popular image of Johnson as an old man by reinserting logically Johnson's youth before his old age. Difficult as it is to imagine a time before we ourselves existed, it is perhaps yet more difficult to imagine great adult figures as children.[37] Most great achievements for which people are remembered occur in their adult years. Thus to examine a great person's childhood is, inevitably, to examine life backwards from the later years. The search for impulses and obstacles to later achievements is all but obligatory after the Romantics and Freud. Yet it is curious how, in the way biography thinks back through its subject, childhood becomes, to all intents and purposes, the effect of the adult accomplishment, the later years become formally prior to the earlier period and hence the lens through which they are viewed. In the case of Johnson, this reverse chronology, at once a problem and an epistemological necessity, is redoubled in direct proportion to the fact that Boswell knew Johnson during the last twenty-one years of his life and because, given his aims and promises to the reader, Boswell appropriately emphasizes these later years. Clifford takes on these challenges directly, not as errors to be corrected but as areas to be examined and filled in. He recreates Johnson from childhood through adolescence and into manhood.

Here lies perhaps the single greatest distinguishing difference between twentieth-century biography and earlier lives. Twentieth-century readers require the biographer to tell us about the formation of the subject's character, personality, peculiarities. Boswell, as Ellmann comments, prefers to give us Johnson's character already formed, because he is interested in the force of that character, not its formation. Post-Freudian readers, however, expect biographers to disclose the "inner compulsions, the schizoid elements" which "lay behind that force."[38] We also tend to suspect and expect the worst of one another.

Boswell did not think of himself as failing to deal with Johnson's private life or covering up his subject's weaknesses. He was, in fact, severely criticized by some for being too frank. But "domestick privacies," Johnson's phrase in *Rambler* No. 60 identifying the realm where biographers often find the most significant and revealing details about their subjects, assuredly did not mean to Boswell what it would come to mean after Freud and Strachey. Decorum was not the only value at stake, nor can the stakes be reduced to a mere prudishness or naïveté. The encompassing issue involves values and knowledge—what counts as valuable knowledge, how one ascertains that knowledge, and how it should be used.

A particular issue in Johnson biography relevant to this matter is Johnson's lifelong struggle with mental illness, a fact not unrecognized by his contemporaries. Sir Joshua Reynolds, for instance, wrote the following comment: "What Dr. Johnson said a few days before his death of his disposition to insanity was no new discovery to those who were intimate with him."[39] Yet not until the mid-twentieth century did scholarship isolate this matter for explicit scrutiny. Katherine C. Balderston's essay "Johnson's Vile Melancholy" (1949) presents a dramatic psychosexual interpretation of some previously unscrutinized evidence. Balderston's interpretation elaborates the twentieth century's growing recognition of the seriousness of Johnson's mental disturbance and the degree to which his insights into passion and pathology were fueled by private experiences, chief among them a supposed sadomasochistic relationship with Mrs. Thrale. Balderston presents a complex of evidence from Johnson's, Thrale's, and Boswell's writings, including reference to a padlock and whip. Brought together and focused on psychoanalytically, she argues, these elements hint "at an untold chapter in Johnson's life" pertinent to explaining the vehemence of his break with Mrs. Thrale when she married Gabriel Piozzi. Balderston interprets Johnson's relations with Thrale using Kraepelin's and Freud's models of the symptoms and structures of psychosexual disorder. Thrale became for Johnson, Balderston argues, "the unrecognized erotic object from whose ministrations his maladjusted libido sought relief and at the same time, to his conscious mind, the revered woman, object of his awed respect and adoration, who by her very virtue could in some mysterious fashion check his abnormalities and exorcise his devils."[40]

Balderston's essay has elicited responses from Johnson's subsequent biographers, James Clifford's being one of the most thoughtful. Clifford refers to a "masochistic strain" in Johnson, forming in early life and manifesting in the later years. He places Johnson's maladjustment in perspective by comparing him with his friend Richard Savage, "a perfect paradigm of the type" of person "emotionally dependent upon pain and disappointment, often self-inflicted."[41] Clifford warns readers at the outset that those expecting "a modern psychological interpretation of Johnson's complexes may be disappointed," since his study avoids using "the technical language of psychiatry" and, while it suppresses "no significant fact," leaves any "reader who so desires [to] make his own analysis" (Clifford, *Young Sam*, x). This passage contains two important embedded observations well worth noting explicitly: first, that a psychiatric or psychoanalytic approach to examining human behavior is now such a familiar biographical tool that its absence makes readers suspicious that the biographer is either ill-trained or attempting to cover up something;

second, that since biographers may now assume readers' familiarity with psychoanalytic methods of interpretation, they may also assume these readers to be, if provided with sufficient accurate information by the biographer, capable of making or choosing not to make their own analyses.

Donald Greene's *Samuel Johnson* (1970) praises Boswell for having written a "great work of art" but "not a biography at all."[42] Greene describes Boswell's *Life* as a compilation from his journal about himself, which included his time with Johnson. Greene also criticizes the quaintness of Boswell's picture of "dear old Doctor Johnson," a phrase difficult to reconcile with Boswell's depictions of Johnson as a gladiator in the lion's den and the new Odysseus. The chief aim of this critical biography is to return the reader to Johnson's writings, his career as writer, and hence to the "fascinating variety" of the man himself. Greene comments that "what the modern reader really needs, to illuminate Johnson for him, is some kind of history of his *intellectual* life, a systematic account of his voluminous and catholic reading, the influences on his thinking on various important subjects, the development of his ideas, and their relation to ideas that preceded and followed them" (Greene, 11).[43] This project inspired Robert DeMaria Jr.'s critical biography, discussed at the end of this chapter.

Paul Fussell's *Samuel Johnson and the Life of Writing* (1971) both follows and departs from Krutch's biography most notably. Fussell, unlike Krutch, writes for an audience of academics and students of the eighteenth century. But, like Krutch, he examines Johnson's behavior as a writer in context of some of the "conceptions about writing that governed Johnson's achievement."[44] These include Johnson's understanding of what literature is and is for, genre, the idea of authorship, and a writer's relation to his predecessors, to name a few, some or all which may no longer be so thoroughly familiar to us as they were to Johnson and his readers. While Fussell attempts to make Johnson the writer and his writings comprehensible and interesting to twentieth-century readers, he does so not by arguing explicitly his contemporary relevance but by making this case indirectly. Fussell locates Johnson squarely in his own time and examines contextual assumptions and knowledge, especially about genre, essential to comprehending him and his writing.

John Wain's *Samuel Johnson: A Biography* (1974) addresses itself, like Krutch's life, to the intelligent general reader, incorporating the work of Johnson scholars while aiming generally to present a "just image of Johnson among a less specialized circle of readers" (Wain, 14). He notes the continuation of Johnson's mistaken reputation for archconservatism and the failure to appreciate the complexities of his thinking about literature, society, politics, and history.

Wain critiques the durable image of Boswell's Johnson, noting its origin in the mind of a man so different from Johnson. Boswell, Wain observes, was a snob and a "sentimental-romantic Tory," who yearned after the dethroned Stuarts and projected these yearnings onto Johnson and the life he wrote about him. This critical and narrative biography is also informed by self-announcedly "documentary interest," by which Wain means an autobiographical motif running throughout. The biographer identifies explicitly with his subject. Both were born in the Midlands, attended Oxford, and spent most of their lives as professional writers in the line of Grub Street hacks. Wain thus claims one aspect of his authority to write about Johnson, a matter central to most biographers' poetics, on the basis of his uniquely personal "position to see [Johnson's] life from the inside" (Wain, 14).

Walter Jackson Bate's *Samuel Johnson* (1975) is an intensively interpretive biography that leaves little room for readers to analyze on their own Johnson's achievement, psychology, values, and beliefs. Reminiscent of Boswell, Bate stands resolutely beside Johnson and the reader, some might even say between Johnson and the reader, making sure that neither Johnson nor the biographer is misunderstood. Bate invokes psychoanalytic method but also urges readers, in reference to Balderston's essay, to beware of the twentieth century's reductive tendency to "leap to sex . . . at the mere mention of anything connected with either 'secrecy' or 'guilt.'"[45] Bate, however, more generally reaffirms the central insight of psychoanalysis, which he finds especially pertinent to Johnson, namely that "a pervasive, incorrigible sense of 'guilt'—as distinct from specific 'remorse'—is the inevitable result of the structural character of the human psyche, in which aggressiveness is taken over by a portion of the ego, and then internalized and directed back against the rest of the ego by a 'superego'" (Bate, 386).

Bate defines his task explicitly as being to confront major problems in preceding Johnson biographies, in particular, and in the genre of life writing, in general. He defines his task implicitly as being to follow in its subject's footsteps, acknowledging by imitation Johnson's love of biography and the high value he placed on its usefulness in helping human beings confront their fears, weaknesses, and insecurities. As a problem solver, Bate, like Wain, feels obliged to take on Boswell. He acknowledges that Boswell's *Life* has been instrumental in making Johnson a "household name," but the cause is Johnson himself, "a heroic, intensely honest, and articulate pilgrim in the strange adventure of human life" (Bate, xx). Bate thus suggests that his biography will depict a Johnson *before* Boswell, a decision with a major associated liability in the extraordinary disparity between the amount of information available about the pre-Boswell years and the mass of information, thanks chiefly to Boswell, available thereafter. This disproportion challenges the biographer substantively and organizationally.

Finally, Bate notes that in biography written since the 1930s a growing separation has occurred between literary biography and literary criticism, as each undertaking has become more specialized. The literary critic avoids biography, the literary biographer avoids critical interpretation, and both avoid judgment. Parenthetically, it is interesting to set this item on Bate's revisionist agenda in the context of Johnson's *Lives of the Poets*, whose other title, *Prefaces Biographical and Critical to the Works of the English Poets*, identifies the distinction between biographical fact and critical interpretation. In each of his literary lives, Johnson writes separate biographical and critical sections, understanding the two, presumably, to be compatible but not intermixable, partaking of different kinds of evidence, relying on different measures of certainty, and offering different kinds of usefulness. Critical judgments, as Johnson demonstrates in his *Preface to Shakespeare*, will never attain final certainty because they are, by the nature of the distinctive kind of thinking involved, always comparative assessments. And comparative assessments not only invite but indeed require rethinking by each generation of readers.

Bate's biography confronts these three problems chiefly by his choice of psychoanalysis as his main biographical tool. First, the biographer as analyst positions himself in between Boswell and Johnson. Second, by approaching Johnson as subject to be analyzed, he gives priority to the early life. Intensity of scrutiny and elaboration of explanation of the extant facts from this lesser known period replace the priority of sheer amount with the intriguing power of significance, putting Bate in charge of the years when Boswell did not know Johnson, emphasizing childhood illness, a powerful mother, eccentric intelligence and curiosity, and financial disappointments as key factors of resistance and motivation defining this heroic life. Finally, psychoanalysis reunites biography and criticism focused through the lens of Freud's notions of the unconscious origins and compensatory functions of creativity.

Clifford's *Dictionary Johnson: Samuel Johnson's Middle Years* (1979), published twenty-four years after *Young Sam*, addresses directly and attempts to rectify Boswell's disproportionate handling of the period 1749 to 1763. Though one-fifth of Johnson's life, this period occupies one-tenth of Boswell's *Life*, a condensation which allowed Boswell to move on to the period he knew best, Johnson's last twenty years. Since these fourteen years were Johnson's most productive period of writing, they serve as chief evidence in any study of Johnson the writer that aims to reconstruct "how and with whom he spent his days" and of his actions and reactions.[46]

Clifford's second volume shifts the emphasis slightly, from origins in the first volume to social, political, intellectual associations and context, as the biographer examines the years of Johnson's greatest work. Clifford announces to the reader his working assumption that in order "to understand the basic motivations of any writer it is necessary to know something about his physical surroundings, the characters of his close associates, and the intellectual, political, and social currents of the day" (Clifford, *Dictionary Johnson*, viii).

Proof that Johnson remains a subject of ongoing interest in the unfinished business of assembling information, particularly about his early years, is Thomas Kaminski's *The Early Career of Samuel Johnson* (1987). Kaminski delimits this biography's time and scope to a systematic examination of Johnson's first years as a professional writer, from his arrival in London in 1737 to his contracting to write the *Dictionary* in 1746. This period has been of somewhat less interest to literary scholars since it does not encompass the major writings by which Johnson would become best known. Kaminski's sociohistorical biography of the first decade of Johnson's career attempts to locate the man in his times, specifically in the newly developing world of commercial publishing. This life, while it does not deny the concept of the individual and individual achievement, does undertake to imagine the self within a set of cultural-material motivations and constraints.

The need for an intellectual-historical biography of Johnson, noted by Greene, motivates Robert DeMaria Jr.'s *Samuel Johnson: A Critical Biography* (1993). DeMaria presents Johnson as a man of opposites: the last of the great continental humanists and the first of the new professional writers, one for whom alienation and compromise were chronically at war with success. This proposition develops a familiar interpretive structure in the history of Johnson biographies, by now a familiar one in this discussion, namely that his life was a battleground of warring opposites, or the *two's syndrome*: Krutch observes that Johnson was a "pessimist with a great zest for living"; Fussell comments on the double combination of opposites, "cunning knowingness and almost unbelievable innocence" with "literary duplicity and literary honesty"; and Bate identifies Johnson's "bisociative thinking."

Two distinct patterns and tendencies in lives of Johnson emerge from the preceding discussion: One is the just mentioned *two's syndrome*; the other, *What's to be done with Boswell?* The explanatory power of the two's syndrome has offered continuing satisfaction. Associated originally with Boswell's depiction of Johnson's tensions and contradictions fueling great accomplishment, this characterization echoes Plato's image of the soul as a charioteer reining in dynamically opposed appetites. With few exceptions, this topos has continued to explain Johnson's character satisfactorily to generations of readers. No biographer of Johnson after Boswell has been able to avoid the question of what's to be done with Johnson's most challenging biographer. Boswell's massive, eccentric life is always there to be reckoned with whether by biographical elaboration, contradiction, or castigation.

More broadly speaking, the architecture of Boswell's *Life* has not provided a model for literary biography in general. Readers have generally preferred narrative biography to his nonnarrative mixture of genres. But Boswell's emphasis on retaining evanescent details of daily life and speech has proved to be a touchstone of life writing. The example of Boswell's avowed teacher, Johnson, particularly in Johnson's allying and interanimating yet not intermixing biographical and critical facts in the *Lives of the Poets*, has continued to be an issue at stake in the writing of modern literary lives. In the twentieth century the two subgenres of literary and critical biography have, to all intents and purposes, gone their separate ways.

Chapter 3

MAJORITY BIOGRAPHY 2: VIRGINIA WOOLF

> But the Victorian biography was a parti-coloured, hybrid, monstrous birth. For though truth of fact was observed as scrupulously as Boswell observed it, the personality which Boswell's genius set free was hampered and distorted.
>
> Woolf, "The New Biography" (1927)

Virginia Woolf, Biographer

On October 5, 1927, Virginia Woolf began writing *Orlando* (1928), a fictional biography based on a real person, which she would later recall having begun "as a joke."[1] Just over three weeks later, on October 30, 1927, Woolf's essay "The New Biography" appeared in the *New York Herald Tribune* (reprinted in *Granite and Rainbow* [1958]). Six years later came *Flush: A Biography* (1933), a comic-scholarly life of Elizabeth Barrett Browning's pet spaniel. In 1935, she began work on a life of Roger Fry (1940). Finally, in 1939, three years after she began *Roger Fry*, Woolf wrote a second essay on life writing, "The Art of Biography" (*Atlantic Monthly*, April 1939). In the pages that follow I will present some of the possible meanings of this sequence of Woolf's engagement with the theory and practice of biography. Among her contemporaries, Woolf was one of the few modernists, Gertrude Stein being a notable exception, to undertake the interdisciplinary challenges of biography, a form more likely to humble than exalt its practitioners.[2] From Woolf's point of view biography had seriously declined since Boswell. Boswell's success in dramatizing personality, while remaining true to the facts, set an example that had proved difficult for the nineteenth century to equal, Woolf believed, much less excel. Assembling facts for the sake of facts, these writers produced huge, shapeless, lifeless tomes.

Woolf's first essay, "The New Biography," assumes an optimistic, progressive tone in proposing the responsibilities and possibilities associated with this genre. She admits the essential challenge of attempting to weld the "granite-like solidity" of truth and the rainbow-like intangibility" of personality into "one seamless whole." She is, however, cheerful, on balance, about the possibilities of improving biography to achieve this union. In the wake of biography's deterioration in the nineteenth century, Woolf identifies new signs that the genre's poetics have been accurately recast to place appropriate emphasis on the imagination. "In the old days," she notes, "biographers told tales of battle and victory. We, by contrast, can no longer maintain that life consists in actions only or in works. It consists in personality."[3]

By Woolf's estimate this new emphasis on the interior life of emotion and thought introduces self-evident improvement in the practice of biography. Victorian biography, with its preconceived emphasis on the exteriorized "idea of goodness" and its corresponding distortion of personality, is now over, she asserts, once and for all. She critiques later nineteenth-century biography, inviting readers to imagine their lives written by a Victorian biographer by posing this question: Does not "all that has been most real" slip through these writers' fingers? Granting that even the new biographers had not entirely solved the problem of capturing the reality of life in words, she praises them for recognizing this to be the foremost aim of biography and for acknowledging the need to enliven biography with imaginative techniques borrowed from the novelist's "art of arrangement, suggestion, dramatic effect."[4]

By contrast with the progressively optimistic tone of "The New Biography," Woolf's "Art of Biography," written eleven years later, gives a more nuanced description of the biographer's task and takes a less youthfully optimistic view of the possibilities of applying fictional techniques to factual writing. The essay opens with an ironic observation about the "high death-rate" of biography: "There it is, whenever a new biography is opened, casting its shadow on the page; and there would seem to be something deadly in that shadow, for after all, of the multitude of lives that are written, how few survive."[5] This high mortality rate results from biographers being "tied" to presenting facts by contrast with the novelist who "is free" to invent details. The *granite* and *rainbow* sides of the issue of the biographer's responsibility to truth (granite), on the one hand, and the imaginative depiction of personality (rainbow), on the other, argued so confidently by Woolf in the earlier essay, are here dramatically revised. Woolf distinguishes between biographer and novelist, the latter who enjoys the delights of perfect freedom, the former who is humbly responsible to truth. On the basis of this new distinction, she then proceeds to characterize the biographer's task as more complex, if less explicitly imaginative, than the novelist's. "He must be prepared," she advises, "to admit contradictory versions of the same fact. Biography will enlarge its scope by hanging up looking-glasses at odd corners."[6]

The centerpiece of "The Art of Biography" is Woolf's comparison of Strachey's biographies of Queen Elizabeth and Queen Victoria. The two, placed side by side, shed "great light," she promises, "upon the nature of biography."[7] In Strachey's life of Elizabeth, since very little was known about this woman, the biographer felt thereby authorized, or at least allowed, to invent this figure novelistically with only occasional constraints posed by the few facts known about Elizabeth. Victoria's life, by contrast, had been heavily documented, and because the biographer's artistic freedom is restricted in direct proportion to the amount of reliable evidence, Victoria's biographers must assume more responsibility to craft and exercise less independent invention. Woolf's observation recalls Boswell's emphasis on not reducing the heterogeneity of his materials and on submitting to the humbling effects of this decision—the "sorted till I was stupefied" principle.

The responsibilities to craft and fact that vary in proportion to the availability and amount of reliable information must somehow unite in the biographer's crafting of fact. Biographers can hope to write effectively only by acknowledging and working within this energizing, if often frustrating, game of constraints. "By telling us the true facts, by sifting the little from the big, and shaping the whole so that we can perceive the outline, the biographer does more to stimulate the imagination than any poet or novelist save the very greatest."[8] Strachey's Victoria, Woolf predicts, "will *be* Queen Victoria, just as Boswell's Johnson *is* now Dr. Johnson" (my emphasis). Woolf's verbs assert her notion of biography's quasi-ontological force born at precisely the moment when the book, having been read, is "tossed aside," but "some scene remains bright, some figure lives on in the depth of the mind, and causes us, when we read a poem or a novel, to feel a start of recognition."[9]

For reasons which she tries to identify, as much to satisfy her own curiosity, perhaps, as to edify readers, biography had come to seem to Woolf, now in late career, a harder taskmaster than either fiction or poetry. It was, she observed, less gratifying to the writer's ego, since, when done well, biography is not remembered for its own sake but for the imaginative traces of the subject's personality left in the reader's memory. Writing a successful biography offers significantly less narcissistic gratification than writing successful fiction or poetry because the sources of the genre's admittedly powerful effects are associated less with the text itself. Rather these effects seem to be a phenomenon of reading, not of textuality, as they characteristically sink deep in the reader's mind to emerge as imaginative memory more forceful than fiction because grounded in fact.

In the years between Woolf's two very different essays on the practice and poetics of biography she wrote three biographies and thus had occasion to rethink biography in practical and theoretical ways. Any explanation of how she came to revise her thinking about the genre must take into account her intervening work and its possible effects on how she thought about life writing. The first two biographical works written after the first essay on biography, *Orlando* and *Flush*, are scholarly-comic fictions, while the third, *Roger Fry*, which appeared shortly after the second essay, is a more conventional life.

Orlando, a picaresque biography, traces the adventures and fortunes of an English nobleman. Born in the Renaissance, Orlando lives on into the twentieth century, changing sex from male to female along the way. A playfully intricate as well as delightful book, this fictional life pays loving homage to Woolf's real-life friend, the novelist Vita Sackville-West. Sackville-West was inspiration and model for Orlando, whose long life, fortunes, and career narrate a tongue-in-cheek history of English manners, morals, and literature and cross-examine traditional biography's conventions, methods, and assumptions. Regarding the matter of time in biography, for instance, the narrator muses on the inadequacy of temporal measurement for depicting identity: "The true length of a person's life, whatever the *Dictionary of National Biography* may say, is always a matter of dispute. Indeed it is difficult business—this time-keeping; nothing more quickly disorders it than contact with the arts."[10] For Woolf, at this moment in her career, time and the imaginative depiction of time were the key to dramatizing personality. Personality was, in turn, she believed, the new biography's primary creative challenge. Its practitioners could no longer justify themselves as mere chroniclers, secretaries to their subjects' lives and times, but rather must rise to the challenge of being coequals. This line of thinking produced *Orlando*.

The *Dictionary of National Biography*, edited by Woolf's father, Sir Leslie Stephen, for sixteen years beginning in 1885, served Woolf well as a source of fertilizing resistance. The *DNB* aimed to give factually accurate accounts of notable figures in British history from the beginnings to the present. Stephen based his editorial principles on a belief in the primacy of facts. Ideas and the discussion of ideas had no place, he argued, in encyclopedic biographical accounts, which could not also undertake to narrate a history of ideas. Stephen wrote several volumes in the *English Men of Letters* series (Thomas Hobbes, Pope, Swift, Johnson, and George Eliot), where the subjects' ideas were acknowledged to have a legitimate place, though here he made a point of distinctly separating information about the subjects' lives from discussions of their ideas.[11]

In the rollicking biographical fiction *Orlando*, Woolf challenges her father's biographical dictionary, scrutinizing, in particular, its predominant commitment to fact, while criticizing Victorian biography generally for its commitment to idealized commemoration and decorum. Woolf's satire proceeds by introducing a series of whimsical yet systematic interrogatory inventions: a protagonist who never dies (hence no place for laudatory eulogy); sexual escapades frankly recounted (hence no decorum); and a sex change (hence no single gender type or stereotype). *Orlando* is filled with uproarious incidents and action, but the novel's emphasis falls, nonetheless, on the namesake character's qualities, the characteristics of the several centuries in which s/he lives, and the felt sense of living more than one life, while somehow embodying, nonetheless, a coherent, recognizable identity. Woolf humorously examines complacent, traditional divisions between thought and action, history and psychology, and public and private life, divisions scrupulously observed in the *Dictionary of National Biography*. She demonstrates by this examination how history is a phenomenological category that invents and is simultaneously driven by a period's conception of personal identity, particularly as identity relates to gender, sexuality, perception, and imagination, as exemplified in the following dinner-table scene (Orlando has become a woman):

> "A little of the fat, Ma'am?" he asked. "Let me cut you just the tiniest little slice the size of your finger nail." At those words, a delicious tremor ran through her frame. Birds sang; the torrents rushed. It recalled the feeling of indescribable pleasure with which she had first seen Sasha, hundreds of years ago. Then she had pursued, now she fled. Which is the greater ecstasy? (Woolf, *Orlando*, 155)

Woolf undertakes to arouse and satisfy the reader's curiosity about what it feels like (physically, emotionally, intellectually, spiritually) to be Orlando at precise moments of her male and female lives (some trivial, some momentous, though which is which is never complacently asserted): when Orlando feels cold, when he falls in love, when she entertains Alexander Pope, when she becomes engaged to be married, when he sits down to begin writing his long poem, *The Oak Tree*, a work-in-progress over three centuries. Since for the modern period real life and genuine identity "dwell in the personality rather than in the act," according to Woolf, and because fictional life has become "increasingly real to us," it follows that biography and fiction assume historically definitive importance.[12]

Flush, a life of Elizabeth Barrett Browning's pet spaniel, has been called "a flip demonstration of what a biographer should do with facts," namely get them right, while at the same time making them appealing emotionally and imaginatively.[13] A list of authorities appears at the end of *Flush*, which, though few, the author admits, prove that she has done her homework on Barrett Browning's dog. In addition there are scholarly notes, simultaneously informative and funny: "'He was stolen.' As a matter of fact, Flush was stolen three times; but the unities seem to require that the three stealings shall be compressed into one. The total sum paid by Miss Barrett to the dog-stealers was £20.'"[14]

For *Orlando*, Woolf created a fictional protagonist, allusively based on a real person who lives an extravagant, supernatural life in order to give the lie to conventional notions of linear time as the mainstay of biographical narration. For *Flush*, Woolf chose a historically real, though nonhuman, protagonist, modeled after Pinka, a cocker spaniel given to Woolf by Sackville-West, who had earlier inspired the figure of Orlando. By choosing a nonhuman subject Woolf motivates a different kind of cross-examination of conventional notions of significance and insignificance, large and small, likeness and difference from a point of view embodying a nonverbal schema of sensation and meaning.

Woolf's dog's-eye view of Elizabeth Barrett, her poetry, courtship, and marriage, anticipates comically her later proposal that biography should hang up mirrors at odd angles to reorient habitual lines of sight. In *Flush*, Miss Barrett, poet, celebrity, and romantic heroine, is depicted in relation to her dog. She is "his mistress," the syntax reversing conventional human priority. Flush comes first syntactically and hence every other way. He is the reader's point of view on all events. His sense of smell, practically nonexistent in humans, affords Flush infinite gradations of subtlety. For him, life is lived chiefly through the sense of smell. "Love was chiefly smell; form and colour were smell, music and architecture, law, politics and science were smell" (Woolf, *Flush*, 130). What, after all, is fear but an overreaction to the misconstruction of difference? As one of Woolf's characters in *The Years* (1935) observes:

> We're all afraid of each other . . . afraid of what? Of criticism; of laughter; of people who think differently. . . . He's afraid of me because I'm a farmer (and he saw again his round face; high cheekbones and small round eyes). And I'm afraid of him because he's clever. He looked at the big forehead, from which the hair was already receding. That's what separates us; fear, he thought.[15]

For Woolf, who throughout her career examined the profoundly damaging effects of fear among human beings, this experiment in creating nonviolent difference in *Flush* must surely have been particularly meaningful. In the following passage Flush and his mistress are described together for the first time: "She spoke. He was dumb. She was a woman; he was a dog. . . . Closely united, immensely divided," Flush and Miss Barrett together each completes "what was dormant in the other" (Woolf, *Flush*, 23, 161). Difference is dramatized as a benign, even benevolent cocreative principle.

When Woolf agreed to write the life of her friend, the artist and art critic Roger Fry (1866–1934), she accepted a variety of constraints and responsibilities. She was approached about writing his biography by Margery Fry, Fry's sister, and Helen Anrep, who lived with Fry from 1926 until his death. This undertaking put her biographical theory to a different kind of test, for a number of reasons, all closely associated with Woolf's touchstone for successful writing, the writer's independence. Facts and the biographer's responsibility to accuracy were the first constraint. The second constraint jeopardizing the writer's essential precondition of freedom came from Fry's relatives, friends, and even Woolf herself, all of whom, in various ways, not all of them conscious or coercive, had stakes in the matter of how his life was depicted.

Woolf describes her life of Fry as a child born of her and Roger's biographical union.[16] She notes further the anxious responsibility she feels in knowing that this portrait may stand for this man for years to come, as Strachey's Victoria became Victoria, particularly since Fry, being dead, could have no say and make no corrections. These matters troubled Woolf greatly. Some critics were disappointed in *Roger Fry: A Biography* (1940). Leonard Woolf, Virginia's husband, commented that the biographer's obligation to deal with facts and arguments at length caused her to write "against the grain" of her talents and temperament and to repress "something which was natural and necessary to her peculiar genius" (Bell, 2:182). Other critics remarked that a life of Fry requires expertise of a trained artist or art historian. Woolf, diversely learned though she was, had neither.

Finally, the challenge of recounting Fry's private emotional life positioned Woolf at odds with her earlier announced ideals of complete biographical candor.[17] When dealing with an actual human being, not to mention a friend, she felt responsible to discretion in certain sensitive matters: Fry's lover's mental illness, for one, and his relationship with Vanessa Bell, Woolf's married sister, for another. Writing about Helen Anrep's illness, Woolf praises Fry's loving care enthusiastically in ways that, ten years earlier in her career, one suspects she might have criticized as a latter-day remnant of the Victorian ideal of self-sacrificing goodness typically associated with wives and mothers, though here associated with a man. Here are two examples: "His patience and sympathy were indefatigable, his resourcefulness beyond belief"; "It is a splendid record of courage, patience and devotion."[18] Woolf calls Fry's and Bell's relationship a "friendship," though it was known they had been lovers. Decorous evasion and panegyric, so roundly criticized by Woolf in "The New Biography," arguably informed her own full-fledged exercise in the genre.

Woolf's reference to work on the Fry biography as "fearful niggling drudgery" (Bell 2:206) recalls her characterization of Fry's attitude toward his own work on Cézanne: "[T]he Cézanne cost its author much drudgery and despair. 'Oh Lord, how bored I am with it . . . it seems to me poor formless stuff'" (Woolf, *Fry*, 286). Turning again to the calendar of the composition of *Fry* (begun in October 1935, completed in 1940) in relation to the date of her second, more complex and sober essay, "The Art of Biography" (April 1939), one may better appreciate how, faced with primary factual materials, a real human subject, her own and other people's intimate acquaintance and friendship with Fry, she might have seen the task of biography somewhat differently. Woolf was a writer on whom experience was not lost. She was drawn imaginatively to theory, yet not traduced by its sleek beauty at the expense of the difficult, out-at-the-seams richness and difficulty of fact. She praises Fry's art criticism for successfully balancing theory and practice:

> For if we allow sensations to accumulate unchecked they lose their sharpness; to test them by reason strengthens and enriches. But fascinating as theories are . . . they too must be controlled or they will form a crust which blocks the way for further experience. Theories must always be brought into touch with facts. The collision may prove fatal to these delicate and intricate constructions. It does not matter. The risk must be run. (Woolf, *Fry*, 228)

Woolf could well be describing the difficult balancing act she, too, tried to maintain between theory and fact, particularly evident in her attitude toward the relevance of psychoanalysis to biography. The best biographical insights often occur when qualities shared by biographer and subject intersect, activating the biographer's curiosity about herself in reflective examination of the subject. Fry's unfinished autobiography includes other such elements, though with some of these Woolf's probing is more reticent.

The central motifs of Fry's unfinished autobiography are a childhood garden scene centered on the image of a red poppy and a painful reproof from his Quaker mother. Here Fry experienced his "first passion and suffered his first great disillusion" (Woolf, *Fry*, 15), two crucial moments of vision whose origins, Woolf comments, even Fry himself, who had traced so many spiritual journeys of other artists, might have found "too deep for analysis" (Woolf, *Fry*, 161). Woolf clearly implies that territory into which Fry would not pass, neither should the biographer.

If latter-day Victorian discretion provides one explanation of Woolf's reticences in writing this life, another explanation might be her humility before the mystery and sanctity of personality, creativity, and free will—elements arguably missing, along with a tolerance for uncertainty, in psychoanalysis. Woolf's skepticism about psychobiography is reminiscent of Bernard DeVoto's caveat:

> [Psychoanalysis] shifts the field of biography from the empirical where the subject mingled with his fellows, lived, worked, struggled, and, it may be, loved. . . . The lay biographer . . . must deal with these as best he may—by the swink of a never-ending labour which terrifies his slumber with the dread that he may have missed something, and which enables him in the end to say only "*a* is more probable than *b*" . . . but if you are an amateur analyst, to hell with uncertainty.[19]

Throughout her career Woolf became increasingly respectful of uncertainty.

In *Roger Fry*, Woolf, like her predecessors Johnson and Boswell, underscores the value of autobiography, its priority and even superiority to biography. Like Boswell, she admits that the most valuable document regarding her subject's life would be a completed autobiography. There being none, Woolf cites heavily from the first-person fragment, a decision for which she has sometimes been criticized. In the case of a figure such as Fry who had a much greater interest in things outside himself than things within (also true of Langston Hughes, discussed in chapter 4), and who often ignored others as thoroughly as he ignored himself, it is scarcely surprising that there were varying accounts of his life, not a few of them unflattering. Woolf's high valuing of autobiography over biography is not based on a naive assumption that autobiography is a transparency on the self. A first-person account is no less complex than third-person biography, as Woolf remarks after citing a passage from Fry's unfinished life: "Obviously the man, looking back at his past has added something to the impression received by a child of seven, and, since it was written for friends who took a humorous rather than a reverential view of eminent Victorians, no doubt it owed a little to the temper of the audience." (Woolf, *Fry*, 22) Yet there is an undeniable, invaluable primacy to an account coming from the subject himself as, for instance, in Fry's depiction of the two sides of his father's personality: one that "'scuttered along' with his coat-tails flying 'all laughter and high spirits'" and the other a "stern man who could in a moment, in a voice of awful gravity, reduce him to a sense of overpowering shame" (Woolf, *Fry*, 22). Whatever Fry's father may have actually been like, however he may have appeared to others, this is how he appeared to his son.

Woolf's life of Fry plots a fairly conventional narrative from birth to death, surveying the familiar topics of Victorian biography (family, schooling, marriage, work) so thoroughly criticized by Woolf ten years earlier. Yet within this encompassing framework there are unconventional digressions. These digressions include the biographer's efforts to suggest the qualities of Fry's mind and to assert, if indirectly, the forces of individual will and freedom embodied in the subject's creative process. Woolf consistently emphasizes the mind of the creator, sometimes even in comically unglamorous ways, as in these remarks on an excerpt from Fry's first essay: "And there his first crude essay in art criticism stops, for, though it is only half-past eight, he is dropping asleep and must go to bed immediately" (Woolf, *Fry*, 53). In a passage describing Fry's first trip to France, Woolf superimposes one time frame on another. One frame is linear-chronological, the other interpretively retrospective: "Yet France was to mean more to Roger Fry than any other country. . . . He was to spend his happiest days there. . . . But he seems in 1892 to have had no premonition what France was to mean to him . . . " (Woolf, *Fry*, 80–81). The several infinitives preserve a historical future yet to be lived, hence, too, contingency and choice, while at the same time identifying the fact that, from the reader's point of view, this time has passed.

To anyone reading this life, Fry and his work are known—and completed—quantities. This decision has long since been made, and the future conditioned by it has manifested. Yet Woolf tries to retain something of the quality of Fry's life at this moment when he, unlike readers of the biography, did not know how things would work out. She aims to preserve the sense of choices yet to be made, desire with an uncertain future, and contingency and freedom still to be negotiated. In so doing, she reminds the reader that history is one of the imagination's most challenging activities, requiring, as it does, stepping aside briefly from ego-centered identity that values theory over fact and risking the humbling challenge of reconstructing fact. "It is difficult," Woolf writes, "to recapture the atmosphere of Chelsea in 1892. The peace was so profound"; "It is difficult in 1939 . . . to realise what violent emotions those pictures [of Cézanne] excited less than thirty years ago" (Woolf, *Fry*, 82, 153). Difficult as such imagining may be, it is not impossible, she believed, and certainly worth the effort.

At the same time Woolf was writing the life of Fry, she began a memoir, the unfinished "Sketch of the Past." Thus she was thinking doubly about childhood, family, education, and work, once in the third person, once in the first person. These parallel compositions, for a writer as perennially alert as Woolf, would have provided the opportunity to sharpen her sense of the similarities and differences between these two kinds of life writing.

Biography was for Woolf clearly more than just a kind of writing, a claim which, by now in this chapter, will come as no surprise to the reader. It was the way she read and wrote, the way she thought about life, and her manner of interrelating all three of these activities. In Woolf's opening note to *The Common Reader: First Series* (1925), a collection of her book reviews and critical essays, she explains the volume's title, borrowed from Johnson's life of the poet Thomas Gray. The "common reader," she observes, reads for private pleasure, not to the critical ends of "imparting knowledge or correcting the opinions of others."[20] "Above all," she continues, "he is guided by an instinct to create for himself, out of whatever odds and ends he can come by, some kind of whole—*a portrait of a man, a sketch of an age, a theory of the art of writing.*" Private, nonprofessional reading for enjoyment is inspired by the creative urge to depict the author, her times, and her poetics in a composite that might be called biographical thinking, a concept shared by Woolf and Johnson.

Elaborating on her title, borrowed from a writer who also recognized the common reader as the source of ultimate literary judgment, Woolf acknowledges in principle what her essays recognize in practice, namely that reading is an encounter of persons and that the critic's job is to identify with the writer as a creative agent, hence to explore the imaginative sources of the work of art. She praises Fry's art criticism for focusing not merely on the finished canvas but on the canvas in the making," just as she criticizes Gosse for "focusing more and more [on] the finished article" and not on "the article in the making."[21] Woolf emphasizes how, for the common reader, as for the critic, reading is fundamentally a biographical-historical activity that involves not merely being "in the presence of a different person—Defoe, Jane Austen, or Thomas Hardy—but . . . living in a different world."[22] The common reader reads in order to enjoy these unsettling pleasures of the imagination.

For Woolf, then, the critic is of necessity a kind of biographer. Critic and biographer alike function as mediums who translate into imaginative presence spirits of the distant or dead. Both must acknowledge imaginative responsibility to reanimate writers' personalities as central to the task of examining their springs of creativity. Personality is, for Woolf, the social face of the artist's creativity, this creativity having, in turn, qualities akin to soul. Hence, for her, literary criticism becomes a kind of spiritual inquiry. In the following passage from "Lives of the Obscure," a literary-critical group portrait of a handful of lesser-known writers, the biographer recovers spirits, much like a medium, from the dusty past:

> For one likes romantically to feel oneself a deliverer advancing with lights across the waste of years to the rescue of some stranded ghost—a Mrs. Pilkington, a Rev. Henry Elman, a Mrs. Ann Gilbert—waiting, appealing, forgotten, in the growing gloom. Possibly they hear one coming. They shuffle, they preen, they bridle. Old secrets well up to their lips. The *divine relief of communication* will soon be theirs. The dust shifts and Mrs. Gilbert—but the contact with life is instantly salutary. Whatever Mrs. Gilbert may be doing, *she is not thinking about us.*[23]

The dead must be invoked by the living if they are to speak again. Yet the ghost's dependence on being addressed first, which might seem to give the upper hand to the living, belies the chastening fact that in this relationship the interest and attention are all directed one way, from the living to the dead. Ghosts never think about the living, she concludes; the interest is all the other way around.

Accompanying Woolf's emphasis throughout her criticism on the personalities of authors and readers and their qualities of mind and imagination, not unlike the imaginative experiments in *Orlando* and *Flush*, are essays epitomized by "On Not Knowing Greek" and "The Strange Elizabethans." These two essays are experiments in cultural biography, imaginative encounters with unbridgeable gulfs of strangeness or *fastness*, the latter being Woolf's word, between the present and the past. We risk foolishness and humiliation in trying to bridge these gulfs. Yet curiosity permits nothing less than the chanciness of wholehearted pursuit: "Very likely the Elizabethans would find our pronunciation of their language unintelligible; our fancy picture of what it pleases us to call Elizabethan life would rouse their ribald merriment. Still, the instinct that drives us to them is so strong and the freshness and vigour that blow through their pages are so sweet that we willingly run the risk of being laughed at, of being ridiculous."[24] Woolf believed that if people could always find such heartening delight and curiosity in the face of difference, the world would be more habitable.[25]

Woolf and Her Biographers

Few if any of Woolf's biographers seem to have been either as awed or as inspired by her theory and practice of biography as Boswell announces having been both humbled and educated by Johnson's. Perhaps they should have been. This difference can perhaps be accounted for by the fact that Woolf has never been so thoroughly identified with biography as Johnson.

The first full-length biography of Woolf, Aileen Pippett's *The Moth and the Star* (1953), proposes a metaphorical thesis about Woolf's personality, "fragile as a moth and enduring as a star."[26] Pippett interviewed many of Woolf's friends and was permitted to read a prepublication version of Woolf's diary entries selected and edited by Leonard Woolf, as well as some private letters written by Woolf to her husband and to Sackville-West. Pippett identifies two questions motivating her biographical study of Woolf and the Bloomsbury Circle: First, did Woolf and her friends shut themselves off eccentrically from ordinary life or did they play an active part in their times? Second, what accounts for the continuing interest in Woolf's writing? Though the chief aim of this literary biography is to examine Woolf as writer and member of a group of intellectuals who, Pippett asserts, were very much engaged with their times, the biographer also focuses on the subject's personality "as apart from the literary artist and the social thinker." This focus allies Pippett's undertaking with Woolf's 1927 version of the new biography's emphasis on depicting personality.

Jean Guiget's *Virginia Woolf and Her Works* (1962) was translated and published by the Woolfs' Hogarth Press in 1965, a fact suggesting at least sanction if not authorization. This biography defines as its aim to "reach the centre, the very core of her being" as artist. Guiget distinguishes his biographical study from conventional biography in the manner by which he arrives at a different center. Conventional biography maps its course to this center along the trajectory of events in the person's life, while his biography tracks Woolf's personality as artist "through isolated gestures and moments, fugitive glimpses," a process reminiscent of Woolf's proposal about hanging up looking glasses at odd angles and her emphasis on capturing the revealing phrase or word.[27] Guiget's method was dictated partly by the unavailability of complete editions of Woolf's correspondence and diaries at the time he wrote, strategic lacks that made a full-scale study of Woolf's life in relation to her work impossible.

The first full-scale life of Woolf and still the authoritative factual account of her life is Quentin Bell's *Virginia Woolf: A Biography* (1972). Bell, Woolf's nephew, was invited by Leonard Woolf to write this life. Bell calls the book a personal history, noting specifically that it is not a critical biography. The aim is to create a reality of its subject "outside the elusive world of her art" (Bell, book jacket). As the authorized biographer, Bell had access to and was given permission to quote from Woolf and Stephen family manuscripts. He undertook this biography as both family insider and professional historian.

BIOGRAPHY

The tables of contents of both volumes (volume 1, 1882–1912; volume 2, 1912–1941) are organized by dates only, in segments of from one to seven years. There are no chapter titles and hence no verbal interpretation of these life segments. Yet this biography is hardly innocent of interpretation, some of which seems chiefly motivated by the need to organize the narrative and, perhaps not inconsequentially, to praise the Stephen side of the family. In the following passage, for instance, Bell proposes in the Stephen family genealogy an eighteenth-century ancestor who began the tradition of writing. James Stephen, imprisoned for debt, "reacted in a manner which was to set an example to his descendants. He took up his pen and argued his case. He was (so far as I know) the first of the Stephens to write a book and from that time on there was scarcely a one who did not publish and never, certainly, a generation which did not add something to the literary achievements of the family." (Bell, 1:1)

Bell, from the outset of his depiction of Virginia, underscores how difficult she was, "incalculable, eccentric and prone to accidents," one who "could vent her displeasure both with words and by creating 'an atmosphere' . . . of thunderous and oppressive gloom, a winter of discontent" (Bell, 1:24). These feelings are attributed to her brothers and sisters, though no specific source is given. Regarding George Duckworth, the half-brother who sexually molested Virginia and her sister Vanessa, Bell uses the quasi-Victorian phrase, "a nasty erotic skirmish." He attributes this interpretation partially to Vanessa Bell (Bell, 1:43), though he does not clearly identify where his mother's interpretation leaves off and his begins.

Woolf's biographers after Bell, like biographers of Johnson after Boswell, typically fall into one of two groups: one which elaborates or develops aspects of Bell's life, the other which corrects his deficiencies or errors. Bell's collected data is compendious, depicting in extraordinary detail, year by year and sometimes day by day, the life of a major writer whom the biographer presents as gifted, difficult, and perceived by all her family, according to Bell, to be mentally unstable. I will return to the issue of Woolf's insanity at the end of this chapter.

Phyllis Rose, in *Woman of Letters: A Life of Virginia Woolf* (1978), defines literary biography as an exploration of the artist's "inner life" and "imaginative world." This undertaking, Rose asserts, rests on the assumption that "a life is as much a work of fiction—of guiding narrative structure—as novels and poems, and that the task of literary biography is to explore this fiction."[28] Rose begins with Woolf's writings, setting each in biographical context. She recognizes that, particularly in the case of a writer like Woolf, so alert to and curious about the intersection of narrative form and the construction of meaning, this priority is crucial. Rose defines an original space apart from the two main tracks of Woolf studies: critical studies of her fiction with emphasis on form and technique, perhaps overemphasizing her self-enclosed devotion to craft, on the one hand, and biographical, historical, and sociological studies of Woolf, her intimates, and friends, including the Bloomsbury associates, on the other. These latter lives include Bell's factual record of his aunt's life, Leonard Woolf's five-volume autobiography, Nigel Nicolson's, *Portrait of a Marriage*, a memoir of his parents, Harold Nicolson and Vita Sackville-West, Michael Holroyd's biography of Lytton Strachey, and Frances Spalding's life of Vanessa Bell, Virginia's sister. Rose observes that these historical-biographical studies have all reinforced, though perhaps not by conscious calculation, E. M. Forster's epithet for Woolf, the Invalid Lady of Bloomsbury. Bell's biography, for instance, gives a detailed account of Woolf's mental illness and the reasons for her suicide, but devotes little attention to the large body of published work. Bell defends this decision by noting that he is not a literary critic. The effect, however, Rose observes, is to obscure the most important aspect of Woolf's life, namely her writing.

In reconstructing Woolf's personal and social history Rose, like Bell, draws on the writer's unpublished memoirs, journals, and correspondence. But Rose uses these materials differently, as evidence of Woolf's self-constructed myths, her resilience and resolve to survive and remain productive in the face of depressive threats of annihilating violence and meaninglessness. Woolf's novels become, for Rose, milestones along the path of heroic achievement.

While Rose writes specifically about Woolf, she also conceives of this biography's emphasis on the writer's resilience as proof of her extraordinary imagination, weighing in against the modern tendency to interpret suicide and despair, especially suicides of women writers, as proof that sensitivity and genius are essentially allied to neurosis. In the foregoing ways Rose conceives of her book as feminist biography written in sympathy, though not in uncritical agreement with its female subject.

Lyndall Gordon's *Virginia Woolf: A Writer's Life* (1984) defines itself as the critical complement to Bell's personal history biography. Gordon proposes to follow Woolf's own recommendation to focus on the work, not the writer, where one may hope to discover "written large" the very secret of her soul and quality of mind. Reminiscent of Woolf's emphasis on Fry's two formative childhood memories, Gordon asserts that the key to Woolf's art lies in her creative response to two childhood memories of the north Cornwall shore and her parents. Gordon describes her critical biography as "rock[ing] back and forth between the life and the work" but "coming to rest always on the work."[29]

A distinct subgenre of Woolf biographies is lives that pair her with a significant relative. George Spater's and Ian Parsons' *A Marriage of True Minds: An Intimate Portrait of Leonard and Virginia Woolf* (1977), Jane Dunn's *A Very Close Conspiracy: Vanessa Bell and Virginia Woolf* (1990), and John Lehmann's memoir *Thrown to the Woolfs: Leonard and Virginia Woolf and the Hogarth Press* (1978) exemplify this approach. Spater and Parsons argue the rationale of their biography on the basis of substantial amounts of new material either edited or catalogued and now available in research library collections, such as the Berg Collection at the New York Public Library, since the publication of Leonard Woolf's autobiography and Bell's *Woolf*. Bell, whose introduction gives an official imprimatur to the book, endorses its usefulness, particularly thanks to the authors' coming from different backgrounds than his. "History," Bell observes, "is something too complex to be written by any one person, it is built—or at least one hopes that it will be built—by historians who approach the facts from different points of the compass and are united only by a common interest and a common integrity."[30] Bell associates biography explicitly with history in a venerably old tradition, which his aunt, it might be noted, had substantially complicated.

Lehmann's *Thrown to the Woolfs* hangs up another looking glass at a different angle to reflect the marriage of Virginia and Leonard, depicting two individuals in the context of their major joint enterprise, the creation of the Hogarth Press. Part memoir, part literary history, part history of a publishing business, Lehmann's memoir focuses on this important independent press during his two periods of association with this enterprise, first as trainee-manager from January 1931 to September 1932, then for eight years as partner, beginning in 1938.

Dunn distinguishes *A Very Close Conspiracy* from "joint biography," describing this life as a study of Virginia's and Vanessa's "essential reciprocity," their interdependency and mutual self-sufficiency, as viewed by others and themselves. Beginning in childhood as defense against loss, continuing into maturity and centering increasingly on their respective artistic work, the sisters' intimate relationship was for each the center of her life. This biography uses techniques partly chronological, partly thematic to organize the narrative.

Susan Rubinow Gorsky's biographical-critical study of Woolf in the Twayne English Authors series, originally published in 1979 and substantially revised ten years later, is an instructive example of how such studies may change over time when important sources become readily available and scholarship booms. Gorsky's *Virginia Woolf* (1989) serves as an introduction chiefly to Woolf the novelist. Gorsky, attempting what she calls a "unified introduction to Woolf as a human being, literary and social theorist, representative of modernism, and especially fiction writer," identifies the novels as touchstones of Woolf's achievement and as locus of the various impulses and drives that motivated her as artist, woman, feminist, individual.[31] The 1989 revised edition takes into account the exponential increase in Woolf scholarship and criticism in the intervening years since the first edition, acknowledging a substantial revaluation of Woolf based on evidence publicly available in the complete edited letters and the diaries then still in progress.

John Mepham's *Virginia Woolf: A Literary Life* (1991) appears in a series of literary lives that examines British and Irish writers as workers by contextualizing their careers in their respective social, political, and professional settings. Examining a writer in the socio-material context of work recasts the definition of the artist (gifted and unique for the Romantics; dead for the postmoderns) by revitalizing the eighteenth-century notion of artists as contributing members of society. Since for Woolf, Mepham asserts, "writing was not an addition to her life but its foundation . . . essential to the integrity of her personality" (Mepham, xiii), an attempt to reidentify her creative character in the texture of historical circumstance and contingency is essential.[32]

Jean Moorcroft Wilson, in *Virginia Woolf, Life and London: A Biography of Place* (1987), proposes that to understand this writer's work, particularly the fiction, one must understand her passion for London, the city where she lived most of her life. London is the touchstone of her novelistic imagination both in its architectural particularity and in its symbolic embodiment of English history and culture. Wilson, Woolf's niece by marriage, organizes her book in a series of descriptions of Woolf's London houses, followed by seven walking tours to guide readers literally into the material setting of Woolf's London life.

To conclude this chapter, I turn to the matter of Woolf's psychology and more specifically to the issue of her mental health which has figured significantly in biographical treatments of this writer. Bell takes Woolf's mental illness as a point beyond dispute, basing this certainty chiefly on Leonard Woolf's account of his wife in his five-volume autobiography (1960–1970). There indeed exists evidence that may be readily construed as symptomatic of instability: the fact of Woolf's death by suicide combined with the record of earlier suicide attempts and several treatments for mental illness at various times in her life. Yet several biographical studies since the late 1970s have called into question unexamined aspects of this assumption about her lifelong pathology.

Roger Poole describes how his biographical study *The Unknown Virginia Woolf* (1978) took its origin in his "sense of unease in the face of all this undefined assertion [regarding Woolf's 'insanity']."[33] Documented serious trauma of childhood and adolescence (molestation by her half-brothers and early death of her mother), followed by her marriage, with its own difficulties, including Leonard's arguably tyrannical caretaking that sometimes, for instance, excluded his wife from discussions with her own doctors, give ample evidence that Woolf's so-called mental illness is a matter for nuanced investigation, not presumption. Such a diagnosis is, Poole argues, perhaps both inaccurate and beside the point.

Poole characterizes his methodology as intended to pay Woolf "the compliment of examining her own subjectivity" by emulating her own remarkable standards for analyzing "inter-subjectivity in language" (Poole, 2). He tries to bridge the gap between literary critics, who take insufficient account of the details of her life, and the dominant historical biographer, Bell, who avoids literary criticism, by reading Woolf's novels as artful documentations of her mental states. Poole argues that in her fiction Woolf attempts to describe, come to terms with, and heal her own illness.

Stephen Trombley's *'All that Summer She was Mad'*: *Virginia Woolf and Her Doctors* (1981) is another unconventional pathography of Woolf. Trombley critiques the lay assumption of Woolf's madness made by Leonard Woolf and subsequently by the biographer and other editors (Nigel Nicholson, Joanne Trautmann, Anne Olivier Bell) authorized by him. Taking a psycho-sociological approach, he examines the factors informing diagnoses of insanity made by Woolf's doctors. Trombley, using analysis that combines Marxist critique and the psycho-sociological work of the Scottish psychoanalyst R. D. Laing, asserts provocatively that these "so-called diagnoses" represent "a magical rather than a medical dispositions . . . nothing more than an attempt on the part of the medical profession to enforce unwritten social codes as if they were the law of the land."[34] He also examines how Woolf might have regarded the notion of her madness, thus diagnosed, and how such matters both figured in her creative process and manifested themselves in her writing, which is quintessentially sane.

Alma Halbert Bond's psychobiography *Who Killed Virginia Woolf?* (1989) examines, in yet another way, how Woolf's mental condition is misunderstood. Noting the "widespread duplicity" which covered up the "real story," Bond focuses on the "family myth" in the Stephen, Woolf, and Bell households whereby it was to the majority's benefit to mask anxieties and guilt feelings by scapegoating Virginia, simultaneously caring for and oppressing her with her symptoms.

These three biographers share two important revisionist views of Woolf: first, that it is implausible to portray her as a difficult, if brilliant, woman cared for by a nobly self-sacrificing husband, and second, that it is equally unsatisfactory to identify her as the preeminent type of the modern suicidal woman writer, precursor of the poets Sylvia Plath and Anne Sexton, whose self-inflicted death shadows her career from the outset, serving as the interpretive lens through which her significance is brought into focus.

By contrast with the depictions of Woolf's emotional life, Johnson's self-described "vile melancholy," recounted by Boswell and elaborated on by subsequent biographers, who renamed this condition according to the medical paradigms of their day, has rarely, if ever, been used against him. Rather, Johnson has generally been admired for the lucidity and courage with which he examined and battled lifelong depression. There are many variables in the cases of Johnson and Woolf. But two elements which invite further consideration, beyond the pages of this book, are the facts that their best-known biographers, Boswell and Bell, each took markedly different attitudes toward the mental difficulties of a man and a woman, respectively, attitudes convincing to many subsequent readers. Johnson is typically honored as the hero of his disabilities, while Woolf is often either pitied or criticized as difficult patient or victim.

Mary Wollstonecraft gives useful anticipatory advice on this matter in *A Vindication of the Rights of Woman* (1792). Men and woman alike, she observes, should renounce pity and charity as guides to behavior, particularly behavior toward women, instituting justice in their place. Wollstonecraft's advice has yet to become outdated as a clarifying perspective on Woolf and her biographers.

Chapter 4

MINORITY BIOGRAPHY:
ALICE JAMES AND LANGSTON HUGHES

Human beings are too important to be treated as mere symptoms
of the past.

Lytton Strachey, Eminent Victorians (1918)

At a 1993 conference on biography, "Life Likenesses: The
Seductions of Biography," held in Cambridge, Massachusetts, participants discussed the impact of "new questions" about
race, class, and sexuality on the theory and practice of biography.
One speaker noted the absence of traditional biographical subjects on the program, the so-called "big boys."[1] This revisionist
agenda would probably not have surprised either Johnson, who
observed that there has rarely passed a life that would not make
a useful biography, or Woolf, who encouraged rethinking unexamined assumptions about conventional hierarchies of importance and value applied to choosing and depicting biographical
subjects.

Conference participants also discussed the new emphasis on
private life, by which sex and sexuality seem almost exclusively
to be meant, in attempting to understand the motives behind

public behavior. A related issue focused on the degree to and manner in which biographers should identify with or share qualities with their subjects in order to write about them with understanding and accuracy. Can a homosexual man portray a heterosexual man, a white woman portray a black woman, and vice versa? When, for example, Martin Duberman was approached by the son of Paul Robeson to write the senior Robeson's biography, Duberman asked if the family knew that their prospective choice was gay, in addition to knowing that he was white and Jewish. Duberman felt that the family should have all this information before choosing an authorized biographer of Robeson, the important twentieth-century African-American singer, actor, and civil rights and political activist, who was black, Christian, and heterosexual. The family apparently did not regard these differences between biographer and subject as impediments. They chose Duberman to write *Paul Robeson* (1988), the authorized life of this celebrated figure.[2]

Contemporary skepticism about the existence of a single, unified identity ("Stable identity is always suspect," one conference participant noted) and this skepticism's effects on the practice of biography was another conference topic. As notions of identity change, so do ideas about the theory and practice of writing lives, a motif running through earlier chapters of this study. The rise of postmodernism in recent decades, with its interpretative paradigms (multicultural, postcolonial, new historicist, and feminist, among them) that assert or imply the absence of any essential, verifiable, reassuring *authenticity* or *authority*, has privileged notions of the instability, uncertainty, and cultural construction of meanings, along with the value of repeated reexaminations of the assumptive ground of interpretation. The watchword of postmodernism seems to be, in other words, "Nothing goes without saying."[3]

From the midst of the Cambridge biography conference's emphasis on postmodern contradiction and uncertainty, two guiding principles of biography were voiced, perhaps surprisingly, by two eminent contemporary biographers. Diane Middlebrook, biographer of Anne Sexton, and Arnold Rampersad, biographer of Langston Hughes and influential theorist of African-American autobiography, proposed *truth* and *judgment* as the biographer's chief responsibilities and benchmarks of reputable biographical research. These words would sound familiar to Johnson, who lived in a period when ideas of uniformity in human nature, common sense (meanings generally agreed upon), and commonly held standards of judgment, concepts scarcely as naive as critics in later periods would make them, still had currency. Woolf, who was skeptical of such traditional-sounding ideas in her early career, found that she could not dispense with them so lightly when she began writing the life of Roger Fry. The examples of Johnson and Woolf suggest that the ideas of truth and judgment are, perhaps, more radical, enduring, and valuable than late-twentieth-century postmodern theory has credited them with being.

The aim of this chapter is twofold: to analyze how issues of race, gender, class, the postmodern descriptions of indeterminate or overdetermined human identity, and the criteria for being biographically notable become foregrounded ideologically in biographies of minority subjects; and to examine some of the distinctive qualities and methods characterizing biographers' relationships with minority subjects. I have chosen two quite different minority subjects for an examination of these issues. The first, Alice James, was a white upper-middle-class woman from a notable American family, who neither married and had children nor worked outside the home. The second, Langston Hughes, was an African-American, who rose from poverty and met the challenge of other adversities to became a major twentieth-century writer both within and beyond the United States.

Jean Strouse, Alice James: A Biography (1980)

Jean Strouse's life of Alice James (1848–1892) could be called a *literary biography manqué* to reflect the fact that the subject is a woman who read, wrote, and thought productively but left no conventional public record of achievement. The author of fascinating letters and a substantial diary, James is in many ways a throwback to the pre-eighteenth-century woman writer described by Woolf in her esssay on Dorothy Osborne, the seventeenth-century letter writer. Born a century earlier, Woolf remarks, Osborne would have written nothing; born a century later, she would have written novels. But because the profession of writing was not yet open to her sex and because the novel had not yet been invented, women like Osborne wrote characteristically in the intimate, domestic forms available to them: the private letter, diary, and memoir. Woman's "I," feminist historians observe, has always been handicapped in a variety of ways. Women's history is thus nearly synonymous with a "history of their specific oppression, of the opposition the system has raised to their fulfillment and the power of resistance they have developed. Hence the biographer of a woman must, with particular care and distinct emphasis, be true to the facts of both the individual life and the condition of women in history, since the meanings, limits, and ideology of woman have been defined by the patriarchal system."[4]

Strouse identifies Alice James, as *the brilliant but neglected younger sister of William and Henry James*. Her epithet announces the author's agenda of feminist revaluation, preparing readers to examine their habits of perception, what they habitually notice and what they do not see, along with their assumed measures of significance and insignificance. This revaluation, as Sandra M. Gilbert, Susan Gubar, Carolyn Heilbrun, Nancy K. Miller, and Linda Wagner-Martin, among others, have noted, sponsors "the woman's quest for her own story," inventing, discovering, and telling the stories of women's lives by finding "the true representations of power . . . the ability to take one's place in whatever discourse is essential to action and the right to have one's part matter."[5] Women's lives, comments Lyndall Gordon, "deviate from the set stories of traditional biography," and the hidden aspect of their lives "may require more transgressive experiment" in order to "elicit the uncategorized ferment of hidden possibilities."[6]

Blanche Wiesen Cook, the author of a life of Eleanor Roosevelt, credits the late-twentieth-century feminist movement with transforming the craft of biography by enlarging the contours of our learning traditions.[7] Feminism recognizes that changing the gender of the subject involves changing "the nature and practice of the biographical craft."[8] Feminist biography, observes Linda Wagner-Martin, is alert to ways "literary history has sometimes prevented women from telling stories—their own, those of their female friends and relatives." It identifies and embraces as part of its task the "problem of being recognized as someone's daughter, someone's wife, or someone's mother rather than as oneself," and it examines "woman's struggle both to fit into her family and her community and to avoid the restrictions that those entities might create for her."[9] The purpose of feminist biography's distinctive agenda thus intends to remedy what the historian Arthur M. Schlesinger Jr. calls "the most spectacular casualty of traditional history, namely women, the group that makes up at least half the human race."[10]

Feminist biography makes a different kind of person eligible for examination, an obscure or minority figure, by virtue of the way this form interrogates conventional biography's selection of publicly lauded, typically male, individuals, brackets the culture's structure of critical or biographical commonplaces, and cross-examines the culture's central notions of plausibility.[11] This genre challenges this mainstream emphasis on the predominating significance of the individual in history, an emphasis that narrates history as a series of episodes in the lives of the great, who are typically men.[12] Feminist biography counterbalances a lives-of-the-great notion of history not only by taking women as its principal subjects, but also by narrating history as group movements rather than acts of individuals.

When traditional celebrity and visibility no longer serve as the only or even chief criteria for selection, retrieval becomes the guiding scholarly method. A record of traditional success may then even count as a liability in choosing a female subject for biography, since familiar notions of greatness are understood to carry, of necessity, the biases of the dominant culture's institutional and ideological values. The template of feminist biography characterizes the individual's life as metonymically representative of larger group structures and conditions affecting the subject as a member of this group. Strouse's biography of James, while focusing on an individual protagonist, reads this woman's life as a sign of her times, representative of conditions and responses of other middle-class women like herself. No biography can focus solely on the protagonist, since this genre is fundamentally social. But feminist biography makes an explicit methodological point of refocusing to compose more explicitly a group picture. Feminist biography argues that, far from being a digression from the main subject, these refocusing and regrouping techniques shed useful light on an otherwise shadowed subject.

Such revisions of conventional notions of achievement and the assumed value of focusing exclusively on the individual have not, it might be noted, edged out such biographical projects as, for instance, the more traditional *Notable American Women*

1607–1950 (1971), with a supplement for the modern period (1980), and *American Women of Achievement* (1987–   ; 50 vols. to date). The latter series, which includes lives of Susan B. Anthony, Katharine Hepburn, Margaret Mead, Anne Hutchinson, and Beverly Sills, among many others, describes its purpose as being to complement feminist revisionist group biography. Lives of women "of achievement" are "inspirational," the series preface notes, offering readers "the example of people with vision who have looked outside themselves for their goals and have struggled against great obstacles to achieve them."[13]

A second characteristic of feminist biography develops from implications of the subject's gender. When a woman is the principal figure, sex and gender typically become the chief consideration, unless the subject's race and class, variables whose effects tend to predominate over gender in life as in life writing, figure more significantly. The biography of a white middle-class man is the biography of a person, while the biography of a white middle-class woman is the biography of a person who is female and a woman, distinctively marked by conditions and circumstances, which include the unique possibility of childbearing. Feminist biography has turned this seeming liability into a methodological asset for examining women's lives differently from men's, particularly in the intersection of private and public life.

Third, feminist biography actively acknowledges, embraces, and often celebrates the subjectivity of biography, arguing that subjectivity is a liability only when it remains unacknowledged or unconscious. Feminist biographers note that, when history is told as serial lives of great men, significant parts of and participants in events are left out. Furthermore, they ask, whose story is it anyway? And how many different stories might there be? And set in how many different scenes? The distinctive quality of subjectivity characterizing women biographers and their women subjects often finds its parallel, so one biographer has noted, in the mother-daughter relationship. Examining the practical implications of Woolf's line of thinking in *A Room of One's Own* about how women think back through their mothers, Bell Gale Chevigny comments that women biographers

> are likely to move toward a subject that symbolically reflects their internalized relations with their mothers and that offers them an opportunity to re-create those relations. . . . When the work is most

intensely experienced as rescue, the fantasy of reciprocal reparations is likely to become an underlying impulse in it. That is, in the rescue—the reparative interpretation and re-creation—of a woman who was neglected or misunderstood, we may be seeking indirectly the reparative rescue of ourselves, in the sense of coming to understand and accept ourselves better."[14]

Eleanor Roosevelt's biographer develops this observation about the therapeutically matrilineal subjectivity of feminist biography in order to redefine the relationship between identification and understanding: "Who do we choose to write about?" Cook asks. "What moves us? What do we care about? For biographers, I think, all choices are autobiographical. . . . There is no reason for selection unless there is a basis for identification—for real understanding."[15] Such identification is typically a complicated affair, perhaps for all biographers, certainly for women biographers writing about women subjects, Heilbrun observes, since both sides have almost certainly

> had to struggle with the inevitable conflict between the destiny of being unambiguously a woman and the woman subject's palpable desire, or fate, to be something else. Except when writing about queens, biographers have not, therefore, been at ease with their subjects—and even with queens, like Elizabeth I of England, *there has been a tendency to see them as somewhat abnormal, monstrous. It is no wonder that biographers have largely ignored women as subjects, and that critics of biography have written as though men were the only possible subjects.*[16] [my italics]

"Why Alice James?" Strouse asks, posing this question in context of a revealing anecdote about her subject. James, on her deathbed, wrote to her brother, the psychologist and philosopher William James: "When I am gone, pray don't think of me simply as a creature who might have been something else, had neurotic science been born."[17] Instead of choosing a subject to fit conventional measures of greatness, Strouse's question, combined with James's own deathbed request not to reimagine her, identifies one of the central tenets of feminist biography, namely to rethink the qualifications for biographical eligibility while retaining accurate emphasis on the individual. James, her biographer remarks, did nothing publicly significant. She produced no significant body of work, as did her brothers William and Henry. Neither did she make any particular contribution to society.

James, unmarried and childless, was, for the greater part of her life, an invalid. She experienced a variety of medical symptoms, resembling the infirmities of many other nineteenth-century women of her social and economic class (Strouse, ix). In terms of this affliction, James was, arguably, a member of a group, the "delicate," "high strung," "nervous" middle- and upper-middle-class women whose lives registered the stressful contradictions affecting female behavior in the late nineteenth century. These societal stress factors include increased leisure time, tacit constraints against public or professional activity, and the idealization of motherhood, to mention only the most obvious.

In addition to locating James in the group of nineteenth-century invalid women, Strouse locates her within one other crucial group, the family within which "she lived with greatest intensity" (Strouse, x). Strouse portrays the dynamic of Alice's family relations as emanating from Henry James Sr.'s underscoring the importance of "being extraordinary" and the greater value of "interesting failure [over] too-obvious success" (Strouse, xi, xiii). His belief in women's inherent goodness and men's inherent but not ineradicable flaws led inferentially to the following paradoxical gender-specific scenario, aimed, consciously or not, to keep women in their place: Although young men have a long and difficult journey on the road to self-improvement, at least there was the interesting, if painful, possibility of going somewhere. Young women, on the other hand, being perfect, have nothing to do and nowhere to go. Strouse presents Alice James as a figure whose family life was characterized by a profound sense of "isolation and irrelevance." Her brothers went off to fight in the Civil War or study at Harvard, while she remained alone at home with her parents, an "'idle and useless young female,'" a situation typical of other middle- and upper-class girls, though she perhaps mused on and wrote about it more than most (Strouse, 79).

Strouse identifies three intersecting challenges that confronted her in writing James's life: first, to identify the unconventional yet convincing interest of James in and for herself; second, not to treat her as a mere symptom of the woman-as-victim sociological phenomenon; and third, not to imagine her as the person she might have become, thereby denying her actual life. Resisting the temptation to reimagine a life might seem to be a contrived measure of biographical achievement. Practice suggests otherwise.

Strouse herself, for instance, comments that "If Alice had been poor" during the Civil War, she would have done "whatever she could to take the wage-earning place of a brother who had gone to fight. If she had been older, she might have volunteered for nursing or relief work" (Strouse, 79). Gloria Steinem in her life of Marilyn Monroe reimagines her subject even more aggressively, picturing the several other Monroes she might have become if she had had a happy childhood or benefited from better psychotherapy. Instead of becoming a "sex goddess," Steinem comments in *Marilyn: Norma Jeane* (1986), Monroe might have become a student, lawyer, teacher, artist, mother, grandmother, defender of animals, rancher, homemaker, sportswoman, rescuer of children, serious actress, or wise comedienne.[18] Steinem, herself a professional woman, thus reimagines the life of another successful career woman, a not uncurious exercise for a feminist to perform on another woman.

Steinem's approach develops out of Strachey's line of thinking about the biographer standing on equal footing with the subject. This assumption permits and even requires iconoclastic examination by authorizing the biographer's projections into the life. Strouse, while arguing the "unique value" of James as an individual, also warns against the dangers of converting her into a stereotyped heroine or victim. Either conversion would distort the individual into an ideological fiction. James, in Strouse's depiction, is a kind of litmus test of social and political issues affecting women. Her brothers' novels and scientific writings, respectively, examine moral, social, and philosophical questions about identity formation and the dangers and delights of private life, public life, and the life of the spirit. Alice investigated these issues in unpublished writings, a diary, and letters, experiencing the strain of these conflicts in her body. She thus exhibits symptoms of the social and political conditions affecting women like herself.

Yet more importantly, her biographer argues, James composed a life with meanings that extend beyond the merely personal when brought into focus by a feminist account. Biographers of minority figures, members of underrepresented groups, or obscure figures often ground the case for their projects in the fact of their subjects' transpersonal, representative interest. The potential liability of this strength is that such subjects sometimes lose the dramatic savor of their individuality in the biographical narrative. Yet the risk has proved to be, on balance, worth taking in feminist biography. Feminist biography does not make the case that it sees from all points of view simultaneously and equally, a case which would indeed weaken the case it does argue for contributing a significant, corrective partial perspective. I now turn to one final related matter to conclude this discussion of feminist biography. Strouse compares James to Judith Shakespeare, fictional sister of William Shakespeare created by Woolf in her feminist literary history, *A Room of One's Own* (1929). Woolf's Judith represents the disadvantaged would-be woman writer of the Renaissance. Woolf uses fiction to focus history's lens on the situation of women before the modern period who wanted to write and for whom the example of Restoration writer Aphra Behn did not yet exist to debate their disapproving fathers. Strouse notes that, although three hundred years separate the hypothetical Judith from the real Alice, both encountered many of the same obstacles to their desires. Family pathology aside, however, characterizing James as a *writer manqué*, on the basis of gender alone, is, from a feminist historical perspective like Woolf's, not the firmest ground for an argument since, after Aphra Behn, history more or less sides with the woman writer.

Langston Hughes by Others and Himself

Samuel Johnson, who was scarcely naive about human beings' capacity for self-delusion, believed, nonetheless, as mentioned earlier, that a person's own life story is always more valuable than that life recounted by another. More truth may be learned from a first-person account, since even untruths in an autobiography are of the subject's own making. In these fundamental differences between the materials and subjectivities of the two genres lies the distinctive value of autobiography.

James Boswell agreed with Johnson on the existential and evidentiary superiority of first-person lives, as discussed in chapter 2, though not to the exclusion of biography, to be sure. For this Boswell may have had several reasons, including the strategic advantage of identifying Johnson as his chief rival since Johnson, by then dead, had not written a full-scale autobiography and thus could be removed from the field of competitors. The case of Langston Hughes, who wrote a two-volume autobiography, *The*

Big Sea (1940) and *I Wonder as I Wander* (1956), and his biographers bears instructive similarities to and differences from the case of Johnson and Boswell.

According to the authorized Hughes biographer, Arnold Rampersad, in his introduction to *The Big Sea*, the first volume of a two-part autobiography, Hughes was a reluctant autobiographer. He wrote the first half of his autobiography in 1939, at age thirty-eight, but had already been asked by his publisher, thirteen years earlier, to write an account of himself to preface his first book of poems, *The Weary Blues* (1926).[19] This early autobiographical essay, entitled by Hughes in French "L'histoire de ma vie," was, according to Rampersad "so dazzling that it set off" yet another brainstorm in the mind of Hughes's editor, Carl Van Vechten.[20] Van Vechten, along with Hughes's publisher, Blanche Knopf, asked the writer to write a full-length autobiography. It could be as "romantic" and "formless as you please," Knopf encouraged him. Disregard chronology, if you wish, she continued, and simply write "a beautiful book, but also one that will *sell*" (Rampersad, 1:112).

Hughes evidently wished to comply, but by his own account hated "to think backwards." He was, he continued, "still too much enmeshed in the effects of my young life to write clearly about it. . . . What moron ever wrote those lines about 'carry me back to the scenes of my childhood'?" (Rampersad, 1:112; cf. Berry, 65–66).[21] Whether written as a critique of sentimental recollection, psychoanalysis, or both, Hughes's remarks are fascinating in their acute emphasis on his dislike of those very psychological elements and the accompanying method of thinking back through one's childhood, identified by Wordsworth's poetic theory and Freud's theory of the unconscious as the ground of creativity and subsequently touchstones of twentieth-century biography.

Freud's thinking, in particular, has displaced subjects' accounts of themselves to secondary interpretive significance relative to the analyst's authoritative position of superior insight. Without the analyst's excavation of meanings, the childhood years, in particular, are considered virtually indecipherable. To this matter I now turn in discussing two lives of Hughes by Rampersad and Faith Berry in the context of Hughes's two-part autobiography. In addition, Berry's *Langston Hughes Before and Beyond Harlem* (1983) and Rampersad's two-volume *Life of Langston*

Hughes: Volume 1: 1902–1941, I, Too, Sing America (1986) and *Volume 2: 1941–1967, I Dream a World* (1988) illustrate several key issues regarding circumstances of writing biography, access to materials, and the amounts of time and money involved in such projects. Hughes's account of himself is powerful precisely to the degree that he expresses feelings matter-of-factly. His two biographers, though differing on many other points, generally agree that this matter-of-factness signals repression or evasion—"the adult mask so carefully constructed to conceal," Rampersad comments, "'the affects of my young life.'"[22] Personal decorum and dignity, like self-sacrifice and generosity, are difficult to bring into view through a Freudian lens. Temporarily bracketing the assumption of repression, another reading of Hughes's words seems equally, if not more highly, probable. Consider the following observation in *The Big Sea*, Hughes's first-person account of the forces, inner and outer, affecting the growth of a poet's mind:

(1) I felt very bad so I wrote a lot of poems.

(2) Upper-class Washingtonians . . . kept insisting that a colored poet should be a credit to his race.

(3) My second book was better because it was more impersonal, more about other people than about myself.

(4) The Negro critics and many of the intellectuals were very sensitive about their race in books. . . . In anything that white people were likely to read, they wanted to put their best foot forward, their politely polished and cultural foot—and only that foot. . . . I personally knew very few people anywhere who were wholly beautiful and wholly good. Besides I felt that the masses of our people had as much in their lives to put into books as did those more fortunate ones.[23]

Hughes's self-scrutiny centers on what he considers to be the major issue confronting him, namely the relation between the personal and private areas of the creative self and the social, public areas of that creative self. For Alice James, these negotiations centered on gender. For Hughes, they centered on race. But class consciousness among blacks is also a powerful factor in how he portrays and expresses race.[24] From the time he decided to spend the rest of his life writing, he had also accepted the task of defining an identity as a poet who was also a *Negro*, as Hughes refers to himself, in relation to the white majority and to his own race. Both races, at different times in his life and in various ways, tempted him to become someone other than himself.

Berry began work on her biography in 1970, three years after Hughes's death, while she was still a graduate student of comparative literature. Berry's original project was a commissioned short life of Hughes for a series of African and African-American biographies. Thirteen years later her critical biography appeared. She makes no claim for her book being definitive, nor could she legitimately make such a claim, because of her long, frustrating experience of restricted access to collections.

The first executor of the Hughes estate was Arna Bontemps, then acting curator of the James Weldon Johnson Memorial Collection at Yale University. When Berry began researching Hughes, Bontemps was preparing to write the biography authorized in Hughes's will. The Yale holdings were thus not open to Berry. When Bontemps died in 1973, leaving no biography, Berry continued her work, although new restrictions imposed by the Hughes estate still prevented her using the Yale materials. Other collections of Hughes's writings at Howard and Fisk Universities were undergoing lengthy cataloguing. Some of his work was also still being held by the Justice Department, dating from 1953 when Hughes had been called to testify before the Senate Permanent Sub-Committee on Investigations, chaired by Senator Joseph McCarthy.

Berry notes that much of her information came, of necessity, from secondary sources recommended to her by Bontemps who, she says, encouraged her work. Berry's reference to Bontemps perhaps give these sources some degree of authority, in addition to underscoring, once again, Berry's disadvantage. Yet she was able to interview a number of "primary sources" among Hughes's friends and acquaintances, from whom she gathered personal recollections, one of Boswell's criteria for biographical authenticity. Berry also mentions meeting Hughes briefly in Paris in 1965 before she began research, though she does not elaborate on this detail.

Biographers, as Berry's account demonstrates, sometimes encounter more obstacles than the obscurities and resistances of their subjects. Berry in her foreword takes several different positions in relation to her subject and to the project of writing "a biographical and critical narrative focusing on the major influences that shaped [Hughes's] life and career" (Berry, x). By this description the biography promises to move back and forth between the life and works, the typifying strategy of critical biography. Berry announces as her principal aim to correct the narrow stereotype of Hughes as "the bard of Harlem" by portraying him accurately as an extraordinarily versatile and internationally influential "man of letters"—poet, translator, essayist, novelist, dramatist, librettist, folklorist, short story writer, journalist. In addition, Berry promises to clarify obscurities and supply omissions in Hughes's autobiography, scarcely a tell-all claim but certainly one that underscores the biographer's frankness and responsible authority over her subject, who remains a hero of achievement if not of self-conscious lucidity. Hughes is, Berry claims, the quintessential hero, one who succeeds against great odds, who endures "every possible hardship and never gave up" (Berry, xi). However much the idea of the hero has been called into question in the modern age, it seems in little danger of disappearing entirely from biography.

Finally, Berry notes that Hughes's "spirit" kept her "going" during the long years of research (Berry, xi). Thus, one of the few quarters from which Berry encountered no opposition in writing Hughes's life was the subject himself or at least his spirit. This spirit she, in turn, calls upon as her muse, invoking a unique brand of nearly unassailable, if empirically unverifiable, authority.

The major challenge confronting biographers writing the life of a minority male or female seems to be how to portray the subject's *minority* status and how to factor in their own ethnic, racial, or gender identity. Is the person hero or victim by virtue of being female, as in the case of James, or of being black, in the case of Hughes? Even when writer and subject belong to the same minority (or underrepresented) group, as do James and her biographer, both women, and Hughes and his biographers, all three African-Americans, other variables may complicate the matter. Hughes's two biographers are African-Americans, but Rampersad is a man and Berry a woman. In the case of Hughes, the crux of examining his personality became, for both biographers, the issue of how to measure the subject's degree of consciousness of his ambivalence about race.

Berry and Rampersad ground their work in the assumption that in his autobiography, as in his life, Hughes was under unconscious orders to present a certain face to the world that concealed as much as it revealed. Biography after Freud, even biography that does not undertake a technical psychoanalytic examination of its subject, identifies the subject's chief characterizing lack (the absence of complete self-understanding in one or more psychological areas) as the biographer's fortunate opportunity and defining responsibility for inquiry. The subject's repression becomes the biographer's rhetorical authority and point of entry into the life, which may be particularly helpful in the case of relations between Hughes and his biographers since Hughes's autobiography places him in competition with all who write about him. Recall, for instance, how Boswell admits that he would have had much less to say and less reason to say it if Johnson had written his own life. An instructive exception to the more typical competitive relationship between biographer and subject, particularly when the subject is also an autobiographer, is the juvenile biography *Langston Hughes: A Biography* (1968) by Milton Meltzer. Meltzer, who was Hughes's collaborator on the *Pictorial History of the Negro in America* (1956),[25] examines Hughes the writer in context of Hughes's own observation "You have to learn to be yourself, natural and undeceived as to who you are, calmly and surely you."[26]

Evidence of how Hughes's two biographers exercise their interpretive authority over the repressed subject occurs in their respective accounts of the poet's break with Mrs. Charlotte Mason, a wealthy, white New York socialite and Hughes's patron. I cite these three accounts in reverse chronological order, leading back to Hughes's first-person narrative, for reasons that will become obvious. Rampersad gives this account:

> Nine years later, in a *reticent* account of their relationship, in which Hughes never identified Mrs. Mason by name (she was still alive), he did not hide his extreme pain in their last meeting. . . . Shattered by her words, *his body betraying a neurotic turmoil* that made his muscles twitch involuntarily and his fingers curl into bizarre shapes, he rode the train to Washington. (Rampersad, 1:185, my emphasis)

Berry gives this account:

> His autobiographical account of the end of their relationship is *more anguished than angry.* . . . *Somewhat naively,* he had believed the latter [retaining their friendship] entirely possible, never realizing that her interest did not extend to any relationship in which she could not

exert control over him, "But there must have been only the one thread binding us together," he confessed later. (Berry, 107, my emphasis)

Rampersad's and Berry's accounts, while not factually inaccurate, would scarcely prepare readers for the differently grounded self-awareness of Hughes's first-person account and might even interfere with their perception of Hughes's insight:

Great wealth had given to a woman who meant to be kind the means to power, and a technique of power, of so mighty a strength that I do not believe she herself knew what that force might become. She possessed the power to control people's lives—pick them up and put them down when and where she wished.

She wished me to be primitive and know and feel the intuitions of the primitive. But, unfortunately, I did not feel the rhythms of the primitive surging through me, and I could not live and write as though I did. . . . So, in the end it all came back very near to the old impasse of white and Negro again, white and Negro—as do most relationships in America. . . . I asked kindly to be released from any further obligations to her . . . but simply let me retain her friendship and good will that had been so dear to me. . . . But there must have been only the one thread binding us together. When that thread broke, it was the end.

I cannot write here about that last half-hour in the big bright drawing-room high above Park Avenue one morning, because when I think about it, even now, something happens in the pit of my stomach that makes me ill.[27]

Rampersad and Berry examine Hughes from the inside out, taking their cue presumably from his failing to describe in revealing psychological detail the scene of his and Mrs. Mason's last meeting. Since Hughes announces this omission and his reason for it, to call the omission reticence, as Rampersad does, seems misleading if not outright inaccurate. To say that Hughes masks his personal pain may not be entirely wrong. But this observation may miss the larger point that Hughes chooses to probe matters he considers more important and perhaps even more painful than mere personal pain: the twin tyrannies of racism and class structure that affect an entire group of people. To call Hughes's decision a cover-up, as Rampersad does, or cite it as evidence of a "failure to come to grips with his personal experience" (Berry, 107), as Berry does, diverges significantly from the subject's position.

A less strained and perhaps more satisfying explanation might be the following: Hughes wrote an exposé identifying a personal experience as a revealing instance of political injustice and abuse by one individual against another. He provides the evidence for this interpretation but ultimately leaves it up to readers to make their own judgments about the powerful lesson to be learned from this incident, not just by Hughes but by anyone who reads his account attentively. Far from slighting the personal or subjective component of his break with Mrs. Mason, Hughes validates its empowering authenticity by emphasizing how a particular event educated him to recognize an abuse of power and a sin against the individual human spirit, each with a long national history.

Collateral support for this revision of Berry and Rampersad comes from Hughes's short story "The Blues I'm Playing" (*Scribner's Magazine*, 1933; *The Ways of White Folks*, 1935). Oceola Jones, gifted black pianist, becomes the protégée of a white patron, Mrs. Dora Ellsworth. The "period of Oceola" is described by the narrator as "one of the most interesting periods in Mrs. Ellsworth's whole experience in aiding the arts." The patron is dead set against anything but classical music in Oceola's repertoire (no blues, church choir music, or jazz) and tries to interfere with the young musician's engagement to a black medical student and eventual marriage. Mrs. Ellsworth is fascinated by her protégée's blackness, admires the "electric strength" of the young woman's "brown-black body," and "if there were a lot of guests at the lodge . . . Mrs. Ellsworth might share the bed with Oceola."[28] Berry notes that this story is the "closest Hughes ever came to give his readers a glimpse of his own former patron" (Berry, 202). William L. Andrews observes more incisively that " 'The Blues I'm Playing' " represents "a brilliant fictionalizing displacement (rather than repression) of Hughes's resentment and hurt over the relationship to Mason and the breakup with her."[29] Hughes in fiction and fact, thus with redoubled emphasis, interprets and powerfully expresses the multiple meanings of his relationship with Mrs. Mason—social, political, aesthetic, economic, and emotional.

Rampersad's life of Hughes belongs to the contemporary line of multivolume scholarly biographies. These lives are typically years in the making, often a decade. Like Bell's life of Woolf, they characteristically narrate the subject's life in dense detail, a few years at a time, these segments marked by watershed formative events in the subject's development. Richard Ellmann's lives of James Joyce and Oscar Wilde and Michael Holroyd's five-volume life of George Bernard Shaw are projects of similar magnitude and indispensable scholarly thoroughness. Readers recognize such definitive lives by characteristics including their size, the many acknowledgments to individuals, libraries, collections, and frequently to granting agencies, centers, and foundations for fellowships which, by providing financial support, indirectly provide the indispensable factor of time essential to this kind of exhaustive research.

Rampersad's biography is, in addition, the authorized life, the commission for which he identifies in acknowledgments recounting the almost accidental origin of the project: "I began the research for this book sometime in the summer of 1979, a few months after being introduced at a concert in Cambridge, Massachusetts to George Houston Bass, a professor of English at Brown University and executor-trustee of the Hughes estate." Rampersad, like Berry, recounts that the biographer designated by Hughes, Bontemps, had died before the life was underway. He adds that subsequently the Yale Hughes collection "had been closed to almost all researchers" (Rampersad, 1:439). Rampersad emphasizes that his agreement to write the authorized biography, details of which remain undisclosed, involved no promises compromising the biographer's responsibility and integrity. Woolf noted, fifty years ago, that Victorian biographies, commissioned by widows, relatives, or other highly interested parties, are notoriously unreliable because there were so many strings attached. Issues involved in authorized lives remain lively, as instanced by this disclaimer in Margaret Walker's life of Richard Wright:

> The executor of the Wright Estate, Mrs. Ellen Wright, however, did not grant me permission to quote many materials that would further illuminate discussions in this book. For nearly a year, I fruitlessly sought her permission. Mrs. Wright would not give further consideration to my requests unless I permitted her to read the manuscript of this biography. Because I view her request as prior restraint tantamount to censorship, I refused. This is not an authorized biography.[30]

Biographers obviously would prefer cooperation from crucial, usually intimate, sources. But they may be unwilling to forego indispensable independence for promised cooperation.

Rampersad, in addition to acknowledging the initial invitation from the second executor of the Hughes estate, also acknowledges four granting agencies and research centers for financial support and concludes with several pages of thanks to libraries and special collections where he researched this life and to individuals who provided information or contributed in other ways to the project. Reading these acknowledgments provides a short course in the mountainous rigors of contemporary scholarly biography, which often involves substantial travel in order to examine the subject's papers and other materials where they are housed. Research for *Langston Hughes* took Rampersad to Connecticut, Georgia, Louisiana, New York, North Carolina, Illinois, and Washington, D.C., to name only a few stops on his itinerary. William Holtz's *Ghost in the Little House: A Life of Rose Wilder Lane* (1993), ten years in the making, took the biographer to France, Switzerland, Germany, Italy, Yugoslavia, Austria, Hungary, Czechoslovakia, and Turkey to retrace Wilder's extensive travels. Leon Edel spent nineteen years on his five-volume life of Henry James. Major investments of time, money, scholarly perseverance, and imaginative energy are among the definitive demands of contemporary scholarly biography.

As a coda to this chapter on minority biography, in context of the discussion above of Rampersad's authorized two-volume life of Hughes, let me return to this scholar's earlier cited important examination of biography and autobiography in African-American culture. Rampersad begins with several major theoretical questions that informed his own undertaking of a life of Hughes to which, he adds, his "formal training as a literary scholar had provided few answers": "Should the biography of a person of African descent differ fundamentally from that of a European? In what specific way or ways is the story different? And how is this difference, perceived in theory, to be rendered in writing a biography itself? What is a black biography?"[31]

In proposing an elegantly complex answer to this question, Rampersad meditates on reasons for the small number of black biographies, written either by black or white scholars in this country, and the predominance, by contrast, of autobiography. He comments that autobiographies succeed "in the modern age almost always in direct relation to their retrospective or their prophetic appeal to community of spirit," that black autobiography "has always preserved something of the flavor of Augustinian

confession," though informed by a distinctive "material dimension in response to the search for political freedom and power,"
and finally that the "very qualities that weakened American
autobiography primed the nation for biography."[32] Rampersad
concludes by assessing the meaning of the contemporary rise of
black biography as symptomatic of "a realignment of the place of
the black individual in the modern world . . . the black has
become more ordinary . . . and even modern."[33]

Rampersad's remarks align with the earlier-mentioned
schema of Jürgen Schlaeger, who posits autobiography and biography as distinctly different kinds of rhetorical constructions
with different legitimizing strategies, grounds of authority, and
points of view. Autobiography is the *discourse of anxiety*, the
insider's view, which posits the speaker's expressed truth to self
as its preeminent aim and value. Biography, by contrast, is the
discourse of usurpation. This genre takes as its truth criterion not
the authenticity of the insider's view but the "consistency of the
narrative and the explanatory power of the arguments" based in
the individual's relatively comfortable relationship with her or
his culture's ground of assumptive value.[34] The rags-to-riches or
success-against-great-odds life story, for instance, perhaps especially this kind of story, assumes the value of everything the protagonist does not have and that therefore does not constitute him
at the outset.

Making sense of a life or lives has always been the aim of biography, though in extraordinarily various ways by different writers in different cultures and different times. James A. Clifton,
analyzing the history of "storylines" created by anthropologists
of Native Americans, has identified two stages of narrative invention: Until the 1950s, the Indian past was depicted "as a time of
stable cultures strongly contrasted with a maladapted disorga-
nized present"; the 1960s storyline used the same elements but
reversed their order, stressing that the period of cultural loss and
disorganization was beginning to give way to the good effects of
recuperative "continuity and persistence." Thus the past "golden
age" of one story becomes the posited future of the subsequent
anthropological narrative. Within the framework of directives
and constraints of these two different storylines, individuals' lives
take on a limited array of interpretations: victim, self-destroyer,
survivor, culture-hero.[35] However challenging the difficulties

may be, Clifton emphasizes, investigators must not renege on the vital reponsibility of "keeping individual humans clearly in mind, of never allowing them to be lost or obscured in anthropological theorizing about abstracted, anonymous collectivities."[36] The next and final chapter, "Group and Collective Biography and Biographical Series," will return to some of the issues of minority biography discussed in this chapter. These biographical forms, by identifying and categorizing individuals according to historical, sociological, racial, ethnic, regional, sexual and gender criteria, to name only a few, and hence actively defining people as members of "groups," address either implicitly or explicitly the question of whose lives are worth writing about and why.

Chapter 5

GROUP AND COLLECTIVE BIOGRAPHY AND BIOGRAPHICAL SERIES

> For the compilers of a biographical dictionary it is a stark necessity "to exclude everything which is redundant and nothing that is significant" imposed by the limits of available space, confronting them with a formidable exercise in eclecticism which is rendered more difficult as each year brings its new crop of celebrities.
>
> J. O. Thorne, preface to *Chambers Biographical Dictionary* (1897)

This study has focused on biography defined as a form that narrates, examines, and interprets individual lives. In this final chapter I return to two previously mentioned variations on the single-book depiction of an individual life, group biography and collective biography with, in addition, brief discussion of biographical series. Collective biography narrates many lives and, while depicting them individually, proceeds by a set of organizational criteria with a cumulative purpose. Group biography depicts the social, personal, and professional interactions of a definable association of individuals, sometimes obscure or lesser known, presented as being interesting in their own right and, perhaps more importantly, to be metaphorically or metonymically revealing of a particular historical period which they influenced or epitomized. Biographical series usually have a single major criterion associating the figures selected for book-length treatment.

Group Biography

Henry James, in his two-volume life of William Wetmore Story, nineteenth-century sculptor and man of letters, proposes a valuable poetics of group biography to accommodate this particular subject. Though not a minor figure, Wetmore was, James believed, better portrayed among a "group of sitters . . . all in their places" to fill the frame. James elaborates this metaphor in the opening chapter of *William Wetmore Story and His Friends* (1903): ". . . our boxful of ghosts 'compose,' hang together, consent to a mutual relation, confess, in fact, to a mutual dependence. If it is a question of living again, they can live but by each other's help, so that they close in, join hands, press together for warmth and contact. . . . The subject is the *period*—it is the period that holds the elements together, rounds them off, makes them right."[1] Group biography characteristically focuses on the historical period, its details and atmosphere, in which the subjects lived.

Leon Edel's *Bloomsbury: A House of Lions* (1979) is a narrative portrait of nine friends (Vanessa and Clive Bell, Roger Fry, Duncan Grant, Maynard Keynes, Desmond MacCarthy, Lytton Strachey, and Leonard and Virginia Woolf) who were recognized as accomplished individuals, while at the same time identified as members of a group, sometimes with acclaim, sometimes with notoriety. Edel proposes that these figures' "network of human relations" continues to serve as "a lesson in modern living."[2] Reminiscent of Woolf in "The Art of Biography," Edel observes that, although the biographer "is not allowed to imagine his facts," the intepretation of those facts requires, on his part, "the imagination of form." His aim in *Bloomsbury* is to make the narrative proceed like "a novel and its subjects characters in a novel," yet remain scrupulously loyal to the facts of the matter (Edel, 13).

Another group biography, R. W. B. Lewis's *The Jameses: A Family Narrative* (1991), tells "the story of a remarkable American family—as regards its literary and intellectual accomplishments, perhaps the most remarkable family the country has ever known—from its eighteenth-century Irish origins to the death of the novelist Henry James in 1916."³ Lewis combines cultural and intellectual history with an examination of this particular family's self-construction. The biographer's announced aim is to describe what it might have meant to be "a native" of the extraordinary James family. This biographer's portrait of the Jameses situates itself in the context of psychoanalytic and new historicist methods, the latter emphasizing the problematic intersection of historical context and modern readings of family dynamics and the history of the family.

Leon Howard's *The Connecticut Wits* (1941) exemplifies group biography as historical recovery. Howard examines six eighteenth- and early-nineteenth-century New England humorists, John Trumbell, Timothy Dwight, Joel Barlow, David Humphreys, Lemuel Hopkins, and Richard Alsop, whose importance as individual writers would be difficult to argue but whose group importance makes a scholarly account worthwhile. This study is called by the author "a sort of test bore through the complex intellectual strata which make the exploration of this period as difficult as it is necessary to the understanding of later cultural developments in the United States."⁴ Since by definition group biography studies several figures, rather than one, this subgenre also tends to emphasize the subjects' historical, intellectual, and cultural contexts within which their significance is perceived.

Lyle Larsen's *Dr. Johnson's Household* (1985) examines a particular group of "minor characters" referred to in Boswell's *Life* as Johnson's *ménage* and identified by Larsen as "that strange collection of people [Anna Williams, poet, Francis Barber, Johnson's black servant, Elizabeth Desmoulins, daughter of Johnson's godfather, Robert Levett, lay physician, and the homeless Poll Carmichael] whom Johnson sheltered and cared for during the last part of his life."⁵ Their association resulted from knowing Johnson, as does their preservation in the historical record. These figures appear in several major eighteenth-century lives of Johnson (Piozzi, Burney, and Hawkins, among them) as shadowy walk-on characters. Though each was presumably important to Johnson and all lived lives of their own, the biographical record tends to merge them with their famous friend. These factors motivated Larsen's curiosity to write a group biography in order to foreground these lesser known friends of Johnson who, except

BIOGRAPHY

for their connections with this famous writer, might have disappeared entirely.

Antonia Fraser's group biography, *The Wives of Henry VIII* (1992), also defines its subjects relationally, as the title indicates, "first and foremost, as wives" of a single husband.[6] From this organizational premise, the historical *donné*, the biographer develops a point-counterpoint illumination of the differences among these eight women, focusing particularly on the distinct pattern in Henry's choices of wives after his first two marriages to strong, defiant women (the twenty-year marriage to Catherine of Aragon and the subsequent brief marriage to Anne Boleyn), which help explain the king's subsequent marked preference for docile women and his commitment to absolute authority over the next six spouses.

The True History of the First Mrs. Meredith and Other Lesser Lives (1972), by the novelist and short story writer Diane Johnson, is a well-researched biography, complete with list of manuscripts consulted and a cast of some forty-six greater and lesser known Victorian figures associated with the obscure Mary Ellen Peacock Meredith. Johnson sets out to reverse the fate of the first Mrs. Meredith, writer and scandalous adulteress who came to be "defined only as an accessory to her father [Thomas Love Peacock, the novelist and poet] and her husband [George Meredith, the novelist and poet]." Enlarging the conventional roles heretofore assigned to this woman in biographies of her husband and father where she functioned as a mere episode in their lives, Johnson recasts Mary Ellen as the central figure of this novelistic story of her own life. Now the protagonist, Mary Ellen becomes, in Johnson's rendering, a revolutionary heroine who dared to break Victorian feminine conventions of submission, fidelity, and decorum, left her husband to live with the painter Henry Wallis, and remained, to the moment of her death, "unfrightened [and] in command."[7]

My underscoring the distinction between lives of individuals and group biography is not intended to blur the fact that biographies of individuals also examine their subjects as members of various groups—family, school associates, fellow-workers, etc. The biography of any individual thus inevitably becomes an account of the person in group settings, since human life is largely characterized by social interaction. Biography, a fundamentally social form, locates and defines its subjects in the presence of others, gathering and evaluating other people's accounts of the person as one of its major constitutive categories of evidence. Inner thoughts and time spent alone are, for reasons of both evidence and rhetoric, more appropriate to autobiography.

Collective Biography and Biographical Series

The other form of multiple-person biography, collective biography, is typically organized like a dictionary with entries, sometimes numbering in the thousands, arranged alphabetically. The word *dictionary* often appears in the title, as, for instance, in the earlier-mentioned *Dictionary of National Biography* (1885–) with 30,000 entries in first edition, and the *Dictionary of American Biography* (1928–), with 15,000 entries. Collective biography dates back to the literate origins of life writing (Suetonius's *Lives of the Caesars*, Plutarch's *Lives*, Aubrey's *Brief Lives*, discussed in chapter 1) and continues to flourish.

The following pages survey representatively, though of necessity selectively, multientry biography. More detailed surveys are available in the following sources: *ARBA Guide to Biographical Dictionaries* (1986), the "Biography" section of the American Library Association *Guide to Reference Books* (10th ed., 1986), and "Biographical Reference Sources: A Selective Checklist" in the "Reference Books Bulletin" section of *Booklist*.

Dictionaries of biography are invaluable and much used reference books in all libraries. There are three principal kinds: general, national or regional, and professional or occupational. Other categories for selection and organization include race, gender, and historical period. Some ongoing series appear with yearly updates. These include *Current Biography* (1940–), published in monthly numbers and bound as an annual, which depicts "some 140 leaders in all fields of endeavor—government, entertainment, business, science, religion, the arts," in profiles of a few thousand words, each including a photograph. Larger works, such as the *Dictionary of American Biography*, are ongoing projects with periodic supplements.

The following brief list of titles of multivolume biographies suggest something of the variety of organizational principles and aims informing such works: Mary Hays's *Female Biography; or, Memoirs of Illustrious and Celebrated Women, of All Ages and Countries*

(6 vols., 1806); *The Universal Biographical Dictionary; or, an Historical Account of the Lives, Characters, and Works of the Most Eminent Persons in Every Age and Nation from the Earliest Times to the Present, Particularly the Natives of Great Britain and Ireland* (n.d., mid–nineteenth century); *Biographie universelle ancienne et moderne* (45 vols., 1843–1865); *Woman's Record* (1853); *Who's Who in America* (1899–   ; with supplements); *Twentieth Century Authors* (1942; with supplements); *The Book of People: Photographs, Capsule Biographies and Vital Statistics of Over 500 Celebrities* (1981); *Dictionary of Scientific Biography* (16 vols., 1970–1980); *Grove's Dictionary of Music and Musicians* (5th ed., 9 vols., 1954); and the *Dictionary of American Negro Biography* (1982). Here are some of the figures chosen for inclusion in two of the foregoing examples: Hays, in her six-volume *Female Biography*, promises to omit "no character of eminence." Entries begin with Abbassa, "the most beautiful and accomplished princess of the East," and end with Zenobia, Queen of Palmyra; in between come Agnes Sorrell; Catherine of Aragon; Dido; Louise Labé; Anne, Countess of Winchelsea; and Margaret Valois, to name only a few. The *Universal Biographical Dictionary*, edited by John Watkins, surveys the "lives, characters, and works" of "the most eminent persons in every age and nation," particularly, as the title indicates, natives of Great Britain and Ireland. Royalty and religious and military figures dominate the premodern entries. Beginning in the late sixteenth century, economic, political, and scientific revolutions that defined the modern age introduced new criteria for achievement and eminence and hence for inclusion in collective biographies. Inventors, mathematicians, writers, and explorers, for example, appear in great number. Relatively few women appear, and those who do, Aphra Behn and Anna Seward, for example, are often substantially identified by their associations with men—fathers and husbands. Men included in such dictionaries are seldom identified by their associations with mothers and wives.

Collective biographies vary in style and intention. Those known as directories present entries of a relatively brief *who's who* or *who's where* kind which include formula data, often solicited from the subjects themselves (birth, education, career, awards and honors, professional memberships, religious affiliation, marriage, children, and usually a mailing address and phone number or, in the case of writers and some other professionals, an agent's name—in short, ways to contact these people).

Some directories are essentially vanity publications, all but requiring purchase in order to be included. The ALA *Guide to Reference Books* recommends alertness to "any evidence of lack of objectivity" in biographical dictionaries or directories. Among the chararacteristics typifying responsible biographical dictionaries are distinguished editorial boards and advisors and well-enunciated, credible criteria for selection based on the interests of users not the self-interest of the subjects or publishers.

Biographical dictionaries tend generally to differ from directories in conception and imagined use. Since the subjects of dictionaries are often no longer living, there is no practical issue of readers trying to contact them, and the matter of assessing the person's importance thus assumes a historical dimension. In addition, dictionary entries are, not infrequently, signed by the individual contributors, who thereby assume scholarly responsibility for the research methods and criteria guiding their work.

A. N. Marquis, founder of *Who's Who in America* at the turn of the twentieth century, defined as the aim of his series to provide "life and career data on noteworthy individuals" whose "achievements and contributions to society made them subjects of widespread reference interest and inquiry." National origin and occupation are the main organizational categories of modern collective biographies. Marquis's language, combining demography with patriotism, identifies the subjects as self-evident candidates for inclusion by virtue of their widespread interest to a large public. The preface to the 1995 *Who's Who in America* (49th ed.) notes that the increased number of entries, from 8,602 names in the first edition to some 75,000 in the 44th edition, reflects "demographic crosscurrents within American society."[8] In the world of biographical directories, "enlarged" is usually synonymous with improved.

Directories typically solicit biographical information from candidates who have first been identified by the publisher's research staff on the basis of media coverage and other accounts in the public record identifying them as noteworthy. These candidates are asked to provide *data*, the word underscoring the directory's announced aim to provide certain uniform information, mentioned above. These data are then checked, the editors note, "to confirm that candidates meet the stringent selection criteria" before being composed as a sketch subsequently returned to the subject for checking. This structure of research places primary emphasis on the subjects themselves, though the overarching editorial policy of uniform entries either excludes or keeps to a minimum certain kinds of variety, including autobiographical self-expression. By contrast, some collective biographies, such as *Twentieth Century Authors*, invite their subjects to contribute autobiographical statements about themselves and their work to be included in the entry.

The purpose of practical utility motivating most directories appears in their titles, which announce the categories of selection: *Directory of American Scholars* (4 vols., 1984); *Who's Who in American Law 1985–1986* (4th ed., 1985); *Biographical Directory of the American Academy of Pediatrics* (1980); *Civil Rights: A Current Guide to the People, Organizations, and Events* (2nd ed., 1974); *Directory of Image Consultants* (1984). For the profession of writing, the two most important collective biographies are *Contemporary Authors: A Bio-bibliographical Guide to Current Writers in Fiction, General Nonfiction, Poetry, Journalism, Drama, Motion Pictures, Television, and Other Fields* (1962–   ), numbering over 111 volumes; and the *Dictionary of Literary Biography* (1978–   ), currently 45 volumes. The *DLB* aims eventually to "encompass all authors who have made significant contributions to literature in the United States, Canada, England, and some other countries as well." Individual volumes focus on a specific period or literary movement, as, for instance, *The American Renaissance in New England* (vol. 1), *American Novelists since World War II* (vol. 2), and *Antebellum Writers in New York and the South* (vol. 3), each edited by a recognized scholar in the field.

Although collective biography dates back to the Greeks, this form's significant growth dates from the latter half of the nineteenth century. The British *Dictionary of National Biography*, founded by George Smith in 1882, is generally considered to be the first major modern biographical tool of the English-speaking world. This dictionary's statement of purpose and criteria is worth citing in full for several reasons, among them its possible salutary surprise to twentieth-century readers with preconceptions about late-Victorian narrowness and rigidity:

> It is believed that the names include all men and women of British or Irish race who have achieved any reasonable measure of distinction in any walk of life . . . every statesman, lawyer, divine, painter, author, inventor, actor, physician, surgeon, man of science, traveller,

musician, soldier, sailor, bibliographer, book collector, and printer whose career presents any feature which justifies its preservation from oblivion. No sphere of activity has been consciously overlooked. . . . Malefactors whose crimes excite a permanent interest have received hardly less attention than benefactors. The principle upon which names have been admitted has been from all points of view generously interpreted; the epithet 'national' has not been held to exclude the early settlers in America, or natives of these islands who have gained distinction in foreign countries, or persons of foreign birth who have achieved eminence in this country.[9]

The announced principle of selection, "any feature which justifies" a person's "preservation from oblivion," underscores newsworthiness, not exemplary behavior, as the informing criterion. Since no living people are included, information was never solicited from the subjects themselves. All entries are signed, this being a distinguishing characteristic of biographical dictionaries which emphasize individual responsibility and accountability on the part of contributors who are urged to do primary research, consult unpublished papers, and provide bibliographies for their entries. The original twenty-two volumes, edited by Sirs Leslie Stephen and Sidney Lee, have been supplemented by subsequent volumes appearing at nine-year intervals from 1901 to 1970.

The United States equivalent of the *DNB* is the *Dictionary of American Biography*, which began appearing in 1928 under scholarly auspices of the American Council of Learned Societies. The *DAB*'s contributing editors, like their British predecessors, identify historical distinction, even negative or notorious distinction (e.g., John Wilkes Booth), as the chief criterion for eligibility and seek primary sources for all entries, which range in length from 500 to 16,500 words (for such notables as George Washington) and are signed.

The *National Cyclopaedia of American Biography* (1891–) is more comprehensive than the *DAB*. Its original statement of purpose, to include biographies of the "founders, builders and defenders of the Republic, and of the men and women who are doing the work and molding the thought of the present time," was later revised to include "not only the biographies of all incumbents of high governmental offices—administrative, legislative and judicial—but also those of persons occupying positions of leadership and distinction in professional, scientific, financial, industrial, educational, literary and religious spheres."[10]

The issues of scholarship and selection distinctly associated with minority collective biography can be usefully surveyed by citing the announced aims and methods of *Who's Who Among Black Americans* and the *Dictionary of American Negro Biography* (1982). The former announces as its aim to stand "as testimony to the strength and survival skills of a people whose genesis began centuries ago in a distant land." This statement which, though it could be made of all Americans except Native Americans, carries a particularly powerful historical subtext in the case of African-Americans who did not emigrate voluntarily from their homelands. This directory focuses on the accomplishments of 20,000 African-Americans, whose forebears arrived as slaves. The directory's list of "leaders, thinkers, artists, pacesetters, and visionaries," terms that combine professional qualifications with inspirational potential, promises to provide role models and to serve as "the logical source" to consult "when gathering facts on a distinguished leader or a favorite celebrity, locating a colleague or a specialist in a particular field, recruiting personnel, or launching a fund-raising effort."[11] Thus ethical, pedagogical, and practical purposes are invoked and served collectively.

The *Dictionary of American Negro Biography*, modeled on the *DAB*, including the convention of signed entries to locate scholarly responsibility, recounts the historical stages in African-American biographical scholarship from the mid-nineteenth century to the present. The editors describe the history of motives and aims for biographical dictionaries of this group. Early collective biographies undertook to "'defend' the Negro against charges of inferiority," to inspire youth by gathering examples of heroes and heroines, and to educate the general public in a history of which they may be ignorant. Increased scholarly interest in African-American history, as an integral part of American historical studies, accompanied the Civil Rights movement of the 1950s. Hence more African-Americans are now included in general collective biographies, such as the *DAB*, as are more women. African-American studies has also developed as a distinct area of inquiry with, like women's studies, characteristic methodologies and interdisciplinary focus.

The editors' discussion of how criteria for inclusion were developed for the *Dictionary of American Negro Biography* identifies several issues distinctive to minority biography. First, the same criteria for selection cannot be accurately applied transhistorically. Achievement by a minority that would have been considered significant in the colonial period might "in many cases" appear "less so a hundred years later." As more minority members enter various fields, standards for inclusion become more exacting. Second, majority categories of "fame" and "national importance" could not be employed with meaningful accuracy since many of those included were unknown to the mainstream white culture of their times, though they played important parts in their separate community. In the earlier periods, the percentages of the African-American community who were involved in certain areas of achievement, education and religion chief among them, were higher than the corresponding percentages of the white community. This disproportion results directly from the kinds of opportunities both denied and permitted by segregation. The editors conclude that they were guided chiefly by "the test of historical *significance*," understood to be a principle of assessment that varies complexly in relation to social and cultural change.

Among the early notable collective biographies of Native Americans are Samuel G. Drake's *Indian Biography, Containing the Lives of More than Two Hundred Chiefs* (1832), the standard nineteenth-century source of Indian biographies, and Charles A. Eastman's *Indian Heroes and Great Chieftains* (1918). Eastman (1858–1939), a South Dakota physician and author, who was raised a Santee Sioux and educated at Beloit, Knox, and Dartmouth Colleges and Boston University, wrote lives of Red Cloud, Spotted Tail, Little Crow, Crazy Horse, Sitting Bull, and others informed by firsthand experience and knowledge.[12] Later important collective biographies are Margot Liberty's *American Indian Intellectuals* (1978) and R. David Edmunds's edited volume of biographical essays, *American Indian Leaders: Studies in Diversity* (1980).[13] The University of Oklahoma Press *Civilization of the American Indian Series* of 219 titles includes a number of individual lives, for example, *Pocahontas* (by Grace Steele Woodward, 1969), *Sitting Bull* (by Stanley Vestal, 1932; rpt. 1957), *Hosteen Klah: Navaho Medicine Man and Sand Painter* (by Franc Johnson Newcomb, 1964), and *Geronimo* (by Angie Debo, 1976).

Notable American Women 1607–1950: A Biographical Dictionary (1971) is the first large-scale scholarly work in its field and an authoritative contribution to the study of women's history. Patterned after the *Dictionary of American Biography* and prepared under the auspices of Radcliffe's Schlesinger Library, this dictionary is the first large-scale work in its field, with 738 contributors having written 1,359 entries. With the exception of Presidents' wives, women were admitted on their own credentials, rather than their husbands', the criterion being distinction in their own right beyond the merely local.

A single-volume dictionary entitled *Women of Achievement: Thirty-Five Centuries of History* (1981) organizes its entries into several areas of accomplishment ("Politics and Power," "Education and Social Reform," "The Written Word," for example). This dictionary chronicles chiefly nineteenth- and twentieth-century Anglo-American and European women, since the rise of the career woman, as we know her, occurs in this 200-year period. The series *Biographical Dictionaries of Minority Women* (Garland, 1994–), which aims to correct oversights in the historical record of lives and achievements of women other than white women, numbers three volumes to date: *Native American Women, African American Women,* and *European Immigrant Women in the United States.*

The readers targeted by various collective and serial biographical works are often members of the group or groups chosen for inclusion in the volumes, as in several of the dictionaries mentioned above, which might be of particular interest to women and minorities, though one would hope, not exclusively so. *The McGraw Hill Encyclopedia of World Biography* (12 vols., 1973) targets secondary–school-age readers and is designed for classroom use. Relatively brief entries of about 800 words are noted to have "a curriculum orientation" and are followed by a brief bibliography of recommended additional reading.

A number of biographical series publish individual volumes cumulatively associated with one another in various ways. The *Radcliffe Biography Series,* for instance, "was sparked," so the series description announces, by the publication of *Notable American Women* (1971). The Radcliffe series commissions new biographies in addition to reprinting earlier titles of note. Subjects include Mary Cassatt (by Nancy Hall), Emily Dickinson (by Cynthia Griffin Wolff), Dorothy Day (by Robert Coles), and Alva Myrdal (by Sissela Bok). Rutgers University Press publishes an *American Women Writers Series. Pandora Press Life and Times* and *Penguin Literary Biographies* are two other valuable series.

Life writing that focuses on sexual orientation as the organizing principle appears in the Chelsea House series *Lives of Notable*

Gay Men and Lesbians. Martin Duberman, the general editor, describes the series aim thus:

> Those who adopt the definition "gay" or "lesbian" soon discover that mainstream culture offers homosexuals no history or sense of forbears. This is a terrible burden, especially during the teenage years, when one is actively searching for a usable identity, for a continuum in which to place oneself and lay claim to a contented and productive life. These series are designed, above all, to fill that huge, painful cultural gap.[14]

Retrieving missing persons or the missing or suppressed portions of their lives in the historical record is the chief aim of minority biography.

Juvenile biography is a plentiful and fascinating subgenre. The Bobbs-Merrill *Childhood of Famous Americans* series is a standard holding of elementary school and public libraries. Readers can research their subjects either by professions and achievements or roles, or by historical periods, including colonial days, struggle for independence, early national growth, and the westward movement. Professions and achievements are subdivided into athletes (Babe Didrikson, Babe Ruth, Jim Thorpe), authors and composers (Eugene Field, George Gershwin, Harriet Beecher Stowe, etc.), businessmen (Alan Pinkerton, Andrew Carnegie, F. W. Woolworth), early settlers (James Oglethorpe, Virginia Dare, William Bradford), entertainers (Annie Oakley, Cecil B. De Mille, Ethel Barrymore), explorers and pioneers (Amelia Earhart, Brigham Young, Buffalo Bill), founders of our nation (Ben Franklin, Crispus Attucks, DeWitt Clinton), noted wives and mothers (Abigail Adams, Dolly Madison, Eleanor Roosevelt), Indians (Black Hawk, Osceola, Pocahontas), and naval heroes (David Farragut, George Dewey, John Paul Jones), to give a sampling. Biographies are subdivided by historical period. Silver Burdett Press publishes Julian Messner's series *Classic American Writers* with lives of Willa Cather, Herman Melville, and Edith Wharton, to date, along with biographical series devoted to African-Americans, Native Americans, American women, and other persons coming from diverse cultural backgrounds, aimed at an audience of young and middle-grade readers.

A small selection of titles of juvenile biographies of Mark Twain alone suggests publishers' understanding of the marketability of biography's instructive pleasures: Jeanette Eaton,

America's Own Mark Twain (New York: William Morrow, 1958; Pflaum, 1967); Harnett T. Kane, *Young Mark Twain and the Mississippi* (New York: Random House, 1966; rpt. 1987); Miriam E. Mason, *Mark Twain: Boy of Old Missouri* (Indianapolis: Bobbs-Merrill, 1942; rpt 1962); May McNeer, *America's Mark Twain* (Boston: Houghton Mifflin, 1962; Eau Claire, Wisc.: Hale, 1966); Sterling North, *Mark Twain and the River* (Boston: Houghton Mifflin, 1961).

The American Library Association's *Guide to Reference Books*, the sourcebook for library acquisitions mentioned above, provides a useful summary to conclude the present chapter's sketch of collective biography and returns us to the scene of a public library where this book began. This guide notes that dictionaries of biography are among the most frequently used reference books in any collection. Even a small library, the editor observes, "will need several works in this class," which fall into three main types: general, national or regional, and professional or occupational. Each of these is, in turn, subdivided into general or retrospective and contemporary.[15]

Recommended basic titles for any United States library, regardless of size, and titles with which the general reader should be familiar are the *Dictionary of American Biography*, the latest edition of *Who's Who in America*, *Current Biography*, *Webster's Biographical Dictionary*, and *Biography Index*, plus appropriate regional dictionaries and, when possible, a core set of professional and occupational volumes such as *American Men and Women of Science* and the *Directory of American Scholars*. International biographical resource materials may be too costly for any but large libraries. But readers may examine their range in bibliographical works, including the earlier mentioned *ARBA Guide to Biographical Dictionaries* and the *Guide to Reference Books*. Master indexes, such as *Biography and Genealogy Master Index*, and the technological advances of microform and online searches now make possible biographical research through extensive sources formerly unavailable except at major libraries or special collections.

With this concluding scene set once again in a library, my study has returned full circle to the preface, a fitting conclusion to an examination of biography, the genre which, next to or perhaps even surpassing the novel, is the most reader centered of all the modern literary forms.

Bibliographic Essay

A useful way to begin examining the range and variety of critical, historical, theoretical, and practical approaches to biography is to browse through Carl Rollyson's *Biography: An Annotated Bibliography* in the Magill bibliographies series (Pasadena, Calif.: Salem Press, 1992). Rollyson organizes this survey of the secondary literature by scope of the study, historical period, method, and occasionally by author and/or biographical subject. He surveys general studies and historical studies (from the Greco-Roman period through the nineteenth century), then proceeds to the twentieth century with separate chapters on psychobiography, feminist biography, and biography in fiction, this last section surveying an aspect of life writing least fully examined in my study and hence of special use to readers of this book. Rollyson devotes separate chapters to studies of Johnson and Boswell and to work by and about the twentieth-century biographer Leon Edel. Since it is unnecessary to duplicate Rollyson's book-length survey, I will emphasize, in the pages that follow, books and some essays which have been most helpful to me in writing this study.

Since even a single good book on a subject directs readers to many other useful titles, these in turn enriching inquiry with other titles, the practical purpose of a bibliography is to set readers on a few paths with as many possible future paths implied as readers to draft their own maps of inquiry. I would also direct readers to consult the endnotes of each chapter to supplement the bibliographic essay. Not every title mentioned previously is repeated in my bibliographical essay, yet the fact that a book or essay has figured constructively in my research makes a self-evident case for my opinion of its worth.

In 1970, Clifford observed that "until recently there has been very little genuine critical work on the art of biography." Nor has there apparently been, on the part of practicing biographers, he continues, much conscious or detailed thinking about their work.[1] In the intervening years since this statement, critical interest in the theory and practice of biography has accelerated. Many of the titles mentioned below postdate 1970.

Of the pre-1970 titles, the single most useful and well-written book on the history and practice of biography is *The Nature of Biography* (New York: Knopf, 1957; New York: Garland, 1985) by John A. Garraty, one of the general editors of the *Dictionary of American Biography*. Paul Murray Kendall's *The Art of Biography* (New York Norton, 1965; rpt. 1985) is useful. Clifford's *Biography as an Art: Selected Criticism 1560–1960* (New York: Oxford University Press, 1962), unfortunately out of print, is an invaluable historical sampler of essays on the genre with an excellent, brief introduction and valuable bibliography. If twentieth-century readers are ever tempted to believe that the only interesting thinking on the poetics and practice of biography dates from the modern period, this collection will educate them otherwise. Edmund Gosse's entry on biography in *The Encyclopaedia Britannica* (11th ed., 1911, 3:952–54) is an important early twentieth-century overview. André Maurois's *Aspects of Biography* (1929; New York: Frederick Ungar, 1966) continues to repay reading as an essay on biography which, because Maurois wrote this book consciously as a contribution to the contemporary context of early-twentieth-century biographical innovation, continues to shed instructive light on this period. Similarly Harold Nicolson's *The Development of English Biography* (London: Hogarth Press, 1927; rpt. 1968) gives useful historical information and is additionally informative to later readers for its reflections of the new ideas informing early-twentieth-century biography. For literary biography, which dates from the eighteenth century, Richard D. Altick's *Lives and Letters: A History of Literary Biography in England and America* (New York: Knopf, 1965; rpt., Westport, Conn: Greenwood Press, 1979) remains a standard reference.

Noteworthy post-1970 overviews or historical introductions are the useful brief survey in Erling A. Erickson's entry on "Biography" in *The World Book Encyclopedia* (Chicago: World Book, 1994, 2:312–14); the section on "biographical criticism" in the general entry on criticism by Hazard Adams, in the *New Princeton Encyclopedia of Poetry and Poetics* (Princeton: Princeton University Press, 1993, 251–52), which registers postmodern skepticism about notions of the author in theory and criticism; and Walter Kendrick's "Parallel Lives: The State of the Art of Literary Biography," which proposes intelligent answers to the question of why, in spite of postmodern theory's announcement that the author is dead, we are still "up to our armpits in literary biography" (*The Village Voice Literary Supplement*, 1992, 10–13). In addition, Reed Whittemore's two-volume study of biography, *Pure Lives: The Early Biographers* and *Whole Lives: Shapers of Modern Biography* (Baltimore: Johns Hopkins University Press, 1988 and 1989) traces the shift from early biography's conceptual alliances with history, drama, and poetry to biography's modern commitment to inclusiveness and the avoidance of theses. Alan Shelston's compact *Biography* (London: Methuen, 1977) astutely approaches the genre from the vantage points of typifying problems, challenges, and solutions. And *Life-Writing: A Glossary of Terms in Biography, Autobiography, and Related Forms* (Biographical Research Center: University Press of Hawaii, 1980) by Donald J. Winslow is useful.

Turning to more specialized period studies, two essential books on classical and early Christian biography are T. A. Dorey's *Latin Biography* (New York: Basic Books, 1967), an edited collection of essays by several historians of the ancient world, and Clyde Weber Votaw's *The Gospels and Contemporary Biographies in the Greco-Roman World* (1915; rpt., Philadelphia: Fortress Press, 1970). Graham Anderson's *Philostratus: Biography and Belles Lettres in the Third Century A.D.* (Dover N.H.: Croom Helm, 1986), though a study of a single author, surveys, as the title indicates, larger terrain of the genre's early history. Thomas J. Heffernan has written an enlightening study of saints' lives, *Sacred Biography: Saints and Their Biographers in the Middle Ages* (New York: Oxford University Press, 1988). For the Elizabethan period, Judith H. Anderson's *Biographical Truth: The Representation of Historical Persons in Tudor-Stuart Writing* (New Haven: Yale University Press, 1984) includes chapters on Cavendish, Roper, and

Walton, biographers crucial for an understanding of the historical shifts that produced early-modern biography. Vivian de Sola Pinto's introduction to *English Biography in the Seventeenth Century: Selected Short Lives* (George G. Harrap, 1951; rpt. Freeport, N.Y.: Books for Libraries Press, 1969) is a classic. Donald Stauffer's *English Biography Before 1700* (Cambridge, Mass.: Harvard University Press, 1930) and *The Art of Biography in Eighteenth Century England* (Princeton: Princeton University Press, 1941) are scholarly models that remain fascinating reading. Another more recent study of eighteenth-century biography is the essay collection, *Biography in the 18th Century*, edited by J. D. Browning (New York: Garland, 1980), with a particularly interesting contribution by James Noxon, "Human Nature: General Theory and Individual Lives." William Epstein applies postmodern theory to readings of Walton, Johnson, Boswell, and Strachey in *Recognizing Biography* (Philadelphia: University of Pennsylvania Press, 1987).

For biography written in the generation after Boswell, Joseph W. Reed Jr.'s *English Biography in the Early Nineteenth Century* (New Haven: Yale University Press, 1966) is informative. So, too, is A. O. J. Cockshut's excellent intellectual-historical study of Victorian biography, *Truth to Life: The Art of Biography in the Nineteenth Century* (London: Collins, 1974; New York: Harcourt, Brace, 1976). The post-Victorian new biographers, including Woolf, Strachey, and Nicolson, are the subject of Ruth Hoberman's *Modernizing Lives: Experiments in English Biography, 1918–1939* (Carbondale and Edwardsville: Southern Illinois University Press, 1987). David Novarr, in *The Lines of Life: Theories of Biography, 1880–1970* (West Lafayette, Ind.: Purdue University Press, 1986) gives a worthwhile survey of the general theory and criticism of biography in England and the United States, from the late Victorian period well into the twentieth century, discussing work of Stephen, Strachey, Woolf, Bradford, Edel, Clifford, Garraty, etc.

The first extensive historical study of American biography was Edward H. O'Neill's *History of American Biography 1800–1935* (New York: A. S. Barnes, 1935; rpt. 1961). O'Neill examines how "the old factual record gave way to the journalistic, psychological form." Dana Kinsman Merrill's *American Biography: Its Theory and Practice* (Portland, Maine: Bowker Press, 1957) surveys the genre up to 1955. Both books offer substantial bibliographies of biography, and Merrill's appendix includes intriguingly informative notes on campaign biographies and on rogue and criminal lives. Donald C. Yelton's *Brief American Lives: Four Studies in Collective Biography* (Metuchen, N.J.: The Scarecrow Press, 1978) usefully examines three major American collective biographies, the *National Cyclopedia of American Biography*, the *Dictionary of American Biography*, and *Notable American Women*. Arnold Rampersad's "Biography, Autobiography, and Afro-American Culture," *The Yale Review* 73:1, Autumn 1983, 1–16, is an important essay on life writing in relation to ethnic and national identities.

Among contemporary critic-biographers, the late Richard Ellmann is, to my mind, the best. He has written variously on biographical theory and practice, all of it stylistically handsome and extraordinarily intelligent. Readers might begin with the brief, fine lecture, *Literary Biography: An Inaugural Lecture Delivered before the University of Oxford on 4 May 1971* (Oxford: Clarendon Press, 1971; New York: Oxford University Press, 1973), proceed to the stimulating essay, "Freud and Literary Biography" (*The American Scholar* 53:4, Autumn 1984, 465–78), and conclude with *Golden Codgers: Biographical Speculations* (New York and London: Oxford University Press, 1973, 1976). James Clifford's *From Puzzles to Portraits: Problems of a Literary Biographer* (Chapel Hill: University of North Carolina Press, 1970) gives an invaluable autobiographical account of the kind of detective work—a combination of training, perseverance, ingenuity, and good luck—that goes into first-rate scholarly biography and in accompanying a fine mind on its reflections back over a lifetime's experience with this genre. As the title of B. L. Reid's *Necessary Lives: Biographical Reflections* (Columbia: University of Missouri Press, 1990) indicates, this author discusses his chosen biographers (Boswell, John Keats, V. S. Pritchett, and Frank O'Connor, among others) from the point of view of a practicing critic-biographer. Park Honan, biographer of Jane Austen, Matthew Arnold, and Robert Browning, writes on the applied theory and practice of biography in *Author's Lives: On Literary Biography and the Arts of Language* (New York: St. Martin's Press, 1990). Carolyn Heilbrun in *Writing a Woman's Life* (New York: Norton, 1988) gives an informative account of feminist critical and compositional issues relating to biography, based on her own experience. Catherine Drinker Bowen, the popular historical biographer, presents her personally developed, but not merely personal, poetics of biography in *The Writing of Biography* (Boston: The Writer, 1950) and *Adventures of a Biographer* (Boston: Little, Brown, 1959). Leon Edel's first critical poetics of biography, *Literary Biography* (Bloomington: Indiana University Press, 1957; rev. ed, 1973), was followed by the volume, *Writing Lives: Principia Biographica* (New York: Norton, 1984, 1989). Phyllis Rose, in the introduction to her biographicalcritical essays on Willa Cather, Frida Kahlo, and Djuna Barnes, among others, *Writing of Women: Essays in a Renaissance* (Middletown, Conn.: Wesleyan University Press, 1985), discusses how biographies "play a special part in the making and sustaining of literary reputations" and reflects on her own "search for a feminine style and for an explanation of it." On critics' skepticism about biography and the uses of a "mingling of biography and criticism," see David Bromwich's "The Uses of Biography" (*The Yale Review*, 73, no. 2, Winter 1984, 161–76).

Steve Weinberg's *Telling the Untold Story: How Investigative Reporters are Changing the Craft of Biography* (Columbia: University of Missouri Press, 1992), written from the point of view of a practicing journalist and biographer, has an informatively economical introductory chapter on Western biography since Plutarch, a fascinating account of Weinberg's eventually successful struggles to write a life of Armand Hammer, and an interesting chapter on "short-form biography," also known as the perodical profile. Janet Malcolm, in *The Silent Woman: Sylvia Plath and Ted Hughes* (New York: Knopf, 1994), examines the intricate melodramas surrounding several biographies of Sylvia Plath and their authors' relations with Plath's husband and sister-in-law. Malcolm returns to some of the metabiographical issues examined in *The Silent Woman* and introduces some others—"biography's lowering imperatives," its "congenital handicaps," and the way "biographical research leads to a kind of insufferable familiarity"—in "A House of One's Own" (*The New Yorker*, June 5, 1995, 58–78). This essay frames its portrait of Vanessa Bell and Virginia Woolf in a discussion of "the legend of Bloomsbury" with reflections on why it has become such a riveting story for our times. For good summary of and response to recent debate over the seedy, gossipy, sordidness of many contemporary biographies, a debate often dated from Joyce Carol Oates's coining of the term "pathography," see James Atlas, "The Biographer and the Murderer" (*New York Times Magazine*, December 12, 1993, 74–75).

Two books which gather a stimulating variety of essays and lectures, many of them by practicing critic-biographers, are

Telling Lives: The Biographer's Art (Washington, D. C.: New Republic/National Gallery of Art, 1979; Philadelphia: University of Pennsylvania Press, 1981), edited by Marc Pachter; and *Studies in Biography* (Cambridge, Mass.: Harvard English Studies 8, 1978), edited by Daniel Aaron. Other worthwhile collections are *The Craft of Literary Biography* (New York: Schocken Books, 1985) and *The Biographer's Art: New Essays* (New York: New Amsterdam Books, 1989), both edited by Jeffrey Meyers; *Biography as High Adventure: Life-Writers Speak on Their Art* (Amherst: University of Massachusetts Press, 1986), edited by Stephen B. Oates, with contributors including Maurois, Edel, Bowen, Justin Kaplan, and Barbara Tuchman; *Extraordinary Lives: The Art and Craft of American Biography* (New York: Houghton Mifflin, 1986), edited by William Zinsser, who assembles essays by presidential biographers Robert A. Caro (Lyndon Johnson) and David G. McCullough (Harry Truman) and by historian Paul C. Nagel (Abigail and Louisa Adams), among others; and *The Troubled Face of Biography* (New York: St. Martin's Press, 1988), a collection with contributions by British critics, historians, biographers, and biographer-novelists, including Victoria Glendinning and Michael Holroyd, edited by Eric Homberger and John Charmley. I single out for particular note John Batchelor's edited collection of essays, *The Art of Literary Biography* (Oxford: Clarendon Press, 1995), a volume of exceptional intelligence, both theoretical and practical, throughout, with contributions by contemporary scholar-critics of biography and practicing biographers including Lyndall Gordon, Hermione Lee, Richard Holmes, Park Honan, and Anthony Storr.

Among the noteworthy collections of essays on biography from feminist perspectives are *The Challenge of Feminist Biography: Writing the Lives of Modern American Women* (Urbana: University of Illinois Press, 1992), edited by Sara Alpern, Joyce Antler, Elisabeth Perry, and Ingrid Winther Scobie; an interdisciplinary and international collection, *All Sides of the Subject: Women and Biography*, The Athene Series (New York: Teachers College, Columbia University, 1992), edited by Teresa Isles; and the thought-provoking *Between Women: Biographers, Novelists, Critics, Teachers and Artists Write About their Work on Women* (Boston: Beacon, 1994), edited by Carol Ascher, Louise DeSalvo, and Sara Ruddick. Linda Wagner-Martin's ranging and instructive *Telling Women's Lives: The New Biography* (New Brunswick: Rutgers University Press, 1994) is substantially informed by the challenges and complications of her own experience of writing a life of Sylvia Plath. See also, Phyllis Rose's introduction to the collection of her own essays *Writing of Women* (mentioned above) and particularly the essay "Fact and Fiction in Biography."

For a specific focus on psychoanalytic method in biography, see *Psychoanalytic Studies of Biography* (Madison, Conn.: International Universities Press, 1987), edited by George Moraitis and George H. Pollock, a large collection based on proceedings of an interdisciplinary conference on this subject. Three studies of biographers and their subjects based on psychoanalytic presuppositions are Elisabeth Young-Bruehl *Creative Characters* (New York: Routledge, 1991); the collection of conference papers collected in *Introspection in Biography: The Biographer's Quest for Self-Awareness* (Hillsdale, N.J.: Analytic Press, 1985), coedited by Samuel H. Baron and Carl Pletsch; and several of the essays in *The Challenge of Feminist Biography*, mentioned above. Alan C. Elms's *Uncovering Lives: The Uneasy Alliance of Biography and Psychology* (New York: Oxford University Press, 1994) asserts that the most dramatic changes in biography took place when biographers began to apply twentieth-century psychological and psychoanalytic theories of personality to their work. Elms applies psychobiographical methods to interpreting the lives of several analysts (Gordon Allport, Freud, Jung, and Abraham Maslow, for instance), selected writers (including Isaac Asimov, Frank Baum, and Vladimir Nabokov), and political figures (George Bush, James Carter, and Saddam Hussein, among them).

Application of contemporary theory to biography is well represented in the collection of essays by several hands, *Contesting the Subject: Essays in the Postmodern Theory and Practice of Biography and Biographical Criticism* (West Lafayette, Ind.: Purdue University Press, 1991), edited by William Epstein. An issue of *Granta* devoted to biography (No. 41, 1992) includes particularly notable essays by Louise Erdrich, "The Names of Women," on three Anishinabe women; and Lorna Sage, who in "Death of the Author," examines the postmodern verity that "writers' lives merely distract us from the true slipperiness and anonymity of any text worth its salt" (235). Douglas Collins's *Sartre as Biographer* (Cambridge, Mass.: Harvard University Press, 1980), though focused on a single writer, opens out onto larger areas of modern biographical theory and practice. Collins examines Jean-Paul Sartre's existentialist biographies of Charles Baudelaire, Gustave

Flaubert, and Jean Genet in the context of his development as a writer and the sources and models that most influenced Sartre's innovative life writing: Theodore Adorno, Roland Barthes, Michel Foucault, R. D. Laing, Claude Levi-Strauss, and Karl Marx. Collins presents Sartre as the only writer since the great age of biography in the eighteenth century to conceive of this genre as not yet "fallen" and still "possible" by virtue of the conscious confrontation it dramatizes between writer and subject in the "dialectic of narcissim."

Anthony M. Friedson's edited collection *New Directions in Biography: Essays by Phyllis Auty, Leon Edel, Michael Holroyd, Noel C. Manganyi, Gabriel Merle, Margot Peters and Shoichi Saeki* (Biographical Research Center: University of Hawaii Press, 1981), which brings an international, multicultural perspective to the theory and practice of the genre, is essential reading. So, too, are the preface and chapter 1, "An Approach to Native American Texts," of Arnold Krupat's *For Those Who Come After: A Study of Native American Autobiography* (Berkeley: University of California Press, 1985). Krupat discusses the bicultural production of Indian autobiographies by a "complex but historically specifiable division of labor" between Indians and whites, which he calls "composite composition." (No Indian autobiographies existed until white settlers decided to make them in the late nineteenth century). In so doing, Krupat also makes extremely valuable comments on the cultural-historical factors producing Euramerican life writing. James A. Clifton's collection of bio-ethno-historiographical essays by several anthropologists, *Being and Becoming Indian: Biographical Studies of North American Frontiers* (Chicago: Dorsey Press, 1989), with its informative preface and first chapter, "Alternate Identities and Cultural Frontiers," epitomizes the way biographical inquiry and form must attempt accurately and responsibly to accommodate the subject.

Ahead of their own time and arguably still ahead of ours in their revisionist thinking about biography are works by Paul Valéry and Jorge Luis Borges. Valéry's "Introducton to the Method of Leonardo da Vinci" (1929; rpt. in *Paul Valéry: An Anthology* [Princeton, N.J.: Princeton University Press, 1977]) examines, in a manner reminiscent of Stein, the compositionally challenging intersection of history, writing, and the representation of identity. Borges, particularly in the essays collected in *Other Inquisitions 1937–1952* (Austin: University of Texas Press,

1964, 1988), applies his characteristically witty and stimulating intelligence to metacritical-biographical speculations on writers including Hawthorne, Poe, Coleridge, Whitman, Wilde, and Kafka. Finally, there are three essential perodicals in the field. *Biography: An Interdisciplinary Quarterly*, edited by George Simson (Biographical Research Center: University Press of Hawaii, 1978–), is a forum for stimulating inquiry into biography and autobiography. The annual fall number of *Biography* surveys the year's books and articles on life writing. *A/B: Auto/Biography Studies*, sponsored by the Autobiography Society (Joyce and Elizabeth Hall Center for the Humanities, Lawrence: University of Kansas, 1985–), publishes scholarship on the theory and practice of autobiography, biography, diaries, letters, and the relations between life writing and other discourse. The annual *Biography and Source Studies*, edited by Frederick R. Karl (New York: AMS Press, 1994–), describes as its aim to gather a variety of biographers' reflections on their craft and to assess the impact of current ideas from related fields on this genre.

Notes and References

Preface

1. For a succinct contemporary statement of this familiar modern definition, see Hilton Kramer, "The Passion of Mark Rothko," review of James E. B. Breslin, *Mark Rothko: A Biography* (Chicago: University of Chicago Press, 1993), *New York Times Book Review*, December 26, 1993, 1, 21. Rachel Gutiérrez usefully observes that biography began in Western culture "to satisfy the curiosity about an individual who stood out among his contemporaries . . . . [Biography]," she continues, "usually offers relevant clues to measure the creative genius of a poet, the original thoughts of a philosopher, the power of a political leader, the gift of an artist, or the achievements of a scientist" (Rachel Gutiérrez, "What Is a Feminist Biography?," 48–55, *All Sides of the Subject: Women and Biography*, ed. Teresa Iles [New York: Teachers College, Columbia University, 1992], 48).

2. Margot Peters, "Group Biography: Challenges and Methods," 41–51, *New Directions in Biography: Essays by Phyllis Auty, Leon Edel, Michael Holroyd, Noel C. Manganyi, Gabriel Merle, Margot Peters and Shoichi Saeki*, ed. Anthony M. Friedson (Biographical Research Center: University Press of Hawaii, 1981), 50.

3. This observation by Noel C. Manganyi, "Biography: The Black South African Connection," 52–61, in Friedson, ed., *New Directions in Biography*, is consistent with remarks by Carolyn Heilbrun, Arnold Rampersad, and Virginia Woolf, to name only a few cited and discussed elsewhere in this study. James R. Kincaid, in an essay on Native American autobiography, expresses a more emphatic version of this observation about the relation of life writing to the structure and institutions of the culture in which it is written: "Even our scientists, our anthropologists [and biographers], invent the idea of a culture they need and then, lo and behold, 'find' it. . . . About Indians, 'they've never been right once," Kincaid quotes Gerald Vizenor, a writer of Chippewa descent, in "Who Gets to Tell Their Stories?," *New York Times Book Review*, May 3, 1992, 1, 24–29. See also, Arnold Rampersad's important essay, "Biography, Autobiography, and Afro-American Culture," *The Yale Review* 73:1 (Autumn 1983), 1–16, to which I am indebted for the discussion of majority and minority biography.

4. Donald J. Winslow, in *Life-Writing: A Glossary of Terms in Biography, Autobiography, and Related Forms*, a Biography Monograph (Biographical Research Center: University Press of Hawaii, 1980), defines literary biography as "a descriptive term for the lives of literary men and women," noting that there is "sometimes confusion in this phrase when it is used to describe the style of a biographical work rather than the subject matter" (25).

5. Andrew Delbanco, "The Man Who Created Hester Prynne," review of Edwin Haviland Miller's *Salem is My Dwelling Place: A Life of Nathaniel Hawthorne* (Iowa City: University of Iowa Press, 1992), *New York Times Book Review*, February 16, 1992, 14, 16.

6. Richard D. Altick, *Lives and Letters: A History of Literary Biography in England and America* (New York: Knopf, 1965), ix, xi.

7. Focusing on possible reasons for the culturally central all-importance of biography in England, by contrast with its marginal importance in Germany, Jürgen Schlaeger cites the anecdote of a colleague's discussion of "the reverential attitude of the English to their national heroes and the complete absence of a desire for ancestor worship in Germans." The

historical reasons for the "obvious neglect of biography in Germany," he continues to cite his colleague's discussion, include: "the 'belated nation'-syndrome, the rigour of historical scholarship, the philosophical tradition, and the misappropriation of hero-worship by the Nazis" (Jürgen Schlaeger, "Biography: Cult as Culture," 57–71, *The Art of Literary Biography*, ed. John Batchelor [Oxford: Clarendon Press, 1995], 57).

Chapter 1

1. Edmund Gosse attributes the first use of *biographia* (in its Greek form) to the early sixth-century writer Damascius, "Biography," 3:952–54, *The Encyclopaedia Britannica*, 11th ed., 29 vols. (New York: Encyclopaedia Britannica, 1910–1911), 3:952.

2. John A. Garraty, *The Nature of Biography* (New York: Knopf, 1957), 33.

3. See Wang Po-hsiang's preface to Szuma Chien, *Selections from Records of the Historian*, trans. Yang Hsien-yi and Gladys Yang (Peking: Foreign Languages Press, 1979), i–vi, from which I paraphrase; hereafter cited in text as Szuma Chien.

4. Xenophon, *Memorabilia and Oeconomicus*, vol. 4 of *Xenophon*, trans. E. C. Marchant, Loeb Classical Library (Cambridge, Mass.: Harvard; London: Heinemann, 1968), 4:81.

5. Clyde Weber Votaw, *The Gospels and Contemporary Biographies in the Greco-Roman World* (Philadelphia: Fortress Press, 1970), 43.

6. Warren Anderson, Introduction, *Theophrastus: The Character Sketches*, xv. Trans. with notes and introductory essays by Warren Anderson (Kent, Ohio: Kent State University Press, 1970).

7. Tacitus, *Dialogus, Agricola, Germania*, trans. Maurice Hutton, Loeb Classical Library (London: Heinemann; New York: Macmillan, 1914), 169, 171; hereafter cited in text as Tacitus.

8. Cornelius Nepos's surviving work includes lives of Cato the Elder, Hannibal, and Atticus, the life of Atticus being based on personal knowledge and generally considered his best.

9. Plutarch, "Alcibiades and Coriolanus," *Lives*, 10 vols., trans. Bernadotte Perrin, Loeb Classical Library (London: Heinemann; New York: Putnam, 1916), 4:5–6.

10. A. J. Gossage, "Plutarch," chapter 3, *Latin Biography*, ed. T. A. Dorey (London: Routledge and Kegan Paul, 1967), 70.

11. For a discussion of the ethics and epistemology of saints' lives, see Thomas J. Heffernan, *Sacred Biography: Saints and Their Biographers in the Middle Ages* (New York: Oxford University Press, 1988), to which my discussion of lives of St. Christina is indebted (284–85).

12. Michael Seidel, *Ted Williams: A Baseball Life* (Chicago: Contemporary Books, 1991), x; hereafter cited in text as Seidel.

13. James A. Clifford, introduction, *Biography As An Art: Selected Criticism 1560–1960* (New York: Oxford University Press, 1962), x.

14. Lee Allen, *Dizzy Dean: His Story in Baseball* (New York: Putnam, 1967), 25.

15. Gosse, "Biography," *The Encyclopaedia Britannica*, 3:954.

16. Harold Nicolson, *The Development of English Biography*, Hogarth Lectures on Literature Series, No. 4 (London: Hogarth Press, 1927), 22. R. W. Southern, in his introduction to Eadmer's *Life of St. Anselm* (Oxford: Clarendon Press, 1979), notes that from the time Anselm became archbishop of Canterbury in 1093, until his death in 1109, he and his biographer Eadmer "were constantly together," that "Eadmer must have begun early to write down what he saw and heard in the archbishop's company," and that "before long he profited by Anselm's habit of talking about his past to form the plan of writing a full biography" (Introduction, ix).

17. Gossage, "Plutarch," *Latin Biography*, 47.

18. Lydia Maria Child, Forematter, *The Freedmen's Book*, rpt. of 1865 ed. (New York: AMS Press, 1980), n.p.

19. Samuel Johnson, *Rambler* No. 60, 3:318–23, *The Rambler*, 3 vols., ed. W. J. Bate and Albrecht Strauss, The Yale Edition of the Works of Samuel Johnson (New Haven: Yale University Press, 1958–).

20. There are many such depictions of the revolutionary changes ushering in the modern age. This particular one is summa-

rized from the informative essay, "Life Studies," by Patrick Coleman, Jill Kowalik, Jayne Lewis, *The Center & Clark Newsletter*, Fall 1994, No. 24:2–3, William Andrews Clark Memorial Library.

21. Gosse, "Biography," *The Encyclopaedia Britannica*.

22. Francis Bacon, *The Advancement of Learning*, ed. G. W. Kitchin (London: Dent, 1973), 74.

23. Thomas Fuller, *The History of the Worthies of England*, 2 vols., ed. John Nichols (London, 1811), 1:8, my emphasis.

24. John Dryden, "The Life of Plutarch," 17:239–88, *Prose 1668–1691*, The Works of John Dryden, 20 vols. (Berkeley: University of California Press, 1971), 17:273.

25. Izaak Walton, *The Life of Mr. George Herbert*, 47–97, in *English Biography in the Seventeenth Century: Selected Short Lives*, ed. Vivian de Sola Pinto (London: George G. Harrap, 1951), 50, 51.

26. Gossage, "Plutarch," *Latin Biography*, 66.

27. Plutarch, *Life of Alexander*, vol. 7, *Lives*, 11 vols., trans. Bernadotte Perrin (London: Heinemann; New York: Putnam, 1914), 7:225.

28. Rampersad, "Biography, Autobiography, and Afro-American Culture," 4–5.

29. Samuel Johnson, *Rambler* No. 60, *The Rambler*, 3:319.

30. This issue of appropriate criteria for choosing biographical subjects remains a subject of debate and practical adjudication as demonstrated by the following passage from the *Dictionary of American Biography* (1928–   ):

Positive qualifications [for selection] were less easily defined. In general, only those are included in the following pages who have made some significant contribution to American life in its manifold aspects. The Dictionary cannot find space for average or merely typical figures, however estimable they may be. The observation of Sir Sidney Lee is quite to the point: "Actions, however beneficent or honourable, which are accomplished or are capable of accomplishment by many thousands of persons are actions of mediocrity, and lack the dimension which justifies the biographer's notice. The fact that a man is a devoted husband and father, an efficient schoolmaster, an exemplary parish priest, gives him in itself no claim to biographic commemoration." (DAB, 1:vii)

31. On Johnson's astute sense of human frailty as the key to his excellence as biographer, see Richard Ellmann, *Literary Biography* (Oxford: Clarendon Press, 1971).

32. Robert W. Creamer, *Babe: The Legend Comes to Life* (New York: Simon and Schuster, 1974), 14.

33. Roger North, *General Preface and Life of Dr. John North*, ed. Peter Millard (Toronto: University of Toronto Press, 1984), 51; hereafter cited in text as North.

34. Donald Stauffer's "Biography and the Novel," chapter 2 of *The Art of Biography in Eighteenth Century England*, 65–131, (Princeton: Princeton University Press, 1941) remains a superb introduction to this subject.

35. Letter from Henry James to Henry Adams, 19 November 1903, 62–63, *The Correspondence of Henry James and Henry Adams, 1877–1914*, 62, ed. George Monteiro (Baton Rouge: Louisiana State University Press, 1992).

36. Elizabeth Gaskell, *The Life of Charlotte Brontë*, ed. Alan Shelston (London: Penguin, 1985), 166.

37. Daniel B. Shea Jr., "The Mathers," chapter 5, 152–81, *Spiritual Autobiography in Early America* (Princeton, N.J.: Princeton University Press, 1968), 152–53 and passim.

38. On several of the Mathers, see *The American Puritans: Their Prose and Poetry*, ed. Perry Miller (Garden City, N.Y.: Doubleday & Company, 1956), Cotton Mather, "A General Introduction to the *Magnalia*," 59–77; Increase Mather, from *Richard Mather*, 230–39.

39. Cotton Mather, "Life of Edward Hopkins," 1:131–35, *Magnalia Christi Americana*, first American ed. from the 1702 London ed., 2 vols. (Hartford, Conn: S. Andrus, 1820) 1:131.

40. Evidence of how pervasive biographical skepticism is in the late twentieth century appears in an article on George Washington in *Highlights for Children*, a magazine for elementary–school-age readers. Cecily Johnson demythologizes the "old familiar story you may have heard about George Washington and the cherry tree," giving historical information about its author, Mason Locke Weems, the publication date and full title of the first enlarged edition of Weems's *Life of Washington* Johnson notes that, though the

story is apocryphal, it serves the purpose of fable, satisfying our love of certain kinds of "stories about our heroes" ("George Washington and the Cherry Tree: An American Fable," *Highlights for Children*, February 1992, 25). The scholarly details in my discussion of Weems's *Washington* are taken from Marcus Cunliffe's Introduction to *The Life of Washington* (Cambridge, Mass.: The Belknap Press of Harvard University Press, 1962).

41. "Biography," 23:282–88, *The Southern Literary Messenger* 23 (October 1856), 23:287.

42. Jorge Luis Borges, "About William Beckford's *Vathek*," *Other Inquisitions 1937–1952*, trans. Ruth L. C. Simms (Austin: University of Texas Press, 1964), 137–40.

43. Ralph Waldo Emerson, "Experience," 3:43–86, *The Complete Works of Ralph Waldo Emerson*, with biographical introduction and notes by Edward Waldo Emerson, Centenary Edition, 12 vols. (Boston: Houghton Mifflin, 1903–1904), 3:60.

44. Gamaliel Bradford, preface to *Union Portraits* (Boston: Houghton Mifflin, 1919), ix.

45. Gamaliel Bradford, *Biography and the Human Heart* (Boston: Houghton Mifflin, 1932), 3, 32.

46. Richard Ellmann, "Freud and Literary Biography," *The American Scholar*, 53 (Autumn 1983/84), 465–78.

47. John Wain, "To Criticize the Critic," *The American Scholar*, 62:4 (Autumn 1993), 606–11.

48. Ellmann, "Freud and Literary Biography," 466–67.

49. Peter Gay, *Freud: A Life for Our Time* (New York: Norton, 1988), 269.

50. Anthony Storr, "Psychiatry and Literary Biography," 73–86, *The Art of Literary Biography*, 73, 78.

51. Walter Kendrick discusses these matters in "Parallel Lives: The State of the Art of Literary Biography," 10–13, *The Village Voice Literary Supplement* (March 1992).

52. Frances Partridge, foreword to Lytton Strachey's *Eminent Victorians*, 6.

53. David Bailey, "Charms and the Man (Michael Holroyd)," 215–42, *Vanity Fair*, September 1991, 236.

54. Lytton Strachey, preface to *Eminent Victorians* (New York: Penguin, 1986), 9; hereafter cited in text as Strachey.

55. Virginia Woolf, "The New Biography," 4:229–35, *Collected Essays*, 4 vols.(New York: Harcourt, Brace, 1967), 4:234.

56. The phrase "artist on oath," attributed to Desmond Mac-Carthy by John Garraty and Michael Holroyd, in addition to Park Honan and others, though none gives the source, is not readily recoverable in any of MacCarthy's published essays. For a thoughtful, incisive statement of this debate regarding which form of writing can tell more of "truth"—biography and autobiography or fiction, see Nicholas Mosley's Foreword to his *Efforts at Truth* (Normal, Ill.: Dalkey Archive Press, 1995). Mosley comments that the situation has "arisen in which there is an almost complete split" between the attitudes regarding life writing and fiction. He attributes this split significantly to the loss of "a framework [religious attitudes] within which human dramas are played out . . . human affairs formed patterns," and concepts of truth beyond the self "worked out in the form of stories" (1–2).

57. Erling A. Erickson, "Biography," Vol. 2, *The World Book Encyclopedia*, 22 vols. (Chicago: World Book, 1993).

58. James L. Clifford, *From Puzzles to Portraits: Problems of a Literary Biographer* (Chapel Hill: University of North Carolina Press, 1970), 84–87.

59. Ellmann, *Literary Biography*, 19.

60. Gutiérrez, "What Is a Feminist Biography?"

61. Michel Foucault, "What is an Author?," *Language, Counter-Memory, Practice: Selected Essays and Inteviews by Michel Foucault*, 113–38, ed. Donald F. Bouchard, trans. Donald F. Bouchard and Sherry Simon (Ithaca, N.Y.: Cornell University Press, 1977); Roland Barthes, "Death of the Author," 142–48, *Image , Music, Text*, selected and trans. Stephen Heath (New York: Hill and Wang, 1977).

62. Kendrick, "Parallel Lives," 10.

63. John Batchelor, Introduction, 1–11, *The Art of Literary Biography*, ed. John Batchelor (Oxford: Clarendon Press, 1995), 2. Park Honan, in his essay "Jane Austen, Matthew Arnold, Shakespeare: The Problem of the *Opus*," in Batchelor's collec-

tion, discusses how biography, in the way it "thrives on variety," is not at odds with, but in fact embraces one of the central tenets of postmodernism, namely the indeterminacy or overdeterminacy of meaning and approaches to the making of meaning (Batchelor, 188). In a related vein that focuses on the knower, the known, and the formulation of knowledge in life writing, John Worthen proposes that all biographers "remain profoundly [and unavoidably] ignorant of many things in the lives of their subjects, but the narrative . . . is in almost every case designed to conceal the different kinds of ignorance from which we suffer," and that these two issues should be brought into discussions of the genre ("The Necessary Ignorance of a Biographer," Batchelor, 227).

64. Schlaeger, "Biography: Cult as Culture."

65. For a soundly informative introduction to autobiography, see James Goodwin, *Autobiography: The Self Made Text*. Studies in Literary Themes and Genres (New York: Twayne; Toronto: Maxwell Macmillan Canada, 1993).

66. My remarks summarize the main points of Shoichi Saeki's essay, "The Curious Relationship Between Biography and Autobiography in Japan," 73–82, in Friedson, ed., *New Directions in Biography*.

67. This description of South African biography and autobiography is summarized from Manganyi's "Biography: The Black South African Connection," in Friedson, ed., *New Directions in Biography*, 52–61.

68. Cited in Kincaid, "Who Gets to Tell Their Stories?"

69. Patricia Nelson Limerick, "Sitting Bull's Last Stand," review of Robert M. Utley's *The Life and Times of Sitting Bull* (New York: Holt, 1993), *The New York Times Book Review*, July 11, 1993, 29.

70. Ward Churchill, "Literature as a Weapon in the Colonization of the American Indian," 17–42, *Fantasies of the Master Race: Literature, Cinema and the Colonization of American Indians*, ed. M. Annette Jaimes (Monroe, Maine: Common Courage Press), 38.

71. Vine Deloria Jr., "Foreword: American Fantasy," *The Pretend Indians: Images of Native Americans in the Movies*, ed. Gretchen

M. Bataille and Charles L. P. Silet (Ames: Iowa State University Press, 1980), xvi.

72. R. David Edmunds, in the introduction to his noteworthy edited collection of biographical essays, *American Indian Leaders: Studies in Diversity* (Lincoln: University of Nebraska Press, 1980), points out that among these distortions was the way colonists, as "citizens of newly emerging nation-states," assumed that Native American political institutions reflected a pattern of "centralized power, kings or princes, and royal lineages" similar to their own. This led them to refer to "'Indian nations,' Indian potentates (*King* Phillip is a good example), and Indian 'princesses' such as Pocahontas" (vii).

Chapter 2

1. Ellmann uses this phrase in *Literary Biography*.

2. Richard Holmes, in *Dr. Johnson and Mr. Savage* (1994), examines Savage as a person, poet, and self-mythologizer, Johnson as Savage's friend and biographer, and the two men's curious, if not inexplicable, friendship. Holmes has also written lives of Percy Bysshe Shelley, Samuel Taylor Coleridge, and Robert Louis Stevenson, among others (see Recommended Biographies: A Selected List).

3. Charles H. Hinnant argues that Johnson is not credulous about Savage's claim and that the ambiguities of his narrative are a purposeful part of its structure, in "Johnson and the Limits of Biography: Teaching the *Life of Savage*," 107–13, *Approaches to Teaching the Works of Samuel Johnson*, ed. David R. Anderson and Gwin J. Kolb (New York: Modern Language Association of America, 1993). See also, Felicity A. Nussbaum, *Torrid Zones: Maternity, Sexuality, and Empire in Eighteenth-Century English Narratives* (Baltimore, Md.: Johns Hopkins University Press, 1995), chapter 2, "'Savage Mothers': Samuel Johnson's *Life of Savage*," 47–66, who argues that this biography exemplifies the period's masculinization of maternity.

4. Samuel Johnson, *Life of Savage*, 2:321–434, *Lives of the English Poets*, 3 vols. (Oxford: Clarendon Press, 1905), 2:433–34; hereafter cited in text as Johnson, *Savage*.

5. Johnson, *Rambler* No. 60, 3:321.

6. John Wain gives this reading of the *Lives* in *Samuel Johnson* (New York: Viking, 1975), 349; hereafter cited in text as Wain.

7. Observed by Joseph Wood Krutch in *Samuel Johnson* (New York: Holt, 1944), 466; hereafter cited in text as Krutch.

8. Allan Cunningham, "Biographical and Critical History of the Literature of the Last Fifty Years," *The Athenaeum*, 14 December 1833, 851–52.

9. Reed Whittemore, *Whole Lives: Shapers of Modern Biography* (Baltimore, Md.: Johns Hopkins University Press, 1989), 101–22, esp. 121.

10. See Robert E. Kelley and O M Brack Jr., *Samuel Johnson's Early Biographers* (Iowa City: University of Iowa Press, 1971) for discussion of this division and for informative comparisons of lives of Johnson before Boswell. For a series of brief, instructive comparisons of accounts other than Boswell's, including Hester Lynch Thrale Piozzi, Sir Joshua Reynolds, Hill Boothby, and others, see Robina Napier's Prefatory Notice to *Johnsoniana: Anecdotes of the Late Samuel Johnson, LL.D.* (London: George Bell, 1884).

11. Kelley and Brack, *Samuel Johnson's Early Biographers*, 120.

12. Anonymous, *The Life of Samuel Johnson, LL.D.*, 223–46, in Kelley and Brack, *The Early Biographies of Samuel Johnson*, 223, 224.

13. Conyers Middleton, preface, 1:xi–xl, *The History of the Life of M. Tullius Cicero*, 1:xi–xl, 3 vols. (London, 1741), 1:xxi.

14. Reed Whittemore, *Pure Lives: The Early Biographers* (Baltimore, Md.: Johns Hopkins University Press, 1988), 130.

15. In Boswell's depiction of Johnson "force of character" lies the principal aim and chief distinction of this biography from twentieth-century biography, so Ellmann remarks in *Literary Biography*, 5.

16. James Boswell, *The Journal of a Tour to the Hebrides with Samuel Johnson, LL.D.*, with Samuel Johnson, *A Journey to the Western Islands of Scotland*, ed. R. W. Chapman (New York: Oxford University Press, 1979).

17. Philip Toynbee, "Novel and Memoir," 21–22, *Nimbus: A Magazine of Literature, the Arts, and New Ideas*, 2:3 (Autumn 1954), 22, my emphasis.

18. James Boswell, *The Correspondence and Other Papers of James Boswell Relating to the Making of the Life of Johnson*, ed. Marshall Waingrow, vol. 2, The Yale Edition of the Private Papers of James Boswell, 5 vols. (New York: McGraw-Hill, 1950–   ), 2:267.

19. James Boswell, *Boswell's Life of Johnson*, 6 vols., ed. G. B. Hill; rev. L. F. Powell (Oxford: Clarendon Press, 1934–1964), 3:64–65; hereafter cited in text as Boswell, *Life*.

20. Prefatory Notice, v–vii, *Johnsoniana: Anecdotes of the Late Samuel Johnson, LL.D. by Mrs. Piozzi, Richard Cumberland, Bishop Percy and Others*, ed. Robina Napier (London: George Bell, 1884), vii.

21. The details of this account appear in Bertram H. Davis's Introduction to his edited and abridged text of Sir John Hawkins's *Life of Samuel Johnson LL.D.* (London: Jonathan Cape, 1962); hereafter cited in text as Hawkins.

22. Whittemore, *Pure Lives*, 10.

23. Boswell, entry dated 22 June 1786, *Correspondence*, 2:lvi.

24. N. John Hall, "A Very Victorian Feminist," review of Jenny Uglow's *Elizabeth Gaskell: A Habit of Stories* (London: Faber and Faber, 1993), *The New York Times Book Review*, November 11, 1993, 27.

25. Parts of this discussion appear in my essay, "Samuel Johnson and Gender," 19–27, *Approaches to Teaching the Works of Samuel Johnson*, ed. Anderson and Kolb (New York: The Modern Language Association of America, 1993); and in an earlier version of this essay, "Negotiating the Past, Examining Ourselves: Johnson, Women, and Gender in the Classroom," *South Central Review* 9:4 (Winter 1992), 71–80.

26. Ellmann, *Literary Biography*, 4.

27. Hesther [*sic*] Lynch Piozzi, *Anecdotes of the Late Samuel Johnson, LL.D.* in *Shaw and Piozzi Memoirs of Dr. Johnson*, ed. Arthur Sherbo (London: Oxford University Press, 1974), 59; hereafter cited in text as Piozzi.

28. Arthur Murphy, Advertisement and "Essay on the Life and Genius of Samuel Johnson," vol. 1, *Dr. Johnson's Works*, 11 vols, rpt. of 1810 ed. (New York: AMS Press, 1970), 1:iii; hereafter cited in text as Murphy.

29. Leon Howard, *Herman Melville: A Biography* (Berkeley: University of California Press, 1951), viii; hereafter cited in text as Howard.

30. A. L. Reade, part 2, preface, *Johnsonian Gleanings*, 10 vols. (New York: Octagon Books, 1968), n.p.; hereafter cited in text as Reade.

31. Paraphrased from L. B. Namier, "History: Its Subject-Matter and Tasks," *History Today* 2:3 (March 1952), 157–62, passim, 161–62.

32. Jay Martin, *Always Merry and Bright: The Life of Henry Miller, An Unauthorized Biography* (Santa Barbara, Calif.: Capra Press, 1978), ix.

33. Thomas Babington Macaulay, "Samuel Johnson," 548–78, *Macaulay Prose and Poetry*, selected by G. M. Young (Cambridge, Mass.: Harvard University Press, 1952), 569; hereafter cited in text as Macaulay.

34. Thomas Babington Macaulay, review of Croker's edition of Boswell's *Life of Johnson* (1831), 70–115, *Critical and Historical Essays*, selected and introduced by Hugh Trevor-Roper (New York: McGraw-Hill, 1965).

35. Walter Raleigh, *Six Essays on Johnson* (Oxford: Clarendon Press, 1910; Folcroft, Pa.: Folcroft Library Editions, 1974).

36. Clifford, in *From Puzzles to Portraits*, discusses how the opening scene of *Young Sam Johnson* (which depicts Johnson in January, 1765, beginning to write a memoir) depends on probable but uncertified dating of this composition. If compelling evidence for a different composition date were to be discovered, Clifford continues, this scene would have to be revised (85).

37. Imagining childhood is Freud's great contribution to the study of human motivation, though the childhood imagined by psychoanalysis is almost entirely an interior drama accessible only through intervention of a trained specialist or imaginative writer.

38. Ellmann, *Literary Biography*, 5.

39. Sir Joshua Reynolds, "Sir Joshua Reynolds on Johnson's Character," 2:219–28, *Johnsonian Miscellanies*, 2 vols., ed. G. B. Hill (Oxford: Clarendon Press, 1897), 2:70.

40. Katherine C. Balderston, "Johnson's Vile Melancholy," 3–14, *The Age of Johnson: Essays Presented to Chauncey Brewster Tinker*, ed. Frederick W. Hilles (New Haven, Conn.: Yale University Press, 1949), 13.

41. James L. Clifford, *Young Sam Johnson* (New York: McGraw Hill, 1955), 290; hereafter cited in text as Clifford, *Young Sam.*

42. Donald Greene, *Samuel Johnson* (New York: Twayne, 1970), 9, 10; hereafter cited in text as Greene.

43. Greene's criticism of Boswell has escalated over the years, beginning with his review of John Wain's *Samuel Johnson*, where he first makes his charge that Boswell's "much-touted 'hero-worship' of Johnson is a mask, disguising from himself and others an unconscious wish to cut Johnson down to size and establish, in the end, the superiority of Boswell, the aristocratic, polished man-of-the world, to the rugged provincial with his uncouth manners and quaint, old-fashioned prejudices—against Negro slavery, for instance," (*The Times Literary Supplement*, November 22, 1974, 1315–16). Greene's essay "The World's Worst Biography" (*The American Scholar* 62:3, [Summer 1993], 365–82) compares the way Boswell handles conversation in the *Life* to Janet Malcolm in her now infamous interview with analyst Jeffrey Masson. Greene proposes that if Boswell were writing today, he would be sued, as was Malcolm in *Masson v. Malcolm*, heard before the Supreme Court, and similarly ruled against on the basis of the decision that a reporter "may make no substantive changes or additions to the person's words" (378).

44. Paul Fussell, *Samuel Johnson and the Life of Writing* (New York: Norton, 1971), xii–xiii.

45. Walter Jackson Bate, *Samuel Johnson* (New York: Harcourt, Brace, 1977), 385; hereafter cited in text as Bate.

46. James L. Clifford, *Dictionary Johnson: Samuel Johnson's Middle Years* (New York: McGraw-Hill, 1979), viii; hereafter cited in text as Clifford, *Dictionary Johnson.*

Chapter 3

1. Quentin Bell, *Virginia Woolf: A Biography*, two vols. in one, (New York: Harcourt, Brace, 1972), 239; hereafter cited in text as Bell by volume and page.

2. Whittemore, *Whole Lives*, 71.
3. Virginia Woolf, "The New Biography," 4:229–35, *Collected Essays* (New York: Harcourt, Brace, 1967), 4:230.
4. Woolf, "The New Biography," 4:234.
5. Virginia Woolf, "The Art of Biography," 4:221–28, *Collected Essays*, 4:221.
6. Woolf, "The Art of Biography," 4:226.
7. Woolf, "The Art of Biography," 4:223.
8. Woolf, "The Art of Biography," 4:227.
9. Woolf, "The Art of Biography," 4:224, 228.
10. Virginia Woolf, *Orlando: A Biography* (New York: Harcourt, Brace, 1992), 305–6; hereafter cited in text as Woolf, *Orlando*.
11. Whittemore, *Whole Lives*, 60–61.
12. Woolf, "The New Biography," 4:234.
13. Whittemore, *Whole Lives*, 72.
14. Virginia Woolf, *Flush: A Biography* (New York: Harcourt, Brace, 1983); 167; hereafter cited in text as Woolf, *Flush*.
15. Virginia Woolf, *The Years* (New York: Random, 1935), 414.
16. Virginia Woolf, *A Writer's Diary*, ed. Leonard Woolf (New York: Random, 1954), 339.
17. Whittemore, *Whole Lives*, 74.
18. Virginia Woolf, *Roger Fry* (New York: Harcourt, Brace, 1976), 103, 146; hereafter cited in text as Woolf, *Fry*.
19. Bernard DeVoto, "The Skeptical Biographer," 181–92, *Harper's Magazine* (January 1933), 185, 186. On the matter of Woolf's familiarity with Freud, the Hogarth Press published James Strachey's translation of Freud beginning in the early 1920s. The *Transactions of the Psychoanalytic Institute* appear in the Hogarth lists.
20. Virginia Woolf, "The Common Reader," *The Common Reader: First Series* (New York: Harcourt, Brace, 1953), 1.
21. Virginia Woolf, "Edmund Gosse," 4:81–87, *Collected Essays*, 4:86.
22. Virginia Woolf, "How Should One Read a Book?," 2:1–11, *Collected Essays*, 2:2.
23. Virginia Woolf, "Lives of the Obscure," 4:120–33, *Collected Essays*, 4:120, my emphasis.

24. Virginia Woolf, "The Strange Elizabethans," 3:32–43, *Collected Essays*, 3:32.

25. Parts of this argument have appeared in Catherine N. Parke, "Virginia Woolf: The Biographer as Medium," *Thought: A Journal of Culture and Idea* 6:251 (December 1988), 358–77.

26. Aileen Pippett, *The Moth and the Star: A Biography of Virginia Woolf* (New York: Kraus Reprint, 1969), viii.

27. Jean Guiget, *Virginia Woolf and Her Works*, trans. Jean Stewart (New York: Harcourt, Brace, 1965), Introduction, 27.

28. Phyllis Rose, *Woman of Letters: A Life of Virginia Woolf* (New York: Harcourt, Brace, 1986), viii.

29. Lyndall Gordon, *Virginia Woolf: A Writer's Life* (New York: Norton, 1993), 8.

30. George Spater and Ian Parsons, *A Marriage of True Minds: An Intimate Portrait of Leonard and Virginia Woolf* (New York: Harcourt, Brace, 1979), xiii.

31. Susan Rubinow Gorsky, *Virginia Woolf*, rev. ed. (Boston: Twayne, 1989), preface, n.p.

32. John Mepham, *Virginia Woolf: A Literary Life* (New York: St. Martin's Press, 1992), xiii.

33. Roger Poole, *The Unknown Virginia Woolf* (Atlantic Highlands, N.J.: Humanities Press, 1990), 1; hereafter cited in text as Poole.

34. Stephen Trombley, *'All that Summer She was Mad': Virginia Woolf and Her Doctors* (New York: Continuum, 1982), 2.

Chapter 4

1. Karen J. Winkler, "Seductions of Biography: Scholars Delve into New Questions about Race, Class, and Sexuality," *The Chronicle of Higher Education*, October 27, 1993, A14. One measure of both a subject's popularity and the degree to which it has become an *issue* to be discussed and theorized (in the academy at least) is its appearance as a conference topic. Other recent notable conferences on biography include "British Biographical Writing: Truth, Subversion, Gender, Ethics" (Schloss Hofen, Lake Constance, 1993) and "The Art of Literary Biography" (University of Newcastle upon Tyne,

1993), proceedings from which are collected in Batchelor, ed., *The Art of Literary Biography*; and "Whose Life Is It Anyway? Biography and the Popular Press Today: A Conference" (University of California at Berkeley, 1995).

2. There have been several notable juvenile biographies of Robeson: Scott Erlich, *Paul Robeson* (New York: Chelsea House, 1988); Eloisa Greenfield, *Paul Robeson* (New York: Crowell, 1975); Virginia Hamilton, *Paul Robeson: The Life and Times of a Free Black Man* (New York: Harper and Row, 1979). Of these, Hamilton's biography is, in many ways, the most interesting, beginning with the fascinating prologue entitled "The Knowledge." Here the author describes how, throughout her childhood, her father passed on to her the knowledge of achievements of African-Americans. Hamilton thus describes the significant interrelationship between autobiography and biography in the African-American community, based on her own experiential information.

3. David H. Richter makes this point usefully in his introduction to the edited collection of essays by several hands on why, what, and how we read in the wake of postmodern theory, *Falling into Theory: Conflicting Views on Reading Literature* (Boston: Bedford Books of St. Martin's Press, 1994), 1–11

4. Gutiérrez. "What Is a Feminist Biography?", 49.

5. Nancy K. Miller, *Subject to Change: Reading Feminist Writing* (New York: Columbia University Press, 1988); citations from Sandra M. Gilbert and Susan Gubar, *The Madwoman in the Attic: The Woman Writer and the Nineteenth-Century Literary Imagination* (New Haven, Conn.: Yale University Press, 1979), 22; and Carolyn Heilbrun, *Writing a Woman's Life* (New York: Norton, 1988), Introduction, 18, 19. An epitomizing feminist rereading of a woman's life is typified by Claire Tomalin's *Mrs. Jordan's Profession: The Actress and the Prince* (Knopf, 1995), about which one reviewer comments: "Ms. Tomalin's life, the first informed by feminism [there had been several earlier biographies; Jordan was thus not precisely obscure and in need of retrieval], reinstates her as a powerful woman as well as an extraordinary talent . . . a remarkable picture of the life of a 'working mother' of 200 years ago" (Stella Tillyard, *The New York Times Book Review*, May 14, 1995, 9).

BIOGRAPHY

6. Lyndall Gordon, "Women's Lives: The Unmapped Country," 87–98, in Batchelor, ed., *The Art of Literary Biography*, 96.

7. Blanche Wiesen Cook, *Eleanor Roosevelt, Volume One 1884–1933* (New York: Viking, 1992), xi; hereafter cited in text as Cook.

8. Sara Alpern, Joyce Antler, Elisabeth Israels Perry, Ingrid Winther Scobie, eds., *The Challenge of Feminist Biography: Writing the Lives of Modern American Women* (Urbana: University of Illinois Press, 1992), Introduction, 6.

9. Linda Wagner-Martin, *Telling Women's Lives: The New Biography* (New Brunswick, N.J.: Rutgers University Press, 1994), preface, x–xi.

10. Matina Horner, "Remember the Ladies," preface to *Gertrude Stein*, by Ann La Farge, American Women of Achievement series (New York: Chelsea House, 1988), 8.

11. Heilbrun, *Writing a Woman's Life*, Introduction, 19, 18.

12. Alpern et al., Introduction, *The Challenge of Feminist Biography*, 13, 15.

13. *American Women of Achievement* series statement of purpose.

14. Bell Gale Chevigny, "Daughters Writing: Toward a Theory of Women's Biography," 375–76, *Between Women: Biographers, Novelists, Critics, Teachers and Artists Write about Their Work on Women*, ed. Carol Ascher, Louise DeSalvo, Sara Ruddick (Boston: Beacon, 1984).

15. Blanche Wiesen Cook, "Biographer and Subject: A Critical Connection," 397–411, *Between Women*, 398.

16. Heilbrun, *Writing a Woman's Life*, Introduction, 21.

17. Jean Strouse, *Alice James: A Biography* (Boston: Houghton Mifflin, 1984), ix; hereafter cited in text as Strouse.

18. Gloria Steinem (text), George Barris (photographs), *Marilyn: Norma Jeane* (New York: New American Library, 1988), 180.

19. Another instance of an autobiographical half-life is John Wain's *Sprightly Running: Part of an Autobiography* (New York: St. Martin's Press, 1962/1965).

20. Arnold Rampersad, *The Life of Langston Hughes*, 2 vols. (New York: Oxford University Press, 1986–1988), 1:112; hereafter cited in text as Rampersad.

21. Compare with Faith Berry's account in *Langston Hughes: Before and Beyond Harlem* (Westport, Conn.: Lawrence Hill, 1983), 65–66; hereafter cited in text as Berry.

22. Rampersad, Introducton to Langston Hughes, *The Big Sea: An Autobiography*, 2nd ed. (New York: Hill and Wang, 1993), xiii–xiv.

23. Hughes, *The Big Sea*, 205, 212, 263, 266–68.

24. I am grateful to William L. Andrews for this observation.

25. Langston Hughes and Milton Meltzer, *A Pictorial History of the Negro in America* (New York: Crown, 1956) is an example of collective biography, discussed in chapter 5. The 5th rev. ed. is entitled *A Pictorial History of Black Americans* (1983).

26. Milton Meltzer, *Langston Hughes: A Biography* (New York: Crowell, 1968).

27. Hughes, *The Big Sea*, 324–25.

28. Langston Hughes, "The Blues I'm Playing," 96–120, *The Ways of White Folks* (New York: Knopf, 1935), 99–100, 108.

29. William L. Andrews, letter to Parke, 29 July 1995.

30. Margaret Walker, *Richard Wright, Daemonic Genius: A Critical Look at His Work* (New York: Warner, 1993), xvi.

31. Rampersad, "Biography, Autobiography, and Afro-American Culture," 1.

32. Rampersad, "Biography, Autobiography, and Afro-American Culture," 10, 3, 14, 11. On the elements and ethos of spiritual autobiography in the Christian tradition that characterize African-American autobiography and on this genre's emphasis on the "growth of authentic, individually authorized selfhood," see also William L. Andrews's Introduction to *Sisters of the Spirit: Three Black Women's Autobiographies of the Nineteenth Century* (Bloomington: Indiana University Press, 1986), esp. 10–16.

33. Rampersad, "Biography, Autobiography, and Afro-American Culture," 15–16.

34. Schlaeger, "Cult as Culture," 59.

35. James A. Clifton's "Alternate Identities and Cultural Frontiers, chapter 1, 1–37, *Being and Becoming Indian: Biographical Studies of North American Frontiers* (Chicago: Dorsey Press,

1989), passim, esp. 3, 5, is a valuably enlightening example of successful cross-disciplinarity in biography, a school of anthropology called *person-centered studies* of other cultures. Ethnographic and ethnohistorical methods are applied to examine the woven strands of cultural, ethnic, and personal identity. Although not conceived of originally as a collection of biographical profiles, this anthropological inquiry into the relationship between borders and identity became such in the making.

36. Clifton, Acknowledgments, *Being and Becoming Indian*," xvii.

Chapter 5

1. Henry James, *William Wetmore Story & His Friends*, 2 vols. in 1, Library of American Art Series (New York: Da Capo, 1969), 16.

2. Leon Edel, *Bloomsbury: A House of Lions* (Philadelphia: Lippincott, 1979), book jacket; hereafter cited in text as Edel.

3. R. W. B. Lewis, Prefatory Word, *The Jameses: A Family Narrative* (New York: Farrar, Straus and Giroux, 1991), n.p.

4. Leon Howard, *The Connecticut Wits* (Chicago: University of Chicago Press, 1943), 59.

5. Lyle Larsen, *Dr. Johnson's Household* (Hamden, Conn.: Archon Books, 1985), xi.

6. Angeline Goreau, "All the King's Women," review of Antonia Fraser, *The Wives of Henry VII* (New York: Knopf, 1992), *The New York Times Book Review*, December 20, 1992, 11.

7. Diane Johnson, *The True History of the First Mrs. Meredith and Other Lesser Lives* (New York: Knopf, 1972), book jacket.

8. Preface, *Who's Who in America*, vi.

9. "A Statistical Account," lxi–lxxvii, *Dictionary of National Biography From the Earliest Times to 1900*, founded in 1882 by George Smith, ed. Leslie Stephen and Sir Sidney Lee (New York: Macmillan; London: Smith Elder, 1885–1901; 22-volume rpt. of the main *Dictionary*, Oxford University Press, 1973), 1:lxvi.

10. Preface, *National Cyclopaedia of American Biography* (New York: James T. White, 1947), vol. 33, n.p. This series, sometimes identified as still in progress, is listed in Sheehy's *Guide to Reference Books* (10th ed.) with the following information: (1893–1984), 64 vols., (in progress?).

11. *Who's Who Among Black Americans*, 8th ed., ed. Shirelle Phelps (Detroit, Mich.: Gale Research, 1994/95), xiii; succeeded by the 9th ed., *Who's Who Among African Americans*, ed. Phelps, 1996/97.

12. Hertha Dawn Wong, in *Sending My Heart Back Across the Years: Tradition and Innovation in Native American Autobiography* (New York: Oxford University Press, 1992), notes that Eastman's biographers "tend to agree" that Elaine Goodale Eastman, Charles Eastman's wife, "provided the initiative and the editing for nine of Eastman's eleven books" (141).

13. For brief informative summary of sources of American Indian biography, see A. LaVonne Brown Ruoff, *American Indian Literatures: An Introduction, Bibliographic Review, and Selected Bibliography* (New York: Modern Language Association of America, 1990), 139–40.

14. Chelsea House Publishers informational flyer on the series *Lives of Notable Gay Men and Lesbians*.

15. *Guide to Reference Books*, 10th ed., ed. Eugene P. Sheehy (Chicago and London: American Library Association, 1986), 279. A 1993 supplement covers materials 1985–1990.

Bibliographic Essay

1. James L. Clifford, *From Puzzles to Portraits*, vii.

Recommended Biographies: A Selected List

The date of first publication in the original language and, when pertinent, composition, appear immediately after each title. My rule of thumb in selecting editions has been to list the best available edition. Biographies awarded the annual Pulitzer Prize (for biography or autobiography) since 1917, listed in standard reference works such as *The World Book Encyclopedia*, also offer a solid introduction to twentieth-century American biography.

Allen, Gay Wilson. *The Solitary Singer: A Critical Biography of Walt Whitman* (1955). Rev. ed. New York: New York University Press, 1967.

———. *Waldo Emerson: A Biography* (1981). New York: Viking, 1981.

———. *William James: A Biography* (1981). New York: Viking, 1967.

Aubrey, John. *Brief Lives* (written mid-seventeenth century; 1813 ed. entitled *Brief Lives*, subsequent enlarged eds. 1898, 1931). Ed. Oliver Lawson Dick. New York: Penguin, 1982.

Backscheider, Paula. *Daniel Defoe: His Life* (1989). Baltimore, Md.: Johns Hopkins University Press, 1989.

Bate, Walter Jackson. *John Keats* (1963; Pulitzer Prize). Cambridge, Mass.: The Belknap Press of Harvard University Press, 1978.

———. *Samuel Johnson* (1978). New York: Harcourt, Brace, 1977. Pulitzer Prize.

Bayle, Pierre. *Historical and Critical Dictionary: Selections* (1697; English trans. 1734–1740). Trans., with introduction and notes by Richard H. Popkin, with assistance of Craig Bush. Indianapolis, Ind.: Hackett, 1991.

Bell, Quentin. *Virginia Woolf: A Biography* (1972). London: Hogarth Press, 1990.

Benstock, Shari. *No Gifts from Chance: A Biography of Edith Wharton* (1994). New York: Scribner's, 1994.

Berry, Faith. *Langston Hughes Before and Beyond Harlem* (1983). Westport, Conn.: Lawrence Hill, 1983.

Blanchard, Paula. *Margaret Fuller: From Transcendentalism to Revolution* (1978). Foreword by Carolyn Heilbrun. Reading, Mass.: Addison-Wesley, 1987.

Boccaccio, Giovanni. *Life of Dante* (written ca. 1351–1355 and early 1360s). Trans. Vincenzo Zin Bollettino. Vol. 40, Series B. Garland Library of Medieval Literature. New York: Garland, 1990.

Bond, Alma Halbert. *Who Killed Virginia Woolf? A Psychobiography* (1989). New York: Human Sciences Press, 1989.

Boswell, James. *The Life of Samuel Johnson, LL.D.* (1791; important 3rd rev. ed. 1799). *Boswell's Life of Johnson*. Ed. R. W. Chapman, rev. J. D. Fleeman. New York: Oxford University Press, 1980.

———. *A Journal of a Tour to the Hebrides with Samuel Johnson, LL.D.* (1785). With Johnson's *Journey to the Western Islands of Scotland*. Ed. R. W. Chapman. London and New York: Oxford University Press, 1979.

Brack, O M Jr., and Robert M. Kelley, eds. *The Early Biographies of Samuel Johnson* (1974). Iowa City: University of Iowa Press, 1974.

Bradford, Gamaliel. *American Portraits 1875–1900* (1922). Port Washington, N.Y.: Kennikat Press, 1969.

———. *Biography and the Human Heart* (1932). Boston: Houghton Mifflin, 1932.

———. *Confederate Portraits* (1914). Boston: Houghton Mifflin, 1914.

———. *Portraits of American Women* (1919). Freeport, N.Y.: Books for Libraries Press, 1969.

———. *Union Portraits* (1916). Freeport, N.Y.: Books for Libraries Press, 1968.

Carlyle, Thomas. *On Heroes, Hero-Worship and the Heroic in History* (1841). Notes and intro. Michael K. Goldberg, text established by Michael K. Goldberg, Joel J. Brattin, and Mark Engel. Berkeley: University of California Press, 1993.

Caro, Robert. *The Years of Lyndon Johnson* (1982). 2 vols. Vol. 1, *The Path to Power*; Vol. 2, *Means of Ascent*. New York: Knopf, 1982.

Cavendish, George. *The Life and Death of Cardinal Wolsey* (written between ca. 4 November 1556 and 24 June 1558; circulated in MS.; first printed 1641). *Two Early Tudor Lives: The Life and Death of Cardinal Wolsey by George Cavendish, the Life of Sir Thomas More by William Roper*. Ed. Richard S. Sylvester and Davis P. Harding. New Haven: Yale University Press, 1967.

Chien. See Szuma, Chien.

Child, Lydia Maria. *The Freedmen's Book* (1865). New York: AMS Press, 1980.

Clifford, James L. *Dictionary Johnson: Samuel Johnson's Middle Years* (1979). New York: McGraw-Hill, 1981.

————. *Hester Lynch Piozzi (Mrs. Thrale)* (1941). 2nd ed. New York: Columbia University Press, 1987.

————. *Young Sam Johnson* (1955). New York: McGraw-Hill, 1981.

Cook, Blanche Wiesen. *Eleanor Roosevelt, Volume 1, 1884–1933* (1992). New York: Viking, 1992.

Cornelius Nepos. *Lives of Eminent Men* (written between 99 and 24 B.C.E., printed Venice, 1471; English trans., Winsted, Oxford, 1904). *Lucius, Annaeus Florus, Cornelius Nepos*. Trans. John C. Rolfe. Loeb Classical Library. London: Heinemann; New York: Putnam, 1929. *Cornelius Nepos: A Selection, Including the Lives of Cato and Atticus*. Trans. Nicholas Horsfall. Oxford: Clarendon Press, 1989.

Creamer, Robert W. *Babe: The Legend Comes to Life* (1974). New York: Simon and Schuster, 1992.

DeMaria, Robert, Jr. *Samuel Johnson: A Critical Biography* (1993). Oxford: Blackwell, 1993.

Diogenes Laertius. *Lives and Opinions of Eminent Philosophers* (written between 200 and 250; first printed Rome, n.d.; Venice, 1475). 2 vols. Trans. R. D. Hicks. Loeb Classical Library. London: Heinemann; New York: Putnam, 1925.

Donaldson, Scott (in collaboration with R. H. Winnick). *Archibald MacLeish: An American Life* (1992). Boston: Houghton Mifflin, 1992.

————. *Fool for Love: F. Scott Fitzgerald* (1983). New York: Dell, 1989.

Duberman, Martin Bauml. *Paul Robeson* (1988). New York: New Press, 1996.

Dunn, Jane. *A Very Close Conspiracy: Vanessa Bell and Virginia Woolf* (1990). Boston: Little, Brown, 1990.

Eadmer. *The Life of St. Anselm, Archbishop of Canterbury* (written ca. 1112–1114; first printed 1551). Oxford Medieval Texts. Ed., trans. R. W. Southern. Oxford: Clarendon Press, 1979.

Eastman, Charles A. *Indian Heroes and Great Chieftains* (1918). Lincoln: University of Nebraska Press, 1991.

Edel, Leon. *Bloomsbury: A House of Lions* (1979). New York: Penguin, 1981.

————. *Henry James* (1953–1973). 5 vols. *Henry James: A Life*. New York: Harper and Row, 1985. Pulitzer Prize.

Edmunds, R. David, ed. *Tecumseh and the Quest for Indian Leadership* (1984). Library of American Biography. Boston: Little, Brown, 1984.

Ehrenpreis, Irvin. *Swift, the Man, His Works, and the Age* (3 vols., 1962–1983). Vol. 1: *Mr. Swift and His Contemporaries*; Vol. 2: *Dr. Swift.*; Vol. 3, *Dean Swift* (not in print). Cambridge, Mass.: Harvard University Press, 1984.

Einhard. *Einhard's Life of Charlemagne* (written between 829 and 836?; 1st ed. 1829, Berlin). Trans. Samuel Epes Turner. Ann Arbor: University of Michigan Press, 1991.

Ellmann, Richard. *James Joyce* (1959). New and rev. ed. New York: Oxford University Press, 1982.

———. *Oscar Wilde.* (1987). New York: Random, 1988. Pulitzer Prize.

———. *Yeats: The Man and the Mask* (1948). New York: Norton, 1978.

Emerson, Ralph Waldo. *Representative Men* (1850). Vol. 4 of *The Complete Works of Ralph Waldo Emerson.* 12 vols. The Centenary Edition. Boston: Houghton Mifflin, 1903–1904. Cambridge, Mass.: The Belknap Press of Harvard University Press, 1987.

Epictetus. *The Discourses as Reported by Arrian* (ca. 60). 2 vols. Trans. W. A. Oldfather. Loeb Classical Library. London: Heinemann; New York: Putnam, 1926.

Fitch, Noël Riley. *Anaïs: The Erotic Life of Anaïs Nin* (1993). Boston: Little, Brown, 1993.

———. *Sylvia Beach and the Lost Generation: A History of Literary Paris in the Twenties and Thirties* (1983). New York: Norton, 1985.

Foxe, John. *Actes and Monuments* (1563; popularly known as the *Book of Martyrs*). Ed. William Byron Forbush. New York: Holt, Rinehart and Winston, 1965.

Freud, Sigmund. *Leonardo da Vinci and a Memory of His Childhood* (1910). Trans. Alan Tyson, ed. James Strachey. New York: Norton, 1989.

Froude, James A. *Thomas Carlyle* (4 vols., 1882–1884). *Froude's Life of Carlyle.* Abr. and ed. John Clubbe. Columbus: Ohio State University Press, 1979.

Fussell, Paul. *Samuel Johnson and the Life of Writing* (1971). New York: Norton, 1986.

Gaskell, Elizabeth. *The Life of Charlotte Brontë* (1857). Ed. Alan Shelston. New York: Penguin, 1985.

Gay, Peter. *Freud: A Life for Our Time* (1988). New York: Norton, 1988.

Gordon, Lyndall. *Virginia Woolf: A Writer's Life* (1984). New York: Norton, 1993.

Goreau, Angeline. *Reconstructng Aphra: A Social Biography of Aphra Behn* (1980). New York: Dial, 1980.

Gorsky, Susan Rubinow. *Virginia Woolf* (1978). Rev. ed. Boston: Twayne, 1989.

Gospels (probable order of composition Mark, Matthew, Luke, John, between ca. 70 and 110). *The Oxford Study Bible.* Rev. English Bible with the Apocrypha. Ed. M. Jack Suggs, Katharine Doob Sakenfeld, James R. Mueller. New York: Oxford University Press, 1994.

Greene, Donald. *Samuel Johnson* (1970). New York: Twayne, 1989.

Guiget, Jean. *Virginia Woolf and Her Works* (1965). Trans. Jean Stewart. New York: Harcourt, Brace, 1965.

Hamilton, Nigel. *JFK: Reckless Youth* (1992). Vol. 1 of life of John F. Kennedy. New York: Random, 1992.

Hamilton, Virginia. *Paul Robeson: The Life and Times of a Free Black Man* (1974). New York: Harper and Row, 1979.

Hawkins, John. *Life of Samuel Johnson* (1787). Ed. and abr., Bertram H. Davis. London: Jonathan Cape, 1962.

Hedrick, Joan. *Harriet Beecher Stowe: A Life* (1994). New York: Oxford, 1994. Pulitzer Prize.

Holroyd, Michael. *Bernard Shaw* (1982–1992). 5 vols. New York: Random, 1982–1992.

———. *Lytton Strachey: A Biography* (1971). Rev ed. New York: Penguin, 1979.

Holtz, William. *The Ghost in the Little House: A Life of Rose Wilder Lane* (1993). Columbia: University of Missouri Press, 1993.

Honan, Park. *Jane Austen: Her Life* (1987). New York: Fawcett Columbine, 1989.

Howard, Leon. *The Connecticut Wits* (1943). Chicago: University of Chicago Press, 1943.

———. *Herman Melville: A Biography* (1951). Berkeley: University of California Press, 1967.

Isocrates. *Evagoras* (written ca. 365 B.C.E.). Vol. 3. Trans. Larue Van Hook. *Isocrates.* 3 vols. Loeb Classical Library. Cambridge, Mass.: Harvard University Press; London: Heinemann, 1945.

James, Henry. *William Wetmore Story & His Friends* (2 vols., 1903). 2 vols. in 1. Library of American Art Series. New York: Da Capo, 1969.

Johnson, Diane. *The True History of the First Mrs. Meredith and Other Lesser Lives* (1972). New York: Knopf, 1972.

Johnson, Samuel. *An Account of the Life of Mr. Richard Savage* (1744). *Life of Savage.* Ed. Clarence Tracy. Oxford: Clarendon Press, 1971.

———. *Lives of the English Poets* (1779–1781). Ed. G. B. Hill. 1968 rpt. Georg Olms Verlagsbuchhandlung. 3 vols. Oxford: Clarendon Press, 1905.

Kaminski, Thomas. *The Early Career of Samuel Johnson* (1987). New York: Oxford University Press, 1987.

Kaplan, Justin. *Mr. Clemens and Mark Twain* (1966). New York: Simon and Schuster, 1990.

Karl, Frederick R. *Franz Kafka, Representative Man* (1979). New York: Ticknor and Fields, 1991.

———. *Joseph Conrad: The Three Lives, a Biography* (1979). New York: Farrar, Straus and Giroux, 1979.

Krutch, Joseph Wood. *Samuel Johnson* (1944). New York: Harcourt, Brace, 1963.

Larsen, Lyle. *Dr. Johnson's Household* (1985). Hamden, Conn.: Archon Books, 1985.

Lehmann, John. *Thrown to the Woolfs* (1978). New York: Holt, Rinehart and Winston, 1978.

Lewis, R. W. B. *Edith Wharton: A Biography* (1975). New York: Fromm International, 1985. Pulitzer Prize.

————. *The Jameses: A Family Narrative* (1991). New York: Farrar, Straus and Giroux, 1991.

Lockhart, J. G. *Memoirs of the Life of Sir Walter Scott*, 10 vols. (1837–1838). New York: AMS Press, 1983.

Macaulay, Thomas Babington. *Samuel Johnson* (1856). "Samuel Johnson," 548–78, *Macaulay Prose and Poetry*. Ed. G. M. Young. Cambridge, Mass.: Harvard University Press, 1952.

Mailer, Norman. *Marilyn: A Biography* (1973). New York: Perigee Books, 1987.

Martin, Jay. *Nathanael West: The Art of His Life*. New York: Farrar, Straus and Giroux, 1970.

————. *Always Merry and Bright: The Life of Henry Miller, An Unauthorized Biography* (1978). New York: Penguin, 1980.

Mather, Increase. *Two Mather Biographies: Life and Death* [of that reverend man of God, Mr. Richard Mather] (1670) *and Parentator* [memoirs of remarkables in the life and death of the ever-memorable Dr. Increase Mather (completed by his son Cotton Mather)] (begun 1685, completed 1724). Ed. William J. Scheick. Bethlehem, Pa.: Lehigh University Press; London: Associated University Presses, 1989.

Maurois, André. *Ariel, the Life of Shelley* (1923). Trans. Ella D'Arcy. New York: Frederick Ungar, 1972.

————. *Lelia, the Life of George Sand* (1952). Trans. Gerard Hopkins. New York: Penguin, 1977.

McCullough, David G. *Truman* (1992). New York: Simon and Schuster, 1992.

Meltzer, Milton. *Langston Hughes: A Biography* (1967). New York: Crowell, 1972.

Mepham, John. *Virginia Woolf: A Literary Life* (1991). New York: St. Martin's Press, 1992.

Middlebrook, Diane Wood. *Anne Sexton: A Biography* (1991). New York: Vintage, 1992.

Mitre, Bartolomé. *Biografias Estudios* (1857). Vol. 11, *Episodios Nacionales, Biografias Estudios y Rectificaciones Historicas. Las Obras Completas*. 17 vols. Buenos Aires, 1938–?.

Murphy, Arthur. *Essay on the Life and Genius of Samuel Johnson* (1792). 1:i–lxxxvi. *Dr. Johnson's Works*. 11 vols. Oxford English Classics. Rpt. of 1810 edition. New York: AMS Press, 1970.

Nepos. See Cornelius Nepos.

Nicolson, Nigel. *Portrait of a Marriage* (1973). New York: Atheneum, 1980.

North, Roger. *General Preface and Life of Dr. John North* (written between ca. 1718 and the 1730s; portions first published 1742 and 1744). Ed. Peter Millard. Toronto: University of Toronto Press, 1984.

O'Brien, Sharon. *Willa Cather: The Emerging Voice* (1987). New York: Oxford University Press, 1988; and New York: Chelsea House, 1995.

Painter, George D. *Andre Gide: A Critical Biography* (1951). New York: Atheneum, 1968.

———. *Proust* (1959–1965). 2 vols. New edition. New York: Penguin, 1990.

Piozzi, Hester Lynch Thrale. *Anecdotes of the Late Samuel Johnson* (1786). In William Shaw's and Piozzi's *Memoirs of Dr. Johnson*. Ed. Arthur Sherbo. London: Oxford University Press, 1974.

Pippett, Aileen. *The Moth and the Star: A Biography of Virginia Woolf* (1955). New York: Kraus Reprint, 1969.

Philostratus. *Life of Apollonius of Tyana* (written late 2nd–3rd centuries; first English trans., 1811). Trans. F. C. Conybeare. 2 vols. Loeb Classical Library. Cambridge, Mass.: Harvard University Press; London: Heinemann, 1960. *Life and Times of Apollonius of Tyana*. Trans. Charles P. Eells. Stanford University Language and Literature Series, 2:1. New York: AMS Press, 1967.

Plato. *The Collected Dialogues of Plato* (written late 4th century B.C.E.). Ed. Edith Hamilton and Huntington Cairns. New York: Pantheon, 1961. See esp. *Charmides, Euthyphro,* and *Ion* also in Loeb Classical Library. *Plato* (vols. 12, 1, 7). Trans. W. M. R. Lamb and Harold North Fowler. Cambridge, Mass.: Harvard University Press; London: Heinemann, 1927, 1914, 1925.

Plutarch. *The Parallel Lives* (written between ca. 46 and 120; 1st ed. of complete works, Paris, 1572; Jacques Amyot's important translation, Paris, 1559; Sir Thomas North's translation of Amyot, 1579). 11 vols. Trans. Bernadotte Perrin. Loeb Classical Library. London: Heinemann; New York: Putnam, 1914–1926. *The Lives of the Noble Grecians and Romans*. Trans. John Dryden, rev. Arthur Hugh Clough. 2 vols. Modern Library. New York: Random, 1992.

Poole, Roger. *The Unknown Virginia Woolf* (1978). Atlantic Highlands, N.J.: Humanities Press, 1990.

Raleigh, Walter. *Six Essays on Johnson* (1910). Folcroft, Pa.: Folcroft Library Editions, 1974.

Rampersad, Arnold. *The Life of Langston Hughes* (1986–1988). 2 vols. *Volume I: 1902–1941, I, Too, Sing America; Volume II: 1941–1967, I Dream a World*. New York: Oxford University Press, 1986–1988.

Reade, A. L. *Johnsonian Gleanings* (privately printed, 10 vols. 1909–1952). New York: Octagon Books, 1968.

Reynolds, David S. *Walt Whitman's America: A Cultural Biography* (1994). New York: Knopf, 1995.

Roper, William. *The Life of Sir Thomas More* (written ca. 1570). *Two Early Tudor Lives: The Life and Death of Cardinal Wolsey by George Cavendish, the Life of Sir Thomas More by William Roper*. Ed. Richard S. Sylvester and Davis P. Harding. New Haven, Conn.: Yale University Press, 1967.

Rose, Phyllis. *Woman of Letters: A Life of Virginia Woolf* (1978). New York: Harcourt, Brace, 1987.

Sandburg, Carl. *Abraham Lincoln: The Prairie Years and the War Years* (1926–1939). 6 vols. New York: Galahad Books, 1993.

Sartre, Jean-Paul. *Baudelaire* (1947). Trans. Martin Turnell. Norfolk, Conn.: New Directions, 1967.

———. *The Family Idiot: Gustave Flaubert, 1821–1857* (1971). 5 vols. Trans. Carol Cosman. Chicago: University of Chicago Press, 1981–1993.

———. *Saint Genet, Actor and Martyr* (1952). Trans. Bernard Frechtman. New York: Pantheon, 1983.

Schoenbaum, Samuel. *William Shakespeare: A Documentary Life* (1975). Oxford: Clarendon Press, 1975; New York: Oxford University Press, 1975.

Seidel, Michael. *Ted Williams: A Baseball Life* (1991). Chicago: Contemporary Books, 1991.

Spalding, Frances. *Vanessa Bell* (1983). London: Macmillan, 1984.

Spater, George, and Ian Parsons. *A Marriage of True Minds: An Intimate Portrait of Leonard and Virginia Woolf* (1977). New York: Harcourt, Brace, 1979.

Spoto, Donald. *The Dark Side of Genius: The Life of Alfred Hitchcock* (1983). Boston: Little, Brown, 1993.

Stein, Gertrude. *The Autobiography of Alice B. Toklas* (1933). New York: Random, 1990.

———. *Four in America* (1947). Freeport, N.Y.: Books for Libraries Press, 1969.

———. *Three Lives* (1908). New York: New American Library, 1989.

Steinem, Gloria. *Marilyn: Norma Jeane* (1986). Text by Gloria Steinem, photographs by George Barris. New York: New American Library, 1988.

Stephen, Leslie. *Samuel Johnson* (1878). New York: AMS Press, 1968.

Strachey, Lytton. *Eminent Victorians* (1918). New York: Penguin, 1986.

———. *Queen Victoria* (1921). New York: Harcourt, Brace, 1989.

Strouse, Jean. *Alice James: A Biography* (1980). Boston: Houghton Mifflin, 1984.

Suetonius. *The Lives of the Caesars* (written 2nd century; 1st ed., Rome, July 1470; Philemon Holland's English trans., London, 1606). *Suetonius*. 2 vols. Trans. J. C. Rolfe. Loeb Classical Library. Cambridge, Mass.: Harvard University Press; London: Heinemann, 1914. *The Twelve Caesars*. Trans. Robert Graves, rev. Michael Grant. New York: Penguin, 1989.

Szuma, Chien. *Selections from Records of the Historian* (written 101–94 B.C.E.). Trans. Yang Hsien-yi and Gladys Yang. Peking: Foreign Languages Press, 1979.

Tacitus. *Agricola* (written between ca. October 97 and January 98; 1st ed. Milan, 1475). *Dialogus, Agricola, Germania*. Trans. Maurice Hutton. Loeb Classical Library. London: Heinemann; New York, 1914. *Tacitus' Agricola Germany, and Dialogue on Orators*. Trans., with an introduction and notes by Herbert W. Benario. Oklahoma Series in Classical Culture. Norman: University of Oklahoma Press, 1991.

Theophrastus. *Characters* (written ca. 319 B.C.E.; important early French ed., Isaac Causabon, 1592; English ed., Joseph Hall, London, 1608). Ed. and trans. Jeffrey Rusten, Ian C. Cunningham, A. D. Knox. Loeb Classical Library. Cambridge, Mass.: Harvard University Press, 1993; *The Character Sketches*. Trans. Warren Anderson. Kent, Ohio: Kent State University Press, 1970.

Traubel, Horace. *With Walt Whitman in Camden* (1914–1992). 7 vols. New York: Kennerly; Philadelphia: University of Pennsylvania Press; Carbondale and Edwardsville: Southern Illinois University Press, 1914–1992.

Trombley, Stephen. *'All that Summer She was Mad': Virginia Woolf and Her Doctors* (1981). New York: Continuum, 1982.

Vasari, Giorgio. *The Lives of the Most Excellent Italian Architects, Painters, and Sculptors* (1550). Trans. George Bull. New York: Viking, 1978.

Wagner-Martin, Linda. *Sylvia Plath: A Biography* (1987). New York: St. Martin's Press, 1988.

Wain, John. *Samuel Johnson* (1975). London: Papermac, 1988.

Walker, Margaret. *Richard Wright, Daemonic Genius: A Critical Look at His Work* (1988). New York: Armistad/Random, 1988.

Walton, Izaak. Lives of John Donne (1640), Sir Henry Wotton (1651), George Herbert (1670), and Bishop Sanderson (1678). *The Lives of John Donne, Sir Henry Wotton, Richard Hooker, George Herbert and Robert Sanderson.* Intro. George Saintsbury. New York: Oxford University Press, 1966.

Watt, Ian. *Conrad in the Nineteenth Century* (1979). Berkeley: University of California Press, 1979.

Weems, Mason L. *The Life of [George] Washington* (1800–1808). Ed. Marcus Cunliffe. Cambridge, Mass.: Belknap Press of Harvard University Press, 1962.

Weinberg, Steven. *Armand Hammer: The Untold Story* (1989). Boston: Little, Brown, 1989; London: Cardinal, 1992.

Wilson, Jean Moorcroft. *Virginia Woolf: Life and London* (1988). New York: Norton, 1988.

Wood, Anthony. *Athenae Oxonienses: An Exact History of All the Writers and Bishops Who Have Had Their Education in the University of Oxford* (1691–1692). 4 vols. Rev. ed. and a continuation by Philip Bliss. London: Lackington, 1820.

Woodress, James. *Willa Cather: A Literary Life* (1987). Lincoln: Universty of Nebraska Press, 1989.

Woolf, Virginia. *Flush: A Biography* (1933). New York: Harcourt, Brace, 1983.
————"Lives of the Obscure." *Collected Essays*, 4:120–33. 4 vols. New York: Harcourt, Brace, 1967.

————. *Orlando: A Biography* (1928). New York: Harcourt, Brace, 1992.

————. *Roger Fry* (1940). New York: Harcourt, Brace, 1976.

Xenophon. *Memorabilia* (written late 4th century B.C.E.; first printed in complete works, Florence 1516, Oxford, 1900; separate ed. of *Memorabilia*, Berlin, 1854). *Memorabilia and Oeconomicus*. In *Xenophon*, 7 vols. Trans. E. C. Marchant. Vol. 4. Loeb Classical Library. Cambridge, Mass.: Harvard, 1968; London: Heinemann, 1968. *Memorabilia*. Rpt. of 1903 ed. Manchester, N.H.: Ayer, 1979.

Index

Augustine, Saint, 32; *Confessions,* 32
Austen, Jane, 79

Bacon, Francis, 13, 16; *The
    Advancement of Learning,* 13
Bainbridge, John: *Biography of an
    Idea: The Story of Mutual Fire and
    Casualty Insurance,* xiv
Balderston, Katherine C., 61, 63;
    "Johnson's Vile Melancholy," 61
Banneker, Benjamin, 11
Barber, Francis, 113
Barlow, James, 112
Barnum, Phineas T., 24
Baratier (Barretier), J. P., 36
Barrymore, Ethel, 123
Barthes, Roland, 30; "The Death of
    the Author," 30
Bass, George Houston, 106
Bate, Walter Jackson, 63-64, 66;
    Samuel Johnson, 63-64
Bayle, Pierre, 11; *Dictionnaire his-
    torique et critique,* 11
Behn, Aphra, 98, 116; *Oroonoko,* xvi
Bell, Anne Olivier, 87
Bell, Clive, 112
Bell, Quentin, 81-83, 84, 86, 105;
    Virginia Woolf: A Biography,
    81-82, 84
Bell, Vanessa, 74, 75, 82, 83, 112
Berry, Faith, 99, 101-6; *Langston
    Hughes Before and Beyond
    Harlem,* 99
*Biographical Dictionaries of Minority
    Women,* 122
*Biographical Directory of the American
    Academy of Pediatrics,* 118
"Biographical Reference Sources: A
    Selective Checklist," 115
*Biographie universelle ancienne et mod-
    erne,* 116
Biography (life writing): compared
    to autobiography, xv, 76-77,
    98-105,108; compared to fiction,
    xvi, 19-20, 28-30, 71; definitions
    and characteristics of, xiii, 13,
    18, 111; hagiography and, 8-9;
    historical development of, 1-34;
    and history (historical writing),

xvi, 2-3, 13; and intellectual
    movements: Darwinism, 25;
    depth psychology and psycho-
    analysis, 25-26, 99; Marxism, 25;
    postmodernism, 90-91;
    Renaissance humanism and
    modern science, 9-10; kinds of:
    authorized, 106-7; collective
    (dictionaries), 10-11, 111,
    115-22; critical, 51; feminist,
    92-98; group, 10-12, 111-15;
    juvenile, 123-24; literary,
    xvii-xviii, 35; scholarly, 105-6;
    other categorizations, 29-30; of
    minorities, xvii, 89-109; motiva-
    tions for, xiii-xiv, 1-2; in non-
    Western cultures, 2, 32-34; ori-
    gins, 1-2; popular form, xiv-xvi,
    2-3; in Western cultures
    (Anglo-American), xviii, 2-29.
    See also Langston Hughes, Alice
    James, Samuel Johnson,
    Virginia Woolf
Biography Index, 124
Black Hawk, 123
Blake, Robert (Admiral), 36
Boccaccio, 10
Boerhaave, Herman, 36
Bok, Sissela, 122
Boleyn, Anne, 114
Bolland, John, 9; *Acta Sanctorum,* 9
Bonaparte, Louis Napoléon, 23
Bond, Alma Halbert, 87; *Who Killed
    Virginia Woolf?,* 87
Bontemps, Arna, 101, 106
Booklist, 115
*Book of People: Photographs, Capusule
    Biographies, and Vital Statistics,
    The,* 116
Booth, John Wilkes, 119
Borges, Jorge Luis, 23
Boswell, James, 12, 17-19, 20, 25-27,
    35, 41, 42-48, 50, 51, 55-64, 68,
    70, 76, 80, 82, 87, 88, 98, 101, 103,
    113; *Journal of a Tour to the
    Hebrides with Samuel Johnson,
    LL.D.,* 44; *Life of Samuel Johnson,*
    12, 35, 42-48, 50, 56, 64
Bradford, Gamaliel, 24

About the Author

Catherine N. Parke teaches English and Women's Studies at the University of Missouri–Columbia. She writes on British and American authors, Jane Austen, James Boswell, Edward Gibbon, Samuel Johnson, Gertrude Stein, and Virginia Woolf, among others, and on biography and autobiography. Her books include *Samuel Johnson and Biographical Thinking*, a critical edition of Zoë Akins's essays on American poetry, entitled *In the Shadow of Parnassus*, and a collection of her own poems, *Other People's Lives*.